new orleans

new orleans

by Michel LaCroix

with maps by Ingo Fast

Longstreet
Atlanta, Georgia

edge guides

Published by Longstreet Press
A subsidiary of Cox Newspapers,
A subsidiary of Cox Enterprises, Inc.
2140 Newmarket Parkway
Suite 122
Marietta, Georgia 30067

Printed in the United States of America
First Printing, 1999

Book design by Sue Canavan

A Balliett & Fitzgerald Book
editor: Vijay Balakrishnan
production editors: Sue Canavan, Maria Fernandez
copy editor: Meagan Backus
proofreader: Donna Stonecipher
associate editors: Kristen Couse, Michael Walters

ISBN: 1-56352-520-8
Library of Congress Catalog Card Number 99-60648

table of contents

introduction   1

french quarter   10
eating/coffee... 17, bars... 38, music/clubs... 42,
buying stuff... 47, sleeping... 68,
doing stuff... 74, body... 85

plus: mardi gras... 40, if you miss the carnival... 65

faubourg marigny   88
eating/coffee...91, bars/music/clubs... 96,
buying stuff... 99, sleeping...100,
doing stuff... 105, body... 107

plus: a revel without a cause... 102

garden districts   108
eating/coffee... 110, bars/music/clubs... 122,
sleeping... 123, doing stuff... 125

plus: architecture... 112, tennessee williams... 120

cbd/warehouse/arts district   130
eating/coffee... 135, bars/music/clubs... 149,
buying stuff... 150, sleeping... 155,
doing stuff... 160

plus: good eats... 134, the dish on dishes... 138

mid-city/ bayou st. john 168
eating/coffee... 171, bars/music/clubs... 181,
sleeping... 184, doing stuff... 188
plus: fire on the bayou: jazzfest... 182,
music music music... 186

uptown 194
eating/coffee... 196, bars/music/clubs... 208,
buying stuff... 210, sleeping... 214, doing stuff... 216

lakeside/ west end 222
eating/coffee... 225, sleeping... 229,
doing stuff...232
plus: tours... 230

magazine street/ irish channel 234
eating/coffee... 236, buying stuff... 242,
sleeping... 255, doing stuff... 256, body... 257
plus: cemeteries... 246

off the edge 258

phone numbers 262

new orleans calendar 264

index 269

introduction

"The devil has a vast empire here."

—Sister Madeleine Hachard, personal diaries, 1728

Louisiana happened March 3, 1699, when French-Canadian explorer Pierre Le Moyne, Sieur d'Iberville, mucked ashore near the mouth of the Mississippi River and, since it was Carnival Day, named the place Pointe du Mardi Gras. Talk about fortuitous! New Orleans followed in 1718 when Le Moyne's brother, Jean-Baptiste, Sieur de Bienville, planted feet and flag and declared the muddy morass around him La Nouvelle-Orléans. He named it after King Louis XIV's brother, Philippe, duc d'Orleans, who had a penchant for wearing ladies' gowns to court. Some local historians insist the city was named for Louis' nephew who was not a fashionable transvestite, but an egomaniacal murderer. Either take seems appropriate for this deliciously loopy town.

Bienville set about battling snakes, alligators, mosqui-toes, hurricanes, and ferocious fevers while carving civi-lization from the nearly impenetrable cypress swamp. Fortunately, the saner heads who warned him against the seriously unhealthy site did not prevail; Paris soon dubbed the place the "wet grave." When the gutsy (or nutty) Bienville defied conventional wisdom, he launched a tradition of nonconformity that continues in New Orleans to this day.

The location is truly improbable. New Orleans lies partly below sea level and stretches for some 363.5 square miles between the Mississippi River and Lake Pontchartrain, almost half underwater. Imagine, the 24,000-acre primeval Bayou Sauvage Wildlife Refuge lies totally within city limits, just 20 minutes from Bourbon Street.

Unable to find quality folk to populate his remote colony, King Louis XIV emptied the Paris prisons and loaded his Louisiana-bound ships with cutthroats, hookers, and thieves, so the struggling town was born amid crime, corruption, public drunkenness, and prostitution. By the 1740s, the wife of Royal Governor Pierre Rigault, Marquis de Vaudreuil, was dealing drugs from the governor's mansion! Rigault's successor, one Louis Billouart de Kerlerec, cleaned up the town's act, and ever since New Orleans has regularly seesawed between order and chaos. Crime has recently been cut 40 percent, mostly due to a new police chief, but Louisiana's last governor was just indicted for the third time. It is the paradoxical legacy of a city famous both for its festivities and for its criminal underside.

After the French and Spanish ownership of the colony ended, New Orleans enjoyed its Golden Age and grew into the nation's fourth-largest city under American rule. It became a major world port, a distinction it retains today. Those were boom times, when the city cemented its reputation as a global pleasure capital. The puritanical American newcomers were shocked by the Creole city's passion for all things sybaritic—a love for opera and theater, dueling and gambling, smart soirées, and serious frivolity.

Visitors shook their heads and wondered: Don't these fun-loving fools ever work? They still wonder, and for good reason. Aside from Mardi Gras, the largest free party on earth, New Orleans also has the Sugar Bowl, Jazzfest, the French Quarter Festival, the Tennessee Williams/New Orleans Literary Festival, gay Southern Decadence, and a host of other festivals saluting everything from William Faulkner, Creole tomatoes, and Easter, to Saints Patrick, Joseph, and Nicholas. It's also held the Super Bowl far more times than any other city. In 1999, FrancoFête begins, a year-long blowout celebrating 300 years of French influence in Louisiana. Just another excuse to party, folks.

But the city is also torn in its identity as party central. Some feel that it is being undone by its own popularity. Although it welcomes the onslaught of visitors every year who fuel the tourist-driven economy, residents are ambivalent about their beloved town slowly turning into a funky Disneyland. The more that money pours in, it seems, the more the old New Orleans is threatened. These days the dilemma is that where there is development there is also a lamentable encroachment of franchise-style homogeneity. The number of permanent residents in the French Quarter, for example, has shrunk by almost a third in recent years, and a few of the most distinguished old krewes [see **mardi gras** sidebar] have withdrawn from what they see as a degradation of the spirit of Mardi Gras. Also, the influx of hundreds of thousands of drunken revelers with money in their pockets has created tension (and crime) in a town

new orleans–speak

More than in any other American city, locals in New Orleans have a vocabulary and pronunciation all their own. Despite efforts of B-movies and bad books to convince you other-wise, New Orleans is not a true Southern city in the sense of, say, Charleston or Savannah. It's been called the South's exotic stepchild because its heritage is Latin Catholic, not Anglo Protestant. Granted, the term Dixie was born here (when illiterate American immigrants, mostly "Kaintocks," mispronounced dix, the local French currency minted in New Orleans), but if you hear a Southern drawl, it's not a native New Orleanian. The true local accent is much closer to Brooklyn's than Birmingham's. Don't be surprised if you hear "dese," "dem" and "dose" or get directions to the "turlet." These are people who wash dishes in the "zink," slather "my-nez" on their po' boy sandwich and like to make a "purnt."

Working-class folks are fond of greeting each other with "Aw-right." If something is exemplary, it's "Mo bettah." If you agree with someone, you'll say, "Yeah, you right." If someone calls you "cher," pronounced "sheh," they're probably a trans-planted Cajun. Be pleased if you get lagniappe (lan-yap); it means an unexpected gift.

New Orleanians can get fighting mad over how you pronounce their city, despite the fact that they can't agree among themselves. You'll hear everything from "N'Awlins" to "Nyawlins" to "N'waluns," as well as "Norluns" and the distinctively uptown intonation, "New Oy-yuns." Never, however, will you hear a local say New Orleenz. That pronunciation is strictly reserved for Orleans Parish, Orleans Avenue and for musicians seeking to rhyme such lyrics as, "Do you know what it means to miss New Orleans?"

Another semantic cause célèbre is the difference between Creole and Cajun. Creole comes from the Spanish word *criollo*, meaning "native," and originally described anyone of French or Spanish ancestry born outside the mother country. Napoleon's Empress Josephine, a native of Martinique, is perhaps the most famous Creole. The intermingling of Europeans with Africans created black Creoles, who were not acknowledged until recent years. The Cajuns come from Acadia, a onetime French colony on Nova Scotia. Cajun is simply a corruption of Acadian. The Creoles were largely city folk, while the Cajuns farmed and fished in bayou country. Both, of course, created distinctive cuisines, although there was some inevitable intermingling.

that still suffers from many varieties of urban poverty. The recent crime stats are encouraging, but New Orleans is still considered one of America's most violent cities; tourists must remain vigilant. The attractions and main drags of the neighborhoods profiled here are safe by day, iffy at night. When in doubt, cab it.

Perhaps all this is only the most modern version of the contradictions that New Orleans has always taken in stride, and somehow triumphed over. Slavery gave birth to jazz here, after all, and the collision of French, Spanish, African, and Caribbean cultures spawned one of the richest cuisines in the world.

And it was also the clash of cultures that produced the distinctive styles of architecture here. Iron galleries are the French Quarter's signature, turning otherwise ordinary structures into frothy, showy fantasies (gilding the lily is a time-honored New Orleans tradition). In the uptown Garden District, glorious antebellum mansions tucked into verdant settings can stun the uninitiated by their gentility.

New Orleans, though, is constantly paying for Bienville's defiant site selection with weather that, some say, only a mosquito or an orchid could thrive in. The humidity can be murder, but what do you expect in a subtropical swamp soaked by almost six feet of rain a year? Because much of the town sits below sea level with a disconcertingly high water table that fluctuates with the Mississippi, every single drop of rain has to be relocated. This explains those monstrous pumping stations, engineering wonders that suck up the water and divert it to Lake Pontchartrain via a vast system of canals Venice would envy. This watery mess lasts from late May to September, a time when many

New Orleanians escape to cooler, breezier places across the lake, or to nearby Gulf beaches. The rest of the year compensates for the crushing heat, allowing as it does January golfing and February fishing.

Navigating the city requires an understanding of special terminology. Traditionally downtown means the French Quarter and uptown is the Garden District, with the sky-

pronunciation guide

New Orleans has named streets for everything from Napoleonic victories to the nine Greek muses, and if you attempt correct French or Spanish, you'll be wrong. Three centuries of polyglot influence have obliterated all traces of both mother tongues.

Just be glad you don't have to ask directions to Kerlerec, Ulloa, Dorgenois, Livaudais, Poeyfarre or Rocheblave streets!

Burgundy: bur-GUN-dy
Calliope: CAL-ee-ope
Carondelet: care-ON-de-LET
Chartres: Chart-uz
Conti: Con-tie
Dauphine: do-FEEN
Decatur: d'CATE-er
Esplanade: ES-plan-aid
Faubourg: FO-berg
Melpomene: Mel-po-mean
Terpsichore: terp-SICK-o-ree
Toulouse: tah-LOOSE or tah-LOOZE
Tchoupitoulas: CHOP-a-TWO-lus
Tremé: Truh-MAY
Vieux Carré: Voo-kuh-RAY

scraping CBD or Central Business District sandwiched roughly in between. Here, we've delineated the areas even further: In addition to the French Quarter, the Garden District, and the Central Business District, there is Faubourg Marigny, directly downriver from the French Quarter; Uptown, upriver from the Garden District; Magazine Street, which stretches through the CBD and the Garden Districts, into Uptown; Mid-City/Bayou St. John, which sprawls above the French Quarter; and Lakeside/ West End on the banks of Lake Pontchartrain. Because the city follows the curvaceous river, standard directions don't make any sense. You'll never hear anyone say north, south, east, or west. Instead, they'll tell you something is simply uptown, downtown, toward the lake or toward the river. If it's across the river, that puts it on the west bank. Confused? It comes easily once you get your bearings. And don't think you've gone crazy when someone claims that the sun rises over the west bank. Courtesy of a grand bend in the Mississippi, it does.

New Orleans may have the trappings of a modern city, but its special charm is that beneath the excitement and problems of urban life, it's pleased to live in the past. It's a still-seductive, slightly jaded grande dame who's seen and done it all. She long ago blew off the aggressiveness of New York and the trendiness of Los Angeles, but never succumbed to the sterility of Houston or the ennui of Phoenix. The city is quite content with its unique status and is happy to let the good times roll through whatever complications history may deliver.

As the city rambles into the next millennium, you can still actually find yourself in one of those mystical French

Quarter fogs, punctuated by the glow of gaslights, the clip-clop of carriage horses, mournful ship's horns, or, if you're lucky, the bluesy wail of a trumpet. You may get a glimpse of New Orleans' special and enduring mystery. The City That Care Forgot. The Paris of the Swamps. The Northernmost Caribbean City. The Westernmost African City. The Crescent City. The Big Easy. Take your pick. It's all these, and and then some.

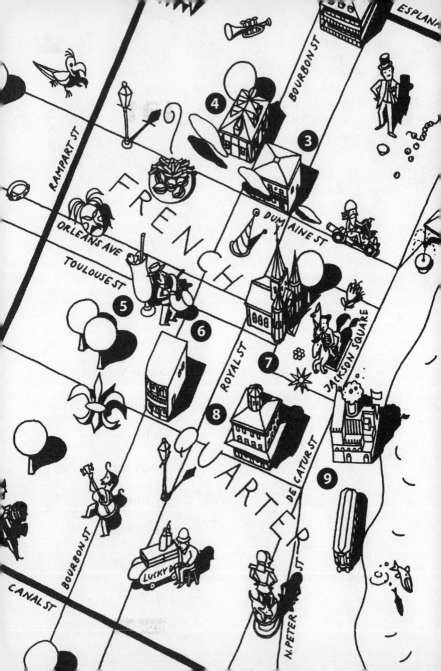

N. PETER ST

french quarter

Only six by thirteen blocks, the French Quarter, also called the Vieux Carré, meaning "Old Square," is a compact grid originally laid out by Bienville in 1718. It's easily walkable, but the sidewalks tend to buckle since the neighborhood is slowly settling back into the swamps. This constant sinking (which has nothing to do with the weight of too many tacky T-shirt shops) is why so much looks out of kilter. It is not unheard-of for doors and windows to have to be refitted into sagging walls and sills.

turn page for map key

The odd perspective is heightened because galleries and balconies slope downward toward the street, allowing for rain runoff. Some visitors claim a cocktail or two puts things back in line, and sometimes it seems an inordinate number of people are testing that theory. (Incidentally, don't be surprised by all those folks toting beer and cocktails on the street—it's perfectly legal as long as they're not in glass containers.)

The Quarter is the oldest and most famous part of town, with the upriver end largely commercial, the downriver section residential. Behind all the shutters, walls, and iron gates is a viable neighborhood where people live and work (drop into the world's smallest A&P at the corner of Royal and St. Peter streets and watch locals "making groceries," as the old-timers say). It's also a wild-card combination of European charm and American tackiness, of punks in slumlord-owned crash pads and high-powered businesspeople in exquisitely restored Creole mansions. Delta Burke, Gerald McRaney, and directors Francis Ford Coppola and Taylor Hackford are among the more famous part-time Quarterites. Other residents are a laissez-faire blend of singles and couples, straights and gays—notice the profusion of rainbow flags—artists, writers, musicians, and plenty of eccentrics.

Maybe you'll see Ruthie the Duck Lady (with or without her pet), who's been painted, photographed, and profiled

map key		
	1 Old U.S. Mint	5 Pat O'Brien's
	2 French Market	6 Preservation Hall
	3 Clover Grill	7 St. Louis Cathedral
	4 Lafitte's Blacksmith	8 The Napoleon House
	Shop	9 Jax Brewery

everywhere in the press. Or the Bead Lady, who'll give you carnival beads if she's on her medication or snarl at you if she's not. Watch for the identical twin sisters of indeterminate age, usually breakfasting at the Clover Grill, who never appear without full makeup and stiletto heels. At 908 Bourbon Street is America's only hardware store honoring drag queens. Mary's Hardware Store used to carry a full line of drag until True Value bought them out. Contractual concessions yielded Mary's True Value Hardware, telephone 525–MARY.

The unabashed commercial trashiness of upper Bourbon Street is countered by the elegance of early 19th-century Creole town houses and cottages, and Victorian shotgun houses dripping with gingerbread, scattered throughout the Quarter. Behind their walls and lacy iron facades lurk secret courtyards with splashing fountains, lotus pools, palms, and banana trees. Peek through iron gates and carriageways for a glimpse of the magic. First-time visitors are struck by the abundance of hibiscus, jasmine, and bougainvillea beckoning from balconies and patios, perfuming the narrow streets and offering respite from urban smells. The Quarter has one of the highest per capita ratios of restaurants in the world, so garbage can be a noxious reality, especially in the steamy summer months. The city tries hard, with vigilant street sweepers and daily garbage pickup, but don't be surprised if that delicious smell of sweet olive is interrupted by a whiff of rotting crawfish. Just pretend you're in old Marseilles.

There are also accusations that the Quarter is dirty. Many residents hose their sidewalks every morning, and bars hire private sanitation companies to augment the city's

daily pickup efforts. But it's a Herculean chore, considering the annual inundation of tourists who often ignore the
strategically placed trash cans. Actually, the Quarter looks
grimy mostly because it's old. Those charming patinas are
the result of centuries of punishing heat and driving rains,
and Quarterites cherish them. Locals still laugh about the
Midwestern tourists who thought the venerable Cabildo
needed a paint job.

The Quarter is anchored at Jackson Square, one of the
most-visited spots in the world. It's dominated by triple-
spired St. Louis Cathedral, named for France's patron saint,
which is flanked by the Presbytère (originally a home for
priests and now an exhibition center) and the Cabildo
(where the Louisiana Purchase was signed). Also on the
Square are the 1849 Pontalba Apartments, the first apartments in America, and still one of the most sought-after
addresses in town, despite daytime noise and nighttime
bums. There are a number of intriguing shops on the
ground floor, as well as the very helpful New Orleans Visitors Information Center. The park within the elegant iron
gates is immaculately maintained with manicured land-
scaping that changes seasonally. In the center is an equestrian statue of General Andrew Jackson, who, with a ragtag
army, defeated the British at the Battle of New Orleans,
making him the city's hero. He went on to remember New
Orleans by giving it a U.S. Mint when he became president.

By day Jackson Square teems with tourists, musicians,
artists, and colorful street entertainers. The gates are locked
at dusk, and by midnight the plaza before the cathedral is
usually overrun by a gamut of punks, drunks, and vagrants.
Grab a carriage on the Decatur Street side of the park and

do your romanticizing elsewhere. Incidentally, don't believe everything the carriage drivers say. The city has tried sending them to school, but they think it's more fun to make things up. If you're lucky, you'll engage one who knows what he or she is talking about. Tip: If they point out the House of the Rising Sun, they're embellishing; that legendary bordello existed only in song. Even better: If they claim the broken glass bottles atop walls were put there to keep slaves from escaping, they're outright liars; those quaint security devices date from this century, and they're meant to keep people from getting in, not out.

Across Decatur from the Square is Jackson ("Jax") Brewery, a multitiered entertainment complex carved from an 1890s brewery. It was home to a honeycomb of local specialty shops until their recent and unfortunate eviction by the behemoth Virgin Records. There are terrific views of the river from the upper floors. Behind the cathedral is Royal Street, boasting one of the best, albeit most expensive, concentrations of antique shops on the planet. And Chartres Street in front of the cathedral also has some superb shops and galleries, as do many of the side streets. With a handful of exceptions, upper Bourbon Street remains a sleazoid stretch of strip clubs, T-shirt and junk shops, cheap eateries, and jazz joints. Pleasure seekers hang here all day, but at night Bourbon blossoms into a tawdry smear of neon, closed to traffic so pedestrians can stroll at their leisure and drunks don't get run over. On weekends it's a steadily flowing crowd of curious tourists, college kids, weekenders, punks, drunks, and those dedicated to separating you from your money. Ah, the early days live on!

Actually, if you keep your wits about you, Bourbon

Street can be a helluva lot of fun, with a few caveats. Beware of pickpockets (they come in all forms) and avoid the aggressively friendly "Party Patrol" accusing you of not having enough fun. They're just con artists out to sell you entertainment crap you don't need. Also shun the unlicensed "Visitor Information Center" next door to the Bank One ATM at Jackson Square, unless you want a time-share. They're banned from the Quarter but occasionally sneak back, like all dedicated con artists. Most annoying are the aggressive dudes betting they know "where you got your shoes." (Answer: "On your feet!") Simply ignore them and move on.

Catch your breath with a leisurely stroll along the Mississippi. The 1984 World's Fair was largely responsible for a renaissance of this area, returning the river to Quarterites who knew it was there only because of ships' horns sounding behind rows of rotting wharfs. It's now lined with esplanades, parks, sparkling streetcars called Red Ladies, one of the nation's best aquariums, and the Moon Walk—named for former Mayor Moon Landrieu, not the Gloved One. As you approach the levee, you'll pass through thick sliding steel doors. Those are part of the flood wall, the city's insurance in case the levee is, God forbid, breached by a hurricane. Benches are strategically scattered about. The Mississippi is its deepest at this point, 197 feet or so, and the volume of ship traffic is a truly awesome spectacle to behold. This is, after all, why New Orleans is here.

eating/coffee

The sheer number and variety of restaurants in the French Quarter is staggering and not a little bewildering. For visitors the dilemma is always the same: So much to eat, so little time; for writers, correspondingly, the problem is: So much to cover and so little space. The following choices represent the breadth and variety available here. Whether you want the elegance of Bella Luna and Louis XVI, the trendy but proven cuisine of Susan Spicer's Bayona and Emeril Lagasse's NOLA, or the lesser but tasty fare of Fiorella's or the Tourist Trap, it's all here for the choosing, with plenty in between. Except for the bargain restaurants, reservations are absolutely essential. Some of these places are booked months ahead—especially if there's a convention of 8,000 cardiologists in town.

New Orleanians love to eat, and you'll find them dining out at all hours. They have sophisticated palates, appreciate good food, and usually tip 15 to 20 percent of the tab (before tax). Dress codes are pretty laid back since this is a tourist town, but it's wise to ask if jacket is required when you make your reservations. Bella Luna probably won't turn you away if you're in jeans, but once you're seated amid all that elegance, you may wish they had.

> **Cost Range** per entree
> $/under 10 dollars
> $$/10–15 dollars
> $$$/15–20 dollars
> $$$$/20+ dollars

asian... If you haven't visited the New York or Miami branch of the notorious **Lucky Cheng's** (720 St. Louis St. 504/529–2045 $$–$$$$), a new experience awaits, and we're not talking about the food. More than one naive tourist has been startled to discover that the exotic Asian waitress is capable of dishing out more than drinks and dinner. This is the home of drag-queen-as-waitress, so be ready for these skilled gender-benders to gleefully plop on your lap and confide their "female" troubles while taking your order. For starters, try the flash-fried calamari in a Thai lemon dipping sauce or tempura sushi roll filled with crawfish and cream cheese. Follow with the pork chop in a coconut crust or tuna crusted with spicy peppercorns. For dessert, order Imelda's Shoe, a chocolate high heel filled with fresh fruit and whipped cream (while in questionable taste, it's very tasty). On Monday and Wednesday nights and weekends, drag shows in the front cabaret feature performers whose professionalism varies wildly. Sadly, so does the quality of food and service at Lucky Cheng's.

cafes/diners... Folks, there just ain't nothing quite like the rowdy **Clover Grill** (900 Bourbon St. 504/598–1010 $), a longtime Quarter institution, where the waiters and clientele are as much fun as the food. The smiles begin with the menu ("Our chili speaks for itself, sooner or later.") and grow when the waiter inexplicably belts out a show tune, or good-naturedly dishes a customer behind his back or to her face. A blackboard lists specials as well as the number of days until Mardi Gras. The famous burgers are cooked under hubcaps (American only, please!), and the fluffy banana or pecan waffles bear cute clover imprints.

This all-night diner is the perfect place for a pick-me-up breakfast after Bourbon Street has worn you down. The Clover Grill's sister diner, **Poppy's Grill** (717 St. Peter St. 504/524–3287 $), has the same fare in a much larger space, including rather uncomfortable booths and a patio for outdoor dining. The walls are adorned with blowups of old romance and movie magazines, and the staff is as zany as Clover's. You can also get cocktails. A serious food bargain and a local fave is **Fiorella's,** with two entrances (45 French Market Place, 1136 Decatur St. 504/528–9566 $–$$), where the decor is truly a hoot and a holler. The French Market side is one cavernous space with tables and worn-out wooden booths. If you sit by the waitresses' station, you may choke on smoke, as they sneak frequent puffs. The Decatur Street end is two small dining rooms with a campy, pseudo-nautical motif including bayou murals, ships' lamps, and captain's chairs. The place reeks and creaks with grease, the result of decades of frying chicken, shrimp, catfish, etc. The waitresses are friendly if a bit slow, but you won't mind because the joint is such a time trip, white bread and all. The food is Southern home-style, but there are Italian touches as well. The fried chicken is super.

Facing the Flea Market, **The Tourist Trap** (91 French Market Place 504/588–1588 $) deserves kudos for the gutsy name. The fare (arrayed on a steam table as in a school cafeteria) is seriously down-home with a dash of soul, and cheap, cheap, cheap. You can indulge in pork chops with macaroni and collards or fried chicken with red beans and rice, all served with cornbread. It's damned good, and afterward, you can go home and wait for your arteries to unclog. Surely you've been there, heard that, and bought a T-shirt already from **Hard Rock Cafe** (*418 N. Peters St. 504/ 529–5617 $$–$$$*), the ubiquitous loud eatery that has multiplied like rabbits from Boston to Bangkok. Actually, the Tennessee ribs in some kind of watermelon sauce are pretty tasty, as is the hickory-barbecued chicken. The kids (or maybe your inner kid) will love it even if you don't.

The long lines of tourists and locals outside **Café Maspero** (*601 Decatur St. 504/523–6250 $–$$*) say it all. This is the place for good, cheap sandwiches, as well as fried-oyster plates and some terrific onion soup. Lowly red-beans-and-rice gets a new spin with a zesty blend of sausage, ham, and spices. **La Madeleine** (*547 St. Ann St. 504/568–9950 $*) is usually jammed with tourists looking for something in the soup-and-salad vein. Since it's a country French café, that means quiche, salads, and French onion soup, or you could try the pizza Provençal topped with chicken, Swiss cheese, and calamata olives. They also have take-out pastries you can enjoy in Jackson Square just outside the big windows.

cajun... Paul Prudhomme almost single-handedly started the renaissance in Cajun food, most notably with his trademark blackened redfish. He brought his talents to New Orleans with **K-Paul's Louisiana Kitchen** (*416 Chartres St. 504/524–7394 $$$$*), which recently underwent a much-needed expansion. Despite the prices, the place is nothing fancy, but what you're paying for is the K-Paul experience, which is pretty unique. By all means try his signature fish, but don't overlook the gumbos. There's a gift shop selling Paul's cookbooks, spices, and other kitchen stuff. If it's Cajun you're after, this is the spot in New Orleans.

Alex Patout's Louisiana Restaurant (*221 Royal St. 504/525–7788 $$$–$$$$*) has been beloved for years by true devotees of Cajun cuisine. Chef Patout's Cajun heritage shows in the attention given to such classic fare as Louisiana court bouillon, made with the freshest-possible shrimp, crawfish, oysters, and Gulf fish in a velvety red sauce. If you've never had *cochon du lait*—slices of pork (the whole pig is slow-roasted) served with a home-style pork gravy—this is the place to try the dish so near and dear to Cajun hearts. Patout's wine list is among the best in town. Gigi Patout is the force behind **Patout's** (*501 Bourbon St. 504/529–4256 $$–$$$*) whose claim to the largest balcony on Bourbon Street is probably true. The can't-miss-it decor has been called zydeco ya-ya, and the food is just as out there. Oysters Gigi, obviously her signature dish, are recommended, along with the "paw paw" platter, which has something from almost every item on the menu.

cajun/creole... For something a little different, try the **Palm Court Jazz Cafe** (*1204 Decatur St. 504/525–0200 $$*), as popular for its music as for its food. The decor is distinctively belle epoque with a beautiful mahogany bar, grand piano, and lots of potted palms. The jazz is provided by veteran musicians who have been there and done that for years, and don't be surprised if someone decides to get up and "second line," including the waiters [see **music music music** sidebar]. The musicians keep your spirits moving while you dine on Crawfish Nantua, a fabulous concoction of crawfish tails in a brandy cream sauce, served over spinach pasta. The Chicken Clemenceau is another recommendation, along with—ah, yes, Shrimp Ambrosia.

One of the best bargains in the Quarter is the **Quarter Scene** (*900 Dumaine St. 504/522–6533 $–$$*). This unassuming neighborhood eatery has a good variety of native dishes including gumbo, superb seafood po' boys, and jambalaya, not to mention pecan-crusted catfish topped with a crawfish sauce. The breakfasts are also super, with such standbys as pain perdu, eggs Claiborne with shrimp and avocado, and the alligator-wrasslin' bayou breakfast with a chicken-fried steak that'll knock your socks off. This onetime haunt of Tennessee Williams (his favorite window table faced Dumaine Street) is a great spot for checking out the neighborhood denizens. Colorful murals by local artists splash the walls, and a fireplace takes the chill off the damp New Orleans winters.

Royal Cafe (*700 Royal St. 504/528–9086 $$$–$$$$*) occupies the Quarter's most-photographed gallery in the historic La Branche House. Chef George Daly is a local who knows his food. Start with his silky oyster/artichoke soup or the shrimp remoulade, and progress to a Caesar salad spiced up with Cajun shrimp. The crawfish-and-spinach salad is another winner, tossed with a vinaigrette made with Dijon mustard and apple-smoked bacon. For dessert, the Chocolate Desire will satisfy exactly that. If possible, grab an upstairs outdoor table so you can enjoy the live music and watch the human menagerie patronizing the tiny A&P across the street. If you're lucky, Doreen's Jazz New Orleans will be playing on the street, and, man, can that lady wail with a horn.

There's an awesome array of New Orleans dishes at **Père Antoine Restaurant & Bar** (*741 Royal St. 504/581–4478 $–$$*), including a good crawfish pie, which can actually be surprisingly hard to find. The crawfish and crab cakes with remoulade are good, as are a variety of gumbos, and there is a good selection of salads. The omelettes are stellar, especially those served with a rich, red Creole sauce that would almost make cardboard palatable. The ideal seats are in the curved area on the corner of Royal and St. Ann streets, separated from the sidewalk by a rail teeming with potted plants.

Original Pierre Maspero's (*440 Chartres St. 504/524– 8990 $–$$*) has Louisiana food from start to finish. Begin with the blackened-shrimp appetizer and head for the jambalaya or shrimp bisque. If you're in breakfast mode, try the French toast. Their muffalettas aren't as good as those at Central Grocery, but then, whose are? Pretty good fare in one of the most historic buildings in the city.

More Cajun/Italian than anything else, **The Napoleon House** (*500 Chartres St. 504/524–9752 $*) is a must-visit. Located in the 1797 Girod House, a National Historic Landmark, it was the site of an obviously failed plot to bring the Little Corporal to Louisiana, and has been a cafe since 1914. The Old World atmosphere is truly pervasive, with ancient patinas on crumbling walls, wooden arches, and overhead fans. A huge favorite with locals, who swear the Pimm's Cups are the best in town, it also offers a variety of fresh po' boys, a hot cheese-drenched ratatouille calzone, spinach-and-artichoke dip, and bruschetta. The jukebox is classical only, with operatic arias a popular choice.

Want to dine amid the sleaze of Bourbon Street? Check out **The Steak Pit** (*609 Bourbon St. 504/525–3406 $*), an unabashedly trashy joint that calls itself the "home of the huge beer." There's live music, and you'll be surprised at how tasty the food is. There are the steaks (that ribeye probably spent the night in tenderizer), but opt for the fried chicken, po' boys, or catfish. If you go with the flow in this place, you'll have a lot of fun, and it's definitely a hot spot for people-watching.

coffee... New Orleans' love affair with coffee is old and enduring. While the average American quaffs 1.5 cups a day, New Orleanians drink more than double that. African women owned the first coffee stands, which quickly became a social center for the Creoles, whose preference was for café au lait. Chicory, a relative of the dandelion, was eventually added, cutting the caffeine but losing none of the body. Packaged by Café Du Monde (CDM) and Community Coffee, chicory coffee is another New Orleans original, and one of the most popular tourist purchases.

The unquestioned granddaddy of all coffeehouses in New Orleans—and maybe the whole country—is the legendary **Café Du Monde** in the French Market **(800 *Decatur* St. 504/525–4544 $)**, whose trademark green-and-white awnings have been flapping in the river breezes for decades. Even the most jaded tourists wouldn't think of leaving without a cup of café au lait and some beignets, those diamond-shaped hole-less doughnuts smothered in powdered sugar. You're asking for trouble if you wear dark colors, a magnet for all that white stuff. The (intentionally) limited menu also lists coffee and hot chocolate. Just across Decatur Street from Jackson Square, with its line of mule-drawn carriages and the venerable Pontalba Apartments, the Café Du Monde is one of the best spots anywhere for watching the world go by. Since the place never closes, the clientele changes by the hour, with some really raunchy characters slithering out in the wee hours. It's pure magic at dawn when the cathedral bells chime, the Quarter is virtually deserted, and those Creole ghosts are skittering home.

The best place to sip a cup of joe while learning about the city's romance with coffee is **Kaldi's Coffee Museum and Coffee House** (*941 Decatur St. 504/586–8989 $*). Housed in an old bank building, the place has been around forever and unashamedly looks it. The ceilings soar two stories with walls bearing a mural of Kaldi himself, that celebrated North African goatherd who was among the first to sing coffee's rejuvenating praises. Kaldi's is another super people-watching spot, frequented mostly by locals who are happily left alone to peruse the *Times-Picayune* or the local free newspapers. If some look like they've spent their last buck on coffee, that's probably the case, but no one would think of asking them to leave.

If you need a break from antiquing, pop into **Café Beignet** (*334–B Royal St. 504/524–5530 $*), kick off your shoes, and relax over a cappuccino. It's a tiny space in the shadow of the ornate Vieux Carré police station, right next door. New Orleans' answer to Starbucks (which has mercifully not overwhelmed the city) is **CC's Gourmet Coffeehouse** (*941 Royal St. 504/581–6996 $*), a creation of the Community Coffee people, who have been slaking New Orleans' coffee thirst for decades. It's a high-ceilinged, airy room with overhead fans, overstuffed couches, and comfy tables and chairs for reading, conversing, or just enjoying the no-problem ambience. There's a wide range of coffees, plus daily specials and something called Mochassippi, fresh espresso blended with a skim-milk sauce, ice, and your choice of flavors. The pastries are tasty too, but if you're there in the afternoon, try the jambalaya quiche with roasted red peppers. CC's is big with local writers, students, and shopkeepers on a break. Weather permitting, which is most of the year, the tall shutters are thrown wide open, bringing you right to the street and vice versa.

A few blocks down the street is **Coffee, Tea Or... (630 St. Ann St. 504/522–0830 $)**, a cozy hideaway that will whisk you away from the Quarter's sometimes crowded sidewalks. You can enjoy the very intimate Spanish-style courtyard or sit indoors in one of two small rooms. They serve one of the best tuna sandwiches in town. Also close by is **Royal Blend Coffee & Tea House** (621 *Royal St. 504/523–2716 $)*, located at the end of a bricked carriageway. Tropical shadows play in the courtyard, pleasant for savoring fare purchased at the squeaky-clean indoor counter, where there are also a few tables in case the skies suddenly part. There are some knockout soups (always ask about the daily special) and salads, including the Caprese, which has vine-ripe tomatoes, baby greens tossed with olive oil and herbs, and fresh mozzarella. Their specialty sandwiches include the High-Rise, a juicy combo of corned beef, pastrami, and Swiss cheese served on fresh seven-grain bread, with generous smears of Creole mustard. Sipping tea here, it's easy to forget the bustle of the Quarter a few yards away.

Tucked so deep in the Quarter that few visitors ever find it is **Croissant d'Or Patisserie** (617 *Ursulines St. 504/524–4663 $)*. It's a sweet secret that should be shared because of its delicious pastries, quiches, sandwiches, and coffees so dear to locals' hearts. The adjacent bakery ensures the freshness of everything in those tantalizing display cases. This onetime Italian ice cream parlor may make you think you're inside a wedding cake, except for the lingering Mardi Gras memorabilia and, for some reason, an antique carousel horse. There's a spacious dining room where patrons play musical chairs as individual parties swell and dwindle. A quiet outdoor courtyard in the rear has a reproduction of Brussels' *Manneken-Pis*, the naughty boy happily tinkling into the fountain.

Cigars are king at **Cafe Havana** (*842 Royal St. 504/ 569–9006 $*), where you can browse the well-stocked humidor for the stogie of your choice. Cheapies or vintage, they're all there for your puffing pleasure in the Latino-flavored café area with its fun faux palms, comfy rocking chairs, and overhead fans. French doors open to the street, allowing for needed ventilation. Patrons can also rent humidor lockers to keep their smokes fresh. Order some café au lait, lean back, and puff away as you contemplate the ceiling painting entitled *Let There Be Light* by artist Charlie Wahrenberger—a smoker's take on Michelangelo's *Creation of Adam* in the Sistine Chapel.

creole... Three grandes dames dominate the Creole restaurant scene. The oldest and most famous is unquestionably **Antoine's** (*713 St. Louis St. 504/581–4422 $$$–$$$$*), which has been under single-family ownership longer than any restaurant in the world. Dating from the 1840s, it's the home of Oysters Rockefeller, Foch, and Bienville, and pommes de terre soufflées, and it has been called a living culinary museum. Actually, it's a vast, labyrinthine establishment with mostly windowless rooms and red walls. Royalty, presidents, and celebrities have made the pilgrimage, but these days, frankly—it's a mess. Busloads of tourists storm the doors, the maître d' can be utterly indifferent (even if you have reservations), and signature dishes like elegant *pompano en papillote* can resemble seafood mush in a paper sack. Sad to say, Antoine's is coasting on its old reputation these days. You'd be much wiser choosing **Arnaud's (813 *Bienville* St. 504/523–5433 $$$–$$$$)**, where tall windows and glistening tile floors beckon warmly, as do chandeliers reminiscent of those grand Mississippi steamboats. The Shrimp Arnaud in a tangy remoulade sauce is an absolute must. Also outstanding are the trout meunière, the aromatic turtle soup, and the grand Chicken Pontalba: ham and veggies sautéed in butter, covered with crisply fried chunks of chicken, and topped with béarnaise sauce. Sundays there's a prix-fixe jazz brunch with wandering musicians who are never too jaded to play "Basin Street Blues" as if for the first time. For the finale, order the Bananas Foster, dramatically flambéed tableside. It's perfect for romance.

The third Creole power player is **Galatoire's (209 *Bourbon* St. 504/525–2021 $$$–$$$$)** which, with its gently whirring overhead fans and white walls, hasn't changed much since it opened in 1905. From the get-go this place has drawn an old-guard clientele of uptown bankers and lawyers. All have their favorite waiters, who greet them by name and hustle them to preferred tables, and both parties would prefer keeping things this way forever. The food is fine, especially the trout Marguery, crabmeat à la maison, and crabmeat Sardou, but unless you're one of the regulars, the service is hardly preferential. Rumor has it Galatoire's is about to start taking limited reservations, but for now you'll have to stand on the street like everyone else.

Breakfast at **Brennan's** (*417 Royal St. 504/525–9711 $$$–$$$$*) is a long-standing tradition, and no wonder. This 1795 French Quarter landmark, with its distinctive pink exterior, houses 12 dining rooms and arguably has the most extensive wine selection in the city. Breakfast is such an extravaganza that you may not want to eat again until the next day, if then. Eggs Hussarde is a classic, with hollandaise and marchand de vin sauce over grilled ham and poached eggs. A classy indulgence, especially washed down with champagne. Don't overlook dinner, your chance to savor Buster Crabs Béarnaise or spicy crawfish Sardou served atop artichoke bottoms and creamed spinach, and drenched in hollandaise sauce. **Mr. B's Bistro** (*201 Royal St. 504/523–2078 $$$–$$$$*) is another reliable Brennan's venture. By day it's noisy with the business crowd; by night, the bar hums and the floor bustles as both mood and clientele change. For starters, there are perfect spring rolls and a tangy smoked-rabbit gumbo. The pasta jambalaya is a perennial fave, as are the gumbo ya-ya and grilled fish. New Orleans–style barbecued shrimp is probably not what you think, so steer clear unless you're prepared to peel them and sop up the peppery butter sauce with hunks of French bread, which is messy, tedious—and, oh yes, worth every bite. Finish things off with profiteroles and café au lait. Try for a window seat on Royal Street with a view of the beaux-arts facade of the old Monteleone Hotel.

Broussard's (*819 Conti St. 504/581–3866 $$$$*) is another hit for traditional Creole fare and a local hangout too. The elegant but understated dining room faces a charming patio thriving with tropical greenness. You might begin with the luscious Louisiana oyster trio before moving on to the tournedos of beef Marcus or grilled pompano Napoleon, which is accompanied by grilled scallops and shrimp layered between puff pastry and drizzled with a mustard-caper sauce. **Tujague's** (*823 Decatur St. 504/525–8676 $$$$*)—pronounced "too-jags"—has been pleasing Creole palates since before the Civil War. This plain, unpretentious place is locally famous for its succulent brisket of beef boiled with onions, peppers, celery, and carrots, and accented with a special horseradish sauce. They also serve their own micro-brewed Tujague's beer, and the menu changes daily.

Emeril Lagasse followed the success of his eponymous uptown eatery with **NOLA** (*534 St. Louis St. 504/522–6652 $$$–$$$$*), the acronym New Orleanians have long used for a return address. The historic charm outside doesn't prepare you for the high-tech industrial interior, but it's appropriate for a chef who's putting his own contemporary spin on haute Creole cuisine. The goodies include Gulf shrimp with bacon and pepperoni made in-house, and delectable duck fajitas. The noise level can sometimes be annoying, but nothing seems to faze Emeril's ever-growing legions of fawning foodies.

The Gumbo Shop (*630 St. Peter St. 504/525–1486 $–$$$*) has been dishing it out for years, and the lines tell you they're doing something right. A carriageway leads through glass doors to a small brick and slate courtyard and a dining room with murals and antique mirrors. The gumbos are excellent, and there's even a vegan version, gumbo z'herbes, created for Lenten abstainers. Also good are the po' boys and the red beans and rice with andouille. Legend says this is one of the buildings to survive the Great Fire of 1788.

Court of Two Sisters (*613 Royal St. 504/522–7261 $$$–$$$$*) has the largest courtyard in the Quarter, the better to accommodate the tourists arriving by the bus-load. Their gimmick is pure atmosphere, with live jazz daily and a vast courtyard swarming with tropical plants, flowers, willows, and even a wishing well. Locals avoid it like a yellow-fever plague, sniffing that the food suffers because it's mass-produced. They're right. This place is all ambience and no substance. The menu may be huge, but it's all done better elsewhere.

eclectic... A longtime Quarter landmark, the tony **Pelican Club** (*312 Exchange Alley 504/523–1504 $$$–$$$$*) is tightly run by chef Richard Hughes, who flirts with a fusion of Louisiana and New American, with a hint of Asian. It rises to new heights with a seared yellowfin tuna served with Gulf shrimp over rice noodles in a red pepper wasabi and teriyaki glaze. Also great is the filet mignon with a merlot-madeira reduction accompanied by local mushrooms, haricots verts, new potatoes, and mashed yams. Incidentally, Exchange Alley was once home to New Orleans' grand fencing masters, who taught self-defense when dueling was in style.

french... Believe it or not, there's only one classic French restaurant in the entire Vieux Carré. By local standards **Louis XVI** in the St. Louis Hotel (*730 Bienville St. 504/581–7000 $$$$*) is a relative newcomer, having opened its doors in 1971, but it's become an award-winner under chef Antoine Camenzuli. It's hard not to be swept up by the quietly calculated elegance—rich striated columns with gilded capitals, a vaulted ceiling, indirect lighting illuminating fine artworks, grand floral arrangements, and exquisite table settings. A Mediterranean-style courtyard provides a final flourish as you savor filet de boeuf Saint Hébert and choose from an impressive wine list. Red meat rules here, but don't overlook the superb filet de poisson Louisiane graced with sautéed bananas, red bell peppers, and beurre meunière, or the escargots Louis XVI, snails sautéed in a light garlic butter with hazelnuts, pecans, and almonds. For the grand finale, choose Cherries Jubilee, Crêpes Suzette or Bananas Foster, all prepared tableside. A romantic evening is as guaranteed as the great service.

international... Susan Spicer of **Bayona** (430 *Dauphine St.* 504/525–4455 $$$–$$$$) is an established star in a galaxy of gifted New Orleans chefs. Her restaurant is housed in a modest but tastefully appointed Creole cottage with some alfresco dining on a patio shaded by banana trees. Her signature grilled duck, thinly sliced and served in a reduction of sherry vinegar and shallots, is accompanied by a spicy pepper jelly and a cashew butter and red-pepper *brunois*. Other recommendations include the grape-leaf-wrapped salmon with couscous and olive vinaigrette, grilled shrimp, and a delicate garlic soup. If you prefer intimate bistro dining, try **DiPiazza's** (337 *Dauphine St.* 504/525–3335 $$$–$$$$). Largely undiscovered by tourists, DiPiazza's is cherished by locals who admire the talents of chefs Chip Martinson and Steve D'Angelo. The menu changes frequently, but recent highlights included smoked seared salmon, seared duck breast with smoked wild mushroom risotto, duck and shrimp pasta, and a humdinger lasagna. Desserts tend to be in the gelato family, which is a perfect finale to such gustatory riches. **The Rib Room** in the Royal Orleans Hotel (*621 St. Louis St. 504/529–7045 $$$$*) is a red-meat lover's oasis in a town largely given over to worshipping everything with fins and shells. Unless you're seated by the windows, the room is large and comfortably dark, with a low-key decor. The prime rib, Chateaubriand and rack of lamb are appropriately succulent, but you might want to begin with the grilled shrimp. Locals pack the place for lunch, but at night it's mostly overrun by tourists. Grab a window seat for some fun people-watching on this antiques-store-packed stretch of Royal Street.

Chef Horst Pfeiffer's **Bella Luna** (*914 N. Peters St. 504/529–1583 $$$$*) has a view seriously competing with his food. Overlooking a grand bend in the Mississippi, it's the most romantic restaurant vista in the Quarter, especially by night, when the glittering riverboats put out for dinner cruises. If you're by the window, you can also see the riverfront streetcars rolling along the levee. Trademark specialties include crab cakes, homemade fettuccine, sautéed redfish, and occasionally a truly memorable chicken-fried venison. A tasty variety of breads is served with butter swirled on a slab of stone, and Pfeiffer's herbs are grown in the garden of the nearby Ursuline convent—these are just two of the touches that make Bella Luna so special. If you're not seated in the upriver dining room, take a peek at the glamorous trompe l'oeil mural.

The Bistro at Maison de Ville (*733 Toulouse St. 504/528–9206 $$$$*) is one of the Quarter's enduring secrets. The tiny dining room will transport you to Paris, with its dark paneled walls, snowy white tablecloths, and fine wine list. The choices are challenging, as country French collides tastefully with south Louisiana, but consider the pan-seared medallions of venison served with pumpkin spaetzle and juniper-berry port glaze. If you're in the mood to go alfresco, request a table in the cozy tropical courtyard in the rear.

G&E Courtyard Grill *(1113 Decatur St. 504/528–9376* **$$$–$$$$)** boasts one of the best courtyards in the Quarter as well as a smart front dining room with Tuscan-type frescoed walls and photos of chef/owner Michael Uddo's Italian ancestors. Overhead fans for summer and mounted heaters for winter make year-round outdoor dining a reality. Uddo has organic produce flown in from California, giving dishes like Caesar salad with flash-fried oysters a startling freshness. Virtually everything, from grilled rainbow trout to seafood pasta, is delicious, but his rotisserie fare really shines. The sesame-crusted duckling is superb.

Peristyle *(1041 Dumaine St. 504/593–9535 $$$$)*, in the Lower Quarter, is another largely undiscovered spot, a comfortable space with a grand bar as you enter and dark, clubby paneled walls throughout. Former Emeril protégée Anne Kearney is the young chef working wonders with such dishes as seared grouper with goat-cheese gnocchi and poached Louisiana oysters. The roasted tuna with pine nuts and celeriac gratin is superb, and the celery root remoulade is definitely a surprise. The iffy neighborhood hasn't deterred the crowds, but it's best to cab it late at night and avoid Rampart Street altogether.

If you like your food served in decor ranging from the sublime to the ridiculous, two venues will suit you just fine. In the former category is **House of Blues** *(225 Decatur St. 504/529–2583 $$–$$$$)*, an inspired restoration—and part of the nightclub of the same name next door [see **music/clubs**]—boasting a mind-boggling art collection. Quarterites usually don't cotton to chain restaurants (basically outlawed in this neighborhood), but this one keeps 'em coming back for more. The reason: The multicultural menu offers barbecued ribs Memphis-style, crawfish cheesecake appetizers, and a chicken sandwich clearly inspired by Indian tandoori cooking. And live music, too!

On the other end of the spectrum is **Planet Hollywood** *(620 Decatur St. 504/522–7826 $$–$$$)*, which looks like a movie star's dream—or nightmare, depending on your take on it. Take it in stride, though, and enjoy a menu that wisely strays from standard P.H. fare. Supposedly Paris and New Orleans are the only two branches allowed to include local fare, and it's really not bad. There's a nice shrimp-and-crawfish lasagna and a well-executed salmon osso bucco with crawfish risotto.

italian... Despite a large Italian population, there aren't that many terrific Italian restaurants in town. An exception is **Bacco** *(310 Chartres St. 504/522–2426 $$$)*, with equally beautiful food and decor. One of the famed Brennan restaurants, this gracefully appointed bistro features delicately lit arches, vaulted ceilings, neoclassical murals and faux-stone floors that quietly transport you back to the old country. The cuisine is Italian-inspired, with a hint of haute Creole. The menu includes a fine traditional antipasto and a sublime grilled pork tenderloin. The very rich tiramisù is a killer, served in a large cappuccino cup and crowned with cocoa-flavored zabaglione. There are three dining rooms, the one on the right with a view of Chartres Street being the noisiest, and if you don't eat in the one on the left, take a peek at the exquisitely executed faux glamor.

The bland, industrial-looking cube at the corner of St. Philip and Chartres streets houses **Irene's Cuisine** (539 St. Philip St. 504/529–8811 $$–$$$). A relative newcomer to the neighborhood, the lines of patrons awaiting entrance haven't let up since it replaced the venerable Miss Ruby's a few years ago. One reason is the portions. Irene really knows how to dish it out, and the surprise is that it's all pretty good. Veal lovers will have trouble choosing among the Marsala, piccata, and sorrentino, all of which are super. Be aware, however, that service can suffer when they get busy, and surly waiters can spoil the tastiest meal. **Mona Lisa** (1212 Royal St. 504/522–6746 $–$$) occupies two narrow rooms with walls flaunting endless repetitions of Leonardo's mysteriously smiling muse. The fare is quite reasonable and includes good, fresh salads served with slices of juicy white pizza pretending to be bread. The spinach lasagna is recommended, and the Mardi Gras pasta—seafood tossed with pasta in a tangy sauce, and almost too much to eat—remains a perennial favorite.

mexican/cuban... One look at the **Country Flame** (620 Iberville St. 504/522–1138 $) and you'll worry you're back in every border town you've ever fled. The flaking, fading terra-cotta-and-turquoise exterior looks absolutely worn out, despite efforts to perk things up with brightly painted flowers and vines. Inside, there's a bleary mish-mash of beer signs, picnic tables, and Mexican stuff, a can-

tina right here in the French Quarter. The floor looks like it
hasn't been mopped since the last Mardi Gras, and don't
hit the restrooms unless you just gotta. So much for appear-
ances. The food is damned good and reasonable too, a standard Mexican menu with the usual combos served with
rice and beans. If anything stands out it's the fajitas, both
chicken and beef, grilled to perfection and served up with
fresh tortillas ready to be stuffed. The clientele is a mixed
bag of tourists and knowing locals, and the proximity of
tables means you may end up yakking with each other.

seafood... One of the newest stars in the Brennan family galaxy is **Ralph Brennan's Redfish Grill** (115 Bourbon
St. 504/598–1200 $$–$$$$), on the first floor of the
Chateau Sonesta. Start with spring rolls and proceed to the
melt-in-your-mouth barbecued oysters or sweet-potato
catfish served with sautéed greens and a tangy andouille
cream drizzle. Ralph definitely knows what he's doing. For
almost a century, **Acme Oyster House** (724 Iberville St.
504/522–5973 $) has been shucking and jiving for tourists
and locals alike. Nothing fancy about this joint, which is
fine with the patrons, who're here for one reason only:
oysters. Although both pollution in the Gulf and hepatitis
warnings have made some people leery, raw oysters are
still a mainstay here, washed down with pitchers of cold
beer. They're also available lightly battered and fried. Here's
your chance to try gumbo poopa, a hollowed-out loaf of
French bread sloshed full of gumbo. There are more of those
slippery, satiny critters at **Felix's Restaurant & Oyster Bar**
(739 Iberville St. 504/522–4440 $–$$). It can be a bit daunt-
ing, with its noisy crowds (almost everyone's a character),

sometimes erratic service, and general air of chaos, but ignore all that and slurp away. If someone in your group is an oysterphobe, steer them to the grilled fish, chicken, steaks, or, as locals say, the spaghettis.

Ralph & Kacoo's (519 Toulouse St. 504/522–5226 $–$$$) is a huge seafood emporium with more seafood variations than you can imagine. The decor starts with nautical touches, but eventually segues into a hodgepodge of taxidermy, assorted flotsam and jetsam, and some grandiose Mardi Gras costumes bound to make you gape. The fare is good, plentiful, and reasonable, and don't load up on those hot hushpuppy starters or you won't have room for the belly-busting seafood platters, crawfish étouffée, or barbecued shrimp. Don't be put off if there's a line; these people know how to move customers as well as satisfy them.

bars

If New York is the city that never sleeps, old New Orleans is notorious for snoozing by day and boozing by night. Many places are open 24 hours a day, meaning "Last call for alcohol" is something you'll never hear. World-famous Bourbon Street (named for French royalty, not the liquor) is unquestionably Party Central, offering both fine music clubs and outright dives. You can sit indoors or out, swill your pleasure in daiquiri shops, strip joints, jazz clubs, and Creole courtyards, or simply grab a brew from a sidewalk cubbyhole and join the hedonistic hordes wandering the tawdry strip between Iberville and Dumaine streets. Bourbon is the street that has seen it all, and then seen it all again.

You can pop into **Pat O'Brien's** (718 St. Peter St. 504/ 525–4823) for refreshments while someone holds your place in line for Preservation Hall [see **music/clubs**] next door, but be warned that you'll want to stay awhile. This place is a tourist magnet, but locals enjoy it simply because it's so much fun. Once those rum-based Hurricanes— served in 29-ounce hurricane-lamp-style glasses—begin to flow, things get festive, especially at the piano bar. The crowd on the patio is pretty jovial, too. Pat O's is no place to be shy.

A rare building left from the French period, and the best way to envision what the old town looked like before the Great Fires of 1788 and 1794, **Lafitte's Blacksmith Shop** (941 Bourbon St. 504/523–0066) is reputedly the oldest bar in America, and one of the most photographed buildings in the city. Take a walk-through and stay for a drink if you like the quaint, decidedly musty atmosphere. It appeared in the film *Walk on the Wild Side* starring Laurence Harvey and Capucine.

The Bombay Club and Martini Bar (830 Conti St. 504/586–0972) is duly celebrated for its martinis. The bar decor is veddy British indeed, complete with memorabilia from the Duke and Duchess of Windsor. Ports, cognacs, single-malt scotches, and over 70 varieties of martini are served. Unfortunately, the kitchen is no longer open, prompting loyal patrons to bring their own hors d'oeuvres.

The Daiquiri Shoppe (911 Decatur St. 504/523–3257) offers a staggering variety of these frozen treats in a near-authentic Vieux Carré setting. The building is actually a reproduction that recently rose from a parking lot and won design awards for its sensitivity to surrounding historical structures. This neat corner spot, opening on two sides,

mardi gras

America's image of Mardi Gras is of a wild weekend of massive crowds mobbing floats for trinkets called "throws" and Bourbon Street revelers flashing, hurling, and getting blind drunk. But this is only a fraction of the whole picture.

Mardi Gras, meaning "Fat Tuesday" in French, is a prehistoric pagan festival created to celebrate the earth's fertility, at which animals and humans were sacrificed in the belief that their spilled blood would replenish the soil. The Greeks and Romans got into the act with their religious Lupercalia, an orgiastic celebration of pleasure and pain. (The word "carnival" comes from the Latin *carne vale* meaning "Flesh, farewell!"; New Orleanians use it to refer to the entire season.) Christianity almost killed it, but Mardi Gras survived by wisely incorporating aspects of the new religion. The first day of the carnival season is Twelfth Night, January 6, which celebrates the Feast of the Epiphany, or coming of the Magi. It ends on Shrove Tuesday, the day before Ash Wednesday, which ushers in Lent, a 40-day period of fasting and self-denial. The length of the carnival season is based on Easter. It may be as short as four weeks or as long as seven. And as soon as one Mardi Gras ends, preparations start for the next.

At Twelfth Night parties, king cakes are served containing a tiny plastic baby representing the infant Jesus. Whoever finds the baby is king or queen for the evening and must give the next party. Krewes are social clubs who stage the parades and balls. Over 60 currently parade in the greater New Orleans area. When they roll, locals studiously avoid the crush of Canal Street, sensibly preferring to watch them uptown or in the burbs. They range from amateurish affairs to the smashing extravaganzas of super-krewes like Bacchus, Endymion, Orpheus, and Rex, with members numbering in the hundreds. There's a krewe for everyone, black or white, male or female, gay or straight—even dog lovers. The Krewe of Barkus includes costumed pets paraded through the Quarter trailed by a clean-up detachment with chrome pooper scoopers.

Then there are the lavish balls reigned over by local royalty. The most exclusive is Comus, restricted to uptown society and a sort of ersatz cotillion. The Endymion ball is held in the Superdome and reaches a fever peak when the parade rolls right into the enormous stadium. The gay Armeinius Ball is a lavish Vegas-style affair with amazingly extravagant costumes and tableaux. Some of the most elaborate costumes are worn by the Mardi Gras Indians, black men parading in honor of the Louisiana Indians who sheltered slaves in the early days. Tribes such as the Wild Magnolias, Black Eagles, and Gold Star Hunters startle motorists and pedestrians when they appear out of nowhere, outrageous feathery visions unlike anything this side of Carnaval in Rio.

In 2000, Mardi Gras will fall on March 7. Tickets are available to most of the balls. All are strictly black-tie.

offers sanctuary when your tootsies are tired from all that
walking. The signature D.O.A. is bound to be restorative, at
least temporarily.

Arnaud's Cigar Bar (813 Bienville St. 504/523–5433)
has a superb selection of tobaccos and fine drink, including rare bourbons, scotches, cognacs, and ports.

music/clubs

The range of the Quarter's music venues is extensive, and
increasingly difficult to categorize due to the ever-growing
varieties of crossover as well as club owners' efforts to
please increasingly larger audiences. But whether your taste
runs to traditional New Orleans jazz, Dixieland, Cajun/
Zydeco, rock 'n' roll, R&B, or country, the choices in the
French Quarter are overwhelming.

Music lover or no, a first trip to New Orleans is incom-
plete without a visit to the legendary **Preservation Hall**
(726 St. Peter St. 504/523–8939), which has been here
since God was a child. It has no a/c, no food or drink service, little standing room, and some of the world's most
uncomfortable wooden benches. You sit so close to your
neighbor you can smell their sweat, but all that means
nothing to those making the pilgrimage to this holiest of
traditional-jazz holies. The admission is $3 and you'll have
to pony up an additional $5 if you want to hear "Saints."
That and the probable wait in line to get in are a small
price to pay for being in the presence of real musical
greatness.

There's more traditional jazz at the **Palm Court Jazz**

Café (1204 *Decatur St.* 504/525–0200), and some good
food, too. Be warned that these old guys knock off fairly
early, meaning come midnight you're gonna be looking
elsewhere for music. Making one of the most flagrant
efforts to sucker the unwary tourist is **Maison Bourbon
Dedicated to the Preservation of Jazz** (641 *Bourbon St.*
504/522–8818). The Dixieland jazz actually turns out to
be genuine and good, but Preservation Hall it ain't. **Funky
Pirate** (727 *Bourbon St.* 504/523–1960) is a quintessential
Bourbon Street joint—loud, smoky, jumping. If the music
doesn't get you, try one of their concoctions, and hope
you'll remember how much fun you had.

Unless you're looking for it, you might miss **Fritzel's**
(733 *Bourbon St.* 504/561–0432), a small, dark spot crank-
ing out some of the best light jazz in the neighborhood.
Housed in an 1836 building, it's been around for a quarter
of a century, and late night can bring in musicians hungry
to jam. They have a good selection of German beers, wines,
and schnapps. Other spots you might want to poke your
ears into include **Andrew Jaeger's House of Seafood**
(622 *Conti St.* 504/522–4964), which has some hot local
R&B nightly, and **21 Supper Club** (329 *Chartres St.* 504/
598–2121), a theater-turned-supper-club featuring traditional and Dixieland jazz.

You'll find a variety of sounds, almost always hot, at
House of Blues (225 *Decatur St.* 504/529–2624), one of
the Quarter's newer clubs and an immediate smash when
it opened. This is the place to see some of the best acts in
the biz, both local and from around the country. You gotta
love that dramatically lit, perfectly detailed shotgun house
facade and the bluesy, albeit a bit self-conscious, atmos-

phere. Here's your chance to see Cowboy Junkies, Beau Jocque and the Zydeco Hi-Rollers, Meat Beat Manifesto, and more. The Sunday gospel brunch became a local tradition almost instantly, making reservations essential.

There's another mixed musical bag at **Howlin' Wolf** (*828 S. Peters St. 504/523–2551*). This is the spot for both local bands and road groups hanging their hats for a couple of gigs. Alternative, blues, jazz, rock 'n' roll—you never know who's going to take the stage. Monday is acoustic open-mike night. Jazz and brass-band aficionados from all over the world flock to **Donna's Bar & Grill** (*800 N. Rampart St. 504/596–6914*). Hit the place any night of the week around eight o'clock and you'll hear traditional brass band music you thought couldn't be found anywhere but on CD. The sound at Donna's is the real deal.

The newest club and talk of the town is **Storyville District** (*125 Bourbon St. 504/410–1000*), a phenomenal 10,000-square-foot music-food complex conjuring the glitzy, tawdry days of Storyville, the former notorious redlight district. **Jazz Alley** is a movie set of bygone glories including a split-level bar in a Creole cottage, oak tables and a storefront mixing faux accessories with the real thing. The smaller **Corner Club** is a jazzy symphony in black, white, and chrome with an enormous jazz mural, and the **Parlor Room** evokes a bordello with red velvet curtains and photos of Storyville denizens by Ernest Belloq. Each room serves fine food by Ralph Brennan. Groove with some jazz while savoring marinated crab claws, spicy fried pecans or tasso and green-onion beignets. This is the best blend of New Orleans food and music you'll find outside Jazzfest itself. A must.

Jimmy Buffet's **Margaritaville** (*1104 Decatur St. 504/592–2560*) is the local aviary for Jimmy's flocks of devoted parrotheads. The walls are splashed with tropical exotica, including parrots of course, and it's the sort of loopy place you can't help but enjoy. The bands start playing around 2 p.m. with a slate including blues, funk, and lots of R&B. Regulars include Eddie Bo, Coco Robicheaux, and the parrot-meister himself when he's in town. An adjacent shop sells Margaritaville memorabilia. The third and newest branch of the Tipitina empire, **Tipitina's French Quarter** (*233 N. Peters St. 504/895–8477*) makes its music more accessible with this location. It hasn't any of the original Tip's colorful funk, but it scores huge with showcase nights starring such luminaries as Cyril Neville and Allen Toussaint. Kermit Ruffins' Big Band Matinee may entertain while you're eating brunch.

Funky Butt at Congo Square (*714 North Rampart St. 504/558–0872*) is a throwback to the honkytonks that once lined this famous street. Named after the legendary Buddy Bolden's hall, it offers hot food, cool jazz, and hard brass. Local music queen Marva Wright plays here, and Irvin Mayfield and Kermit Ruffins have been known to drop in for a late-night jam or two.

gay clubs... The corner of St. Ann and Bourbon streets is ground zero for gay clubs. **Oz** (*800 Bourbon St. 504/593–9491*) is arguably the best dance club in town, a cavernous space that's usually packed with shirtless dudes buffed to the max. Nearly naked male go-go dancers commandeer the upper levels. The light shows are glitz city and lots of fun. Literally across the street is the **Bourbon Pub**

(803 Bourbon St. 504/529–2107), a huge bar opening onto St. Ann Street as well as Bourbon. There's a constant flow of people, both watchers and watched, streaming through the French doors thrown wide to the sidewalks, and the crowd runs the gamut from twinkies to daddies with a dash of Quarter clones, lesbians, and straights. Upstairs is the **Parade Disco** *(entrance beneath the Fleur De Lis sign)*, a good-sized dance space that's popular for special events. On weekends, the overflow crowds from these two bars turn the intersection into a noisy gay block party.

A block down Bourbon is **Lafitte's-In-Exile** *(901 Bourbon St. 504/522–8397)*, the city's most famous and popular gay bar. It's almost exclusively male and usually jam-packed with guys busily fraternizing, watching the TV monitors (a campy mix of music videos, TV sitcoms, and old movie clips), or playing pool upstairs, where patrons over-whelmed by the smoke and noise can also find refuge on the spacious wraparound galleries. An eternal flame burns in memory of their homophobic ousting from the original site, now Lafitte's Blacksmith Shop. These guys may for-give, but they sure don't forget. **Good Friends** *(740 Dauphine St. 504/566–7191)* is an inviting space boasting a huge, handsomely carved mahogany bar complete with urns containing neon calla lilies. It's a friendly neighbor-hood bar, good for meeting locals and enjoying the upstairs piano bar on Sundays. The enthusiastic singalongs some-times blow the roof off with show tunes dating back to the year one. The Levi's/leather crowd heads for **Rawhide 2010** *(740 Burgundy St. 504/525–8106)*, as do cowboys, college kids, and a smattering of curious tourists. Recently renovated, Rawhide has pool tables and video poker, but no dancing. This is the turnaround point for pub-crawling gay men who work their way back and forth from Lafitte's-In-Exile.

buying stuff

The Quarter is a shopper's paradise. The choices are almost endless, the variety exhilarating, and best of all, there's something for everyone's pocket. Whether you want to pay $38,000 for a fussy Louis XIV commode or a couple of bucks for a voodoo doll, it's all here, and then some.

Royal Street is synonymous with antiques shops, almost solid from Bienville Street to St. Louis Street, and indeed there's an awesome selection of some of the most glamorous objets d'art you'll find this side of Paris. For most, unfortunately, the cost is somewhere in the stratosphere. Hang around in one of these places and check out the gasps of disbelief when unsuspecting tourists turn over a price tag—especially when they learn the item's a reproduction. Obviously these prices are what the market will bear, because Royal Street has been booming for years, but remember it doesn't cost a cent to browse through all that faded glory. During the day, it's a pedestrian mall, and thus closed to traffic.

Astronomically priced antiques aside, there are also plenty of colorful specialty shops with down-to-earth prices. Talented Louisiana artists abound, and their fine work is on display everywhere from tony galleries to quirky boutiques. These unique pieces pay homage to everything from jazz, cemeteries, Mardi Gras, and hot sauce, to crawfish, alligators, and even mosquitoes. And don't forget voodoo. So here's a selection of what's available, but remember the true charm of the Quarter is only discovered by serendipitous exploring. This is especially true of its stores.

antiques... The venerable **Dixon & Dixon** *(237 Royal St. 504/524–0282, 319 Chartres St. 504/528–3680)* is perhaps the most famous New Orleans antiques emporium, with a vast collection of European furniture, paintings, and clocks. Prices are just what you'd expect, and then some. **Gerald D. Katz** *(505 Royal St. 504/524–5050)* is another venerable institution, with antique jewelry and precious objets. The **French Antique Shop, Inc.** *(225 Royal St. 504/524–9861)* is exactly that, a madhouse jumble of Gallic merchandise that would take forever to sift through. Browsing just might yield something you've been after for years. **Keil's** *(325 Royal St. 504/522–4552)* has been around for a hundred years with English as well as French antiques.

Harper's *(610 Toulouse St. 504/592–1996)* showcases European and American pieces from the 18th, 19th, and 20th centuries, plus pianos, paintings, silver, crystal, and more. It's a vast emporium well worth exploring for unusual treasures. **Harris Antiques** *(623 Royal St. 504/523–1605)* offers a large collection of furniture with a special focus on statuary, bronzes, and epergnes. **M.S. Rau** *(630 Royal St. 504/523–5660)* has fine American, English, and Asian pieces, plus glassware, silver, and a truly dazzling selection of stock chandeliers to choose from. At **Manheim Galleries** *(403–409 Royal St. 504/568–1901)* you can buy reproductions made on the premises or select from a vast collection of vintage French, English, and Continental pieces. Excellent jade. At **L.M.S. Fine Arts and Antiques** (729 *Royal St.* 504/529–3774) the focus is on Russian antiques. **Animal Art Antiques** (617 *Chartres St.* 504/529–4407) houses an enormous and captivating menagerie of majolica, palissy, massier, furniture, paintings, and objets, all with animal themes. These one-of-a-kind pieces are stunning indeed, but the prices for these rare beasties may give you apoplexy. **Lucullus** (610 *Chartres St.* 504/528–9620) specializes in culinary antiques for cooking, dining, and imbibing. Where else but New Orleans would you find an antiques store devoted to food?! Or one where you can get a psychic reading? Try **Madam Laveau's Antiques** (1000 *Bourbon St.* 504/581–4000). Ask for Arthur.

books/records...
The French Quarter was once famed for its variety of quaint, vintage bookstores brimming with beguiling out-of-print and rare books. Only a handful remain, charming reminders of a world before slick chains began dispensing cappuccino alongside books. These quiet islands are a perfect retreat from the sudden tropical rainstorms that periodically rush in from the Gulf to send everyone scurrying. **La Librairie** (823 *Chartres St.* 504/525–4837) is just off Jackson Square and has been in business for over three decades. In addition to antiquarian books, it also has a small selection of old postcards and prints, splendid browsing, and a helpful staff. Its much larger partner, **Beckham's Bookshop** (228 *Decatur St.* 504/522–9875) has two stories of secondhand books—some 50,000 volumes—plus 10,000 classical records. You

could spend an entire day here and barely scratch the surface. For scholarly tomes, try **Crescent City Books** (*204 Chartres St.* 504/524–4997). **Dauphine Street Books** (*410 Dauphine St.* 504/529–2333) has a good selection of old and out-of-print books and usually a box of cheapies perched out front to entice passersby.

Tucked away on Pirate's Alley by the cathedral is **Faulkner House Books** (*624 Pirate's Alley* 504/524–2940), a tiny, tidy shop in a house where William Faulkner briefly lived and wrote. In addition to his works, it carries contemporary books as well as rare and first editions. Deep in the Lower Quarter is **Kaboom Books** (*901 Barracks St.* 504/529–5780), a veritable rabbit warren of raw wooden shelves with an amiable staff who somehow know where everything is and are always ready to shepherd you through the maze. One corner has chairs and stacks of *The New York Times Book Review* for your perusal, and a pleasant view of Cabrini Park across the street. This is an especially good place to find that old mystery you wanted to read.

clothing... Gentlemen's Quarter, Ltd. and Ladies Quarter (*232 Royal St.* 504/522–7139) once catered to the

carriage trade. Although this smart shop still carries a few men's items such as vests, ties, shirts, and cuff links, it's now primarily for women. Owner Jerry Graves makes frequent buying trips to New York, and what he brings back flies off the rack. The look is urbane chic, but the prices aren't. A much smaller **Ladies Quarter** (*427 Royal St.* 504/596–3000) carries more jewelry than clothes.

Fleur de Paris (*712 Royal St.* 504/525–1899) is the unquestioned favorite for local ladies and tourists alike.

There is an amazing amount of merchandise draped, propped, and hung in this charming corner store. They carry both designer and vintage clothing, one-of-a-kind hats, and fancy silk lingerie. The inspired window displays have been stopping traffic for years, whether it's big-hatted ladies on the Titanic or blood-dripping vampiras inspired by that famous horror writer uptown. Don't miss this one. **French Connection** (416 N. Peters St. 504/522–0014) which has been in the Quarter for a decade, is a London-based outfit selling smart clothing for the urban man and woman. **Wise Buys** (534 Chartres St. 504/524–3004) offers designer women's clothing at sometimes surprising discounts. You can find Ann Taylor and Gruppo Americano, among others, so take your time and look a bit. The red walls and high ceilings of **Trashy Diva** (829 Chartres St. 504/581–4555) are hung with a fab collection of vintage clothing. Check out the 1890s corsets, which they advise you to put on before trying certain period clothes. A few doors down is **Violet's** (808 Chartres St. 504/569–0088), which carries fancy dress-up duds, including some smashing beaded bags, jewelry, and other unique accessories.

   Pippin Lane (217 N. Peters St. 504/671–8900) carries a fascinating selection of imported children's clothing, shoes, hand-painted furniture, toys, and wonderful linens. The price range should please everyone. Light, summery fashions and accessories for women are the thing at **Royal Ltd.** (936 Royal St. 504/524–0949), a fun spot for browsing. There's more of the same, as well as marvelous costumes, at **Royal Rags** (627 Dumaine St. 504/566–7247), where a helpful staff will help you accessorize or create the perfect ensemble. Just rifling through their racks is inspirational.

Shushan's Ltd. (536 St. Peter St. 504/586–1188) carries
casual duds and an amazing collection of hats for men and
women. The name says it all at **California Drawstrings**
(812 Royal St. 504/523–1371), which has light summer
fashions for men and women. There's more casual wear
across the street at the **Cotton Market** (819 Royal St. 504/
525–2227), which also has lots of denim.

collectibles... Casa del Corazon (901 Chartres St.
504/569–9555) is a tiny corner shop with lots of heart,
literally. Most of the merchandise is from Latin America,
and ranges from junky knickknacks to beautiful one-of-a-
kind artworks. There is the to-be-expected collection of
hearts, including an especially dazzling array of silver
designs to be worn as pins or necklaces, or just admired.
There are also colorful Mexican folk masks, milagros, and
a smattering of religious art. The place is perfect for gift-
shopping, with a staff that's friendly and helpful.

If you're not looking for it, you might miss **Barakat**
(934 Royal St. 504/593–9944), and that would be a shame.
The sign says "Found Objects and Vintage Furnishings,"
but there's more than that in this small emporium with its
ever-changing inventory. This is where you might finally
find those sconces you've wanted for years, or maybe an
unusual vase or table. This place is a treasure trove if you
take the time to explore. The same might be said of **Sigle's
Antiques and Metalcraft** (935 Royal St. 504/522–7647),
a larger space crammed with goodies. Take your time, or
you might miss something. Their metal section contains
reproductions of some of New Orleans' most famous and
enduring ironwork designs, such as acorns, grapevines,

and acanthus leaves. There's fine junking to be found at **The Hombres** (605 *Toulouse St. no phone*), a secondhand shop just made for browsing. There's more of the same, but with a focus on vintage clothing, at **Le Garage** (1234 *Decatur St.* 504/522–6639), a must for those with a passion for wonderful used things.

Vintage 429 (429 *Royal St.* 504/529–2288) is a cinemaphile's dream. It stocks an amazing array of film-related merchandise, from posters to movie stills and glamour shots of your favorite stars (some signed). You'll also find estate jewelry, vintage decorative pieces, and historical and political memorabilia. It's fun to poke around this one, although you might be put off by the hugely indifferent staff. **Importicos** (736 *Royal St.* 504/523–3100, 517 *St. Louis St.* 504/523–0306) has gift items from all over the globe, as does **A Different Approach** (824 *Chartres St.* 504/ 588–1978), which emphasizes handicrafts.

La Petit Soldier Shop (528 *Royal St.* 504/523–7741) will bring out the little boy in adult male shoppers. The storefront is bound to entice, with its armies of tiny handpainted soldiers from different nations and periods of history. These expertly crafted pieces are almost too beautiful to be toys, and are really designed to be passed down through the generations. **Lord Jim** (618 *Royal St.* 504/524–0914) has a stunning collection of miniatures, porcelains, vintage and new pillboxes, and a huge selection of blownglass paperweights. This place bears serious exploring and has a staff who can answer all your questions.

Civil War Store (212 *Chartres St.* 504/522–3328) has an extensive inventory of money, ammunition, documents, and other historical memorabilia. **James H. Cohen &**

Sons (437 Royal St. 504/522–3305) specializes in antique
weapons, rare coins, gold jewelry, and more. Both shops
are for serious collectors.

Angel Wings (710 St. Louis St. 504/524–6880) is a charming little shop with miniature gewgaws, as is **Black Butterfly** (727 Royal St. 504/524–MINI), which carries just
about every Lilliputian thing imaginable and is another
must-visit for serious collectors. They claim to have the
largest miniatures collection in the South, and when you
start browsing you probably won't disagree. Doll collectors
won't want to miss **Oh, Susannah** (518 St. Peter St.
504/586–8701), which has an astonishing assortment of
antique and new dolls that'll blow you away. It's worth a
visit even if you're not shopping. There are still more at
Hello Dolly (815 Royal St. 504/522–9948), with one of the
largest doll collections in the South. It shares half a duplex
with **Crafty Louisianians** (813 Royal St. 504/528–3094),
a genuinely fascinating emporium crammed with local
folk art. You'll find some of the cleverest, most whimsical
creations anywhere here, made of everything from Spanish
moss to Mississippi mud.

Fischer Gambino (637 Royal St. 504/524–9067) is hard
to categorize because they carry such an intriguing inventory. Art glass is a mainstay, whether in the form of figurines,
Tiffany lamps, an exceptional collection of chandeliers, or
mirrors. This is the place for that hard-to-find Venetian-
glass stemware in the shape of a pink flamingo, or maybe
a carousel horse. It's also wonderful for original artworks,
made of glass of course. **Concepts** (621 Toulouse St.
504/529–4405) is another shop difficult to slot. The prod-
uct line includes jewelry, statuary, and one-of-a-kind works

by Louisiana artists. A while back they carried some extraordinary objets modeled after mausoleums in New Orleans' famous Cities of the Dead. This is the place to look if you want something uniquely local. Their sister store, **Image Gallery** (738 Royal St. 504/558–0059), has more of the same.

food... Laura's Candies & Creole Gourmet (600 Conti St. 504/525–3880), is New Orleans' oldest candy store. They've been pushing diet-destroying confections since 1913, so they've obviously found their market. They make several varieties of pralines and carry a selection of French Quarter comestibles they'll happily ship.

Aunt Sally's Original Creole Pralines (810 Decatur St. 504/524–3373) seems to have been here forever, and there's something comforting about that. Bright and always bustling, this cheerful place does a brisk business beyond those sweet candies with the killer calories. Check for other local foodstuffs, including the ubiquitous hot sauces and Café Du Monde products, as well as cookbooks, dishes, and more. You can ship it or schlepp it. The **Café Du Monde Shop** (1039 Decatur St. 504/581–2914) nearby is the retail outlet for the famous Creole coffee with chicory and mixes for the accompanying beignets. They ship all over the world.

A few doors down is **Central Grocery** (923 Decatur St. 504/523–1620), home of the famous muffaletta and a Quarter institution for decades. Foodies will love browsing the well-stocked shelves for exotic condiments like Creole mustard, shrimp boil, and a variety of remoulade sauces. The serious shopper will find some surprising bargains for carrying home or shipping. Just for fun, pick up a muffaletta and have lunch down by the river, a very short stroll away. **La Marquise Pastry Shop** (625 *Chartres* St. 504/524–0420) has scrumptious pastries in the true French manner. Their croissants melt in your mouth.

A bakery for dogs? You bet! **Three Dog Bakery** (827 *Royal* St. 504/525–BAKE) has all-natural treats for Fido and Rover, including custom-made birthday cakes, if that's your pet's desire. You can't browse this happy place without chuckling at such inspired goodies as Pup Tarts, Beagle Bagels, Boxer Brownies, and more. Dogs are welcome of course (maybe more than people). Even if you don't have a pooch, it's worth a look.

There are a couple of places on Jackson Square worth checking out. **Creole Delicacies** (533 *St. Ann* St. 504/ 525–9508) carries a long line of tasty treats, the inevitable pralines, plus coffee, preserves, sauces, and soups. They also have gift baskets. The delicious smells waft right out into the arcade. In addition to the obvious, you'll find New Orleans' largest hot-sauce selection at the **Sugar & Spice Company** (532 *St. Peter* St. 522–5516). Collected from all over the world, there's everything from gentle, to incendiary, to suicidal. The unusual bottles with colorful, sometimes naughty labels have become collectibles for many people and make inexpensive fun gifts for others.

french market...
This long arcade with its awnings and distinctive squat pillars is the nation's oldest continuously operated public market; the site was used as a market by the Indians long before the arrival of the French. Beautifully restored and maintained, it contains every-

thing from candy stores and tie shops to music-related boutiques and Louisiana food products. Just start at one end and work your way to the other. It sprawls three full blocks, from the Café Du Monde at St. Ann Street to Ursuline Street, where it becomes the **Farmer's Market**, at which you'll find fresh local produce at only slightly inflated prices—Creole tomatoes and satsumas, mirlitons, pickled okra, and huge necklaces of garlic. There's also an extensive array of hot sauces from Louisiana and around the world, some of which are insanely incendiary.

At Governor Nicholl's Street, the Farmer's Market flows into the indoor/outdoor **Flea Market**, which continues to Barracks Street and the Old U.S. Mint. This bustling place doesn't necessarily have all the crap you've seen at similar emporiums. Sure, there are the usual T-shirts and sock bargains, watches, shades, pens, purses, belts, jewelry, and so forth, but there's lots of other stuff too. There's some fine jewelry by local artists, notably Oscar, whose innovative plastic pins of zydeco musicians, flamingoes, and more are always big sellers at Jazzfest. Also look for voodoo dolls, feathered Mardi Gras masks, glittery harlequins and pierrots, plus neckties with jazz, alligator, crawfish, and hot-sauce themes. The aisles are usually crowded, so look closely or you might miss something.

galleries/framing... Most visitors, and not a few locals, are surprised to learn the extent of the New Orleans art market, which is among the top ten in the nation. The city has inspired more artists and boasts far more art galleries than any other American city its size, and there's no end in sight to the burgeoning scene. The proof is in the staggering number of galleries lining Royal Street, Magazine Street, and the Warehouse District in the CBD.

Michalopoulos (617 Bienville St. 504/558–0505) showcases the works of local painter James Michalopoulos, who dazzled the art world with his unusual New Orleans cityscapes. Their perspective is amusingly and daringly warped—gelatinous houses heaving and pulsing against the confines of the canvas—as if the city were caught in the midst of an earthquake. It could also be called the vision of someone who's swilled one too many Hurricanes. Michalopoulos is also a brilliant color innovator with a unique style. If the canvases are over your budget—and they sure ain't cheap—pick up one of his postcards or a box of stationery, the perfect memento. He also designed the official 1999 Jazzfest poster.

As Gypsy Rose Lee always said, "You gotta have a gimmick!" Clearly heeding her words is George Rodrigue, whose paintings of his deceased pet Tiffany are familiar to visitors from all over the world. If you're among his legions of fans, don't miss **Rodrigue Studios** (721 Royal St. 504/581–4244), packed with endless, ad nauseum variations on his trademark blue dog. Not everyone loves his work. Locals still chuckle over another local artist who painted a red German shepherd humping a startled blue dog and displayed it in his Royal Street gallery. Not to mention one especially irreverent Mardi Gras krewe whose throws included blue rubber dog poop one year. You may dismiss Rodrigue's paintings as garbage, but you gotta admit the guy's found his niche, and a very lucrative one at that. Crafty devil, he's even trademarked the phrase "The Blue Dog."

Earl Hébert's superb Cajun genre paintings have thrilled, amused, and moved art lovers for years. Whether he's capturing a fais-do-do, courir du Mardi Gras, music legend John Lee Hooker, or Tante Nanine lounging on the front porch, his touch is true and from the heart. The cozy **Earl Hébert Gallery** (1035 Royal St. 504/523–3400) is also his home. Just knock on the door if you want to check out his talent, or look for him working in front of the upriver Pontalba Apartments on Jackson Square. **Photo Works** (839 Chartres St. 504/593–9090) is a sleek, airy gallery showcasing fine photographic works. Their window photo of Dennis Hopper shooting a bird was such a crowd pleaser, they had to put up a sign asking people not to photograph a trademarked work.

Bergen Galleries (730 Royal St. 504/523–7882) has posters and prints galore, plus the Quarter's biggest selection of posters by local artists. **Hanson Galleries** (229 Royal St. 504/524–8211) specializes in contemporary masters, new originals, and graphics, and occasionally showcases some dazzling Haitian art. **Kurt E. Schon, Ltd.** (510 St. Louis St. 504/524–5462, 523 Royal St. 504/523–5902) has classic landscapes and portraits from the 17th to 20th centuries. **Black Art Collection** (309 Chartres St. 504/529–3080) focuses on African-American art, as does **Eye on the Square** on Jackson Square (no phone). **Barrister's Gallery** (526 Royal St. 504/525–2767) carries tribal and Southern folk art. **Southern Expressions** (521 St. Ann St. 504/525–4530) is a print gallery primarily centered on Southern themes, meaning you'll get the usual plantations, romantic Quarter scenes, moonlight, magnolias, and belles.

The Frame Shop & Gallery (1041 Bourbon St. 504/581–1229) does some of the most beautiful custom framing in town. They also have a fine collection of old posters and prints by a variety of artists with plenty of New Orleans–themed works to choose from. Locals love **Spilled Ink** (734 Orleans St. 504/523–5543), which does quality framing at a reasonable price. Owner/artist Matt will work closely with you to deliver just what you want.

jewelry... Stop in to be dazzled at **Bedazzle** (635 St. Peter St. 504/529–3248), which carries the works of more than a hundred Louisiana and national jewelry designers. They're not exaggerating when they describe their inventory as art. Be sure and check out the interesting works of Soren Pederson. **Rumors** (513 Royal St. 504/525–0292) and **Rumors-Too** (319 Royal St. 504/523–0011) flaunt the most astonishing array of earrings imaginable. From tiny posts to elaborate metal confections Carmen Miranda would've killed for, it would take hours to inspect them all closely. These shops also have some truly phantasmagorical masks at equally fabulous prices, but, oh, are they knock-outs. This ain't the kinda stuff that would be approved by the P.T.A. **Brass Lion** (516 Royal St. 504/525–9815) has a dazzling array of jewels sparkling beneath an equally glitzy collection of chandeliers. This just may be the place to find a sumptuous Victorian piece fit for first-class passage on the Titanic.

Joan Good Antiques (809 Royal St. 504/525–1705) has a rainbow selection of semiprecious gems. Garnets are her specialty, but she also carries topaz, cameos, and interesting art deco marcasite pieces. You just may be inspired to throw a *Great Gatsby* party when you get home. **Sabai Jewelry/Gallery** (*924 Royal St. 504/525–6211*) also has some fine one-of-a-kind pieces, and on Jackson Square is **Salloum's Contemporary Jewelry** (*524 St. Peter St. 504/522–7554*). **Dashka Roth Contemporary Jewelry** (*332 Chartres St. 504/523–0805*) specializes in Judaica.

leather...
You can probably get that hard-to-find leather item at **Second Skin** (*521 St. Philip St. 504/561–8167*), which offers a wide selection of vests, chaps, jackets, pants, and caps for those who have a sado-masochistic bent, or just want to look as if they do. There's also a consciousness-raising selection of adult toys and novelties. There's more of the same at **Gargoyle's** (*1205 Decatur St. 504/529–4387*), plus plenty of racy '90s and retro '60s duds.

masks/mardi gras...
Forget those hopelessly tacky masks inundating the Quarter and get the real thing at **Masquerade Fantasy** (*1233 Decatur St. 504/593–9269*). These truly ingenious leather confections are handmade by local artist Jim Gibeault and others, and are all one-of-a-kind. You won't believe the extent of their imaginative power until you gawk at the walls overflowing with fero-cious, funny, and fabulous creations. Considering the man-hours involved, the prices are surprisingly reasonable. **Serendipitous Masks** (*831 Decatur St. 504/522–9158*) can create just about any feathery fancy you can dream up, or you can choose from those froufrou fancies on display. Grand entrance guaranteed if you're wearing one of these plumed beauties.

Mardi Gras Center (831 *Chartres St.* 504/524—4384) has all sorts of carnival fixings, plus plenty of stuff for masquerading. You can get new, used, and custom-made costumes as well. The first thing greeting you when you walk in the door at **Accent Annex Mardi Gras Headquarters** (633 *Toulouse* St. 504/592—9886) is a giant Peter Pan draped in feather boas, and why not? This is the Quarter branch of a citywide chain that's been supplying carnival krewes and revelers for years. It's all here—masks, beads, crowns, jewelry, doubloons, wreaths, indoor/outdoor decorations, fans, boas, parasols—everything you need to throw that Mardi Gras party back home. It's a lot of fun to browse, but after a while all that gold, purple, and green can make you cross-eyed.

The Vieux Carré Hair Store (805 *Royal* St. 504/522—3258) always stops pedestrians with its windows towering with masks and wigs. They not only have one for you, they'll make a costume to go with it. If you want to go barefaced, they've got theatrical makeup to put you over the top.

perfume... Hové Parfumeur, Ltd. (824 *Royal* St. 504/525—7827) has been scenting New Orleans ladies and gentlemen since 1932. This local, family-run business will create oils, soaps, sachets, and of course, fragrances to your individual specifications. **Bourbon French Parfums** (525 *St.Ann* St. 504/522—4480) has been creating custom-blended signature scents since 1843. They also carry a complete line of commercial colognes, eau de cologne, body lotions, foaming bath gels, toiletries, and more. Once your body is beautiful, you'll want to cool it off with one of their gorgeous fans.

serendipity... **Grace Note** (*900 Royal St. 504/ 522–1513*) is the store you hope to find while browsing the Quarter, with its thrilling assortment of artworks, architectural and religious fragments, and one-of-a-kind luxe objets. There are clothes and hats fashioned by owner/ designer Jan Dryer from vintage materials and based on old designs, ancient ironwork forged into iron crosses by artist Skip Henderson, large kallitypes by Luther Gerlach, and Robert Reicher's garden shrines, evocative of Asian spirit houses. The window displays are among the most imaginative in the city.

There are few shops in the world like **Little Mex** (*1019 Decatur St. 504/529–3397*), a labyrinth of merchandise you simply have to see to believe. The entrance is hardly engaging, but once you're in the door, the call to browse is irresistible. There's shelf after shelf, room after room, cubicle after cubicle of stuff, stuff, and more stuff. Many goods are from Mexico—leather, baskets, tin, brass, and copper— but you'll also find Mammy cookie jars, flowery '60s casseroles, the cheapest postcards in town (10 for $1), statuary, gumbo mixes, and even a suit of armor.

The clouds of bubbles warn that you're approaching **Postmark New Orleans** (*631 Toulouse St. 504/529–2052*), which carries an outrageous line of greeting cards and a diverting selection of stationery, candles, lamps, a limited furniture line, and unique gift items. Owners Starkey Kean and Earl Joiner have a stock of beautiful things that would delight "Ab/Fab"'s Edina. Everything's either fun, fab, or frivolous and sometimes all three. **Quarter Moon** (*918 Royal St. 504/524–3208*) has an interesting assortment of masks and jewelry, plus some hand-painted things. Poke around and see what you can unearth. You can find **Mystic Curio** (831 *Royal St.* 504/581–7150) by following the wind chimes. Inside is all sorts of astrological, mystical, magical, and New Age-y stuff. They have a great collection of tarot cards and can arrange for tarot, palm, and astrological readings if you're so inclined. Big fun here.

It's always Christmas at **Santa's Quarters** (1025 *Decatur St.* 504/581–5820), a series of rooms packed to the max with Yuletide goodies. There's everything you'd expect and much more, including exquisite nativity sets and Louisiana ornaments—so you can have jazz trumpets, streetcars, fleurs de lis, crawfish, and alligators dangling on your tree. Speaking of local customs, don't miss their dazzling Mardi Gras tree bedecked with carnival golds, purples, and greens. **Idea Factory** (838 *Chartres St.* 504/524–5195) is hard to miss with its trademark potty rocking chair out front—it rocks sideways! This is just a hint of the whimsical merchandise inside, but there is some fine work by serious artists too. Wood is the dominant material here, and it's fashioned into everything from windmills to imaginative figures. Check out the creative window displays.

Fifi Mahoney's (828 *Chartres St.* 504/525–4343) is a cosmetics emporium with all sorts of things to aid milady (or mi "lady") in her or his transformation. Aside from makeup, they carry custom wigs and feather boas in a rainbow of colors. What would you expect from someone with a name like that? **Louisiana Loom Works** (822 *Chartres St.* 504/558–0901) carries fine rugs and such, mostly handwoven. **Ma Sherie Amour** (517 *St. Ann St.* 504/598–1998) is a seriously romantic shop carrying a variety of precious

if you miss the carnival

If you don't visit during the heady carnival season, you can glimpse the real thing at **Blaine Kern's Mardi Gras World** (233 Newton St., Algiers, 225/361–7821). Kern and his family have been building floats for years, and this is where you can see their works in progress. It's a magical world of gigantic alligators, clowns, mermaids, and other wild things. The $7.75 adult admission includes coffee and a slice of king cake. At the foot of Canal Street take the Mississippi River ferry to Algiers. It's best not to walk through the industrial area, so arrange for a Kern shuttle to pick you up.

The **Mardi Gras Museum at Rivertown** (421 Williams Blvd., Kenner, 504/ 468–4037) is also worth a look. It includes a good history/timeline of Mardi Gras with maps showing all the parade routes, a Queen of Carnival gown, a Mardi Gras Indian costume, antique invitations, and a replica float you can clamber over if you like. Don't miss the Chevy Gremlin completely covered in throws.

A much smaller, but still high-quality collection of Mardi Gras memorabilia is the **Germaine Cazenave Wells Mardi Gras Museum** at Arnaud's restaurant (813 Bienville St. 504/ 523–5433). There's also a scattering of elaborate carnival costumes in the rear dining rooms of **Ralph & Kacoo's** (519 Toulouse St. 504/522–5226). Just walk in either restaurant and ask to have a look.

items including stained-glass sun catchers, porcelain fig-urines, and exquisite tea sets. Romance also reigns at **Rendezvous Linen & Lace** (522 St. *Peter* St. 504/522–0225) with a beautiful selection of linens (some lacy, some not), tablecloths and napkins, tea cozies, tea towels, and baby clothes for the fussiest moms. **Quarter Stitch** (630 *Chartres* St. 504/522–4451) carries a complete line of supplies for knitting, crocheting, needlepointing, and the like. **The Kite Shop on Jackson Square** (542 St. *Peter* St. 504/524–0028) has, well, kites. And lots of 'em!

The **Coghlan Gallery** (710 *Toulouse* St. 504/525–8550) sells concrete, terra cotta, and metal decorative pieces for gardens, porches, and lawns, all reasonably priced. Tucked behind a wall surmounted by twin lions, it has fountains and large sculptures in the courtyard and smaller pieces up the stairs. There's a lot to see. **The Gothic Shop** (830 *Royal* St. 504/558–0175), has a wild collection of concrete masks, statues, columns, angels, sphinxes, gargoyles, and more. There are fun, inexpensive reproductions of all sorts of Roman, Greek, Egyptian, medieval, and, yes, Gothic good-ies to grace your home, indoors and out. These folks are almost always having huge sales, marking down their already reasonable prices. Some items are tiny enough to tote home, but if you buy something oversized, just take it a block down the street to the **French Quarter Postal Emporium** (940 *Royal* St. 525–6651). An earth-motherly but professional staff will work with you on secure pack-ing and finding the best rates. Beats schlepping.

southwestern art... Who knows why anyone would come to New Orleans to shop for Southwestern art,

but if you get the urge, there's a good selection at **Vision Quest** (1034 *Royal St.* 504/523–0920). This nicely done shop stocks masks, dolls, sand paintings, pottery, books, artifacts, and all sorts of other things associated with Southwestern Native American cultures. If you've never been in that neck of the woods, it's a good sampling of what's available. On the upscale end is **Southwest Designs** (230 *Chartres St.* 504/522–4345), a gallery showcasing fine art and sculpture by celebrated Southwestern artists.

voodoo... There are three emporia catering to those interested in this much-misunderstood religion. Whether you're a serious practitioner or just want to put a harmless (?) hex on somebody, these are the places to go. They stock everything from voodoo dolls to that hard-to-find John the Conqueror root (not to be confused with St. John's wort). Don't go in if your intention is to ridicule, or you may find yourself on the receiving end of some bad gris-gris.

With all those colorful African flags flying, it's hard to miss the **Voodoo Museum** (724 *Dumaine St.* 504/523–7685). It has all the fixings to cast spells, remedy sex problems, or smooth emotional waves. There are also interesting permanent displays, an occult library, and an authentic temple in the rear. Ask about their cemetery tours. Named for New Orleans' infamous voodoo queen, **Marie Laveau's House of Voodoo** (739 *Bourbon St.* 504/581–3751) carries a complete stock of voodoo essentials, including gris-gris for casting spells and plenty of love potions. They also give lectures and can arrange tours. **Reverend Zombie's House of Voodoo** (725 *St. Peter St.* 504/486–6366) has more of the same.

sleeping

The Quarter has been welcoming visitors for a couple of centuries, so when it comes to inns, hostelries, and B&Bs, they've got the system down. Whether you want a big luxury hotel with all the amenities, a 19th-century Creole town house with a decidedly European flavor, or something modest but clean and respectable, you can find it with no problem. Keep in mind that New Orleans' hotels offer a variety of rates related to various special events. Obviously, rooms are more expensive during Mardi Gras, the Sugar Bowl, and Jazzfest, and lower during the inferno of summer. Plan accordingly, and if you want to come to carnival, book well ahead.

Cost Range for double occupancy per night on a weeknight. Call to verify prices.
$/under 100 dollars
$$/100–150 dollars
$$$/150–200 dollars
$$$$/200+ dollars

Consistently rated as one of the most charming small hotels in the world, the **Maison de Ville** (*727 Toulouse St.* *504/561–5858 $$$$*) is truly a step back in time. For many years, its low-key elegance has been a magnet for celebrities who know they'll be managed and coddled with the utmost discretion. All rooms and suites are furnished with 19th-century antiques and have access to a lush tropical courtyard complete with trickling fountain.

Tennessee Williams often stayed in Room 9. The seven Audubon Cottages on nearby Dauphine Street, where the great bird painter lived in 1821, are also part of the hotel. Tariff includes continental breakfast served in the room, plus complimentary beverages in the courtyard at dusk.

The Omni Royal Orleans (621 St. Louis St. 504/ 529–5333, 800/843–6664 $$$) opened in 1960 on the site of the old St. Louis Hotel, which it sort of replicates. It has more than 300 very spacious rooms reflecting 19th-century taste; supposedly no two are alike. All have marble baths with phones, and, speaking of marble, check out the lobby, which teems with glitzy chandeliers, gold leaf, sconces, and graceful fanlight windows. There's 24-hour room service, valet parking, a barber and beauty salon, and fitness facilities. The rooftop pool seven stories up has gorgeous views. During the final weekend of Mardi Gras, the luxurious lobby is a great place to spot some extraordinary costumes, but unless you're a guest or know someone who is, you won't get past the doors, which are manned by security guards.

The baroque dowager, **Hotel Monteleone** (214 Royal St. 504/523–3341, 800/535–8585 $$$) is the oldest hostelry in the Quarter, built in 1907, restored in 1996, and operated by the same family for four generations. You sense the tradition, from the liveried doormen and gracious concierge to the slowly revolving Carousel Bar, which has been a local watering hole for decades. There are 600 rooms, all of them exceptionally spacious and well appointed, and 35 suites. There is a rooftop pool, an exercise room, and the other usual amenities. **Hotel St. Louis** (730 Bienville St. 504/581–7300 $$) surrounds one of the prettiest tropical courtyards in the Quarter and has a Parisian elegance that's irresistible. There are crystal chandeliers, antique furnishings, and fine paintings in abundance. Some rooms have balconies overlooking the central courtyard, while a few suites even have private courtyards. The St. Louis likes to call itself an intimate full-service hotel with all the perks of a big convention hotel, and that's fair enough. Amenities include a full-time concierge, gourmet room service, and a complimentary newspaper daily, plus a staff trained to deliver just about anything you want. The big surprise is that it has some amazing off-season bargains.

The Soniat House & Maisonettes (1133 *Chartres St. 504/522–0570 $$$–$$$$*) are tucked away so discreetly in the Lower Quarter, you'll pass them unless you're paying attention. The main building is a beautifully restored Creole mansion with a shady, capacious courtyard and well-appointed public areas. Operated by Rodney and Frances Smith, the service is decidedly detail-oriented, with a knowledgeable concierge, Crabtree & Evelyn soaps, Egyptian-cotton sheets, and down pillows. The Soniat also has seven luxury suites with hot tubs in 1830s townhouses right across the street.

You leave behind the ongoing bacchanalia of Bourbon Street the moment you retreat to the serene marble lobby of **The Royal Sonesta Hotel** (*300 Bourbon St. 504/586–0300,800/766–3782 $$$$*) with its chandeliers and coolly manicured jungle. This is a huge place, with 500 rooms and 32 suites, all with mini-bars, some with balconies and patios. Unless you enjoy noise, request a room facing the pool or courtyard, or beneath the rooftop dormers. Amenities include restaurant, cocktail lounge, bar, health club/spa, and concierge. **The Inn on Bourbon Street** **(541 Bourbon St. 504/524–7611, 800/535–7891 $$$)** is a Best Western hotel, meaning you could be anywhere in America except for what's outside your door. There are 186 rooms and two suites with on-premises bar, restaurant, cafeteria, health club/spa, and exercise room. If you really want to wallow in the revelry, there are 32 rooms with balconies overlooking Bourbon, and you'd better believe they're hot tickets during Mardi Gras.

The Olivier House Hotel (828 *Toulouse* St. 504/525–8456 $–$$) is an 1836 Creole mansion carved into 42 rooms, no two alike. Most are rather simple; others have antiques, balconies, and kitchenettes with microwaves. This place gets a lot of repeat business from Europeans and traveling theatrical companies, so you'll probably meet some interesting folks. There are two tropical courtyards, one with pool, the other with chattering birds that can occasionally work your last nerve. **The Dauphine Orleans** (415 *Dauphine* St. 504/586–1800, 800/521–7111 $$$) is pleasant enough, with a fun bar aiming at bordello ambience and a poolside exercise room tucked into a 19th-century Creole cottage. The 104 rooms and seven suites are average, and include hair dryers, irons, and ironing boards. Other amenities include an outdoor hot tub, lounge, and business services.

Right by the historic Ursuline Convent, **Le Richelieu** **(1234 *Chartres* St. 504/529–2492 $–$$$)** has 69 rooms and 17 suites, with modest rates despite some luxury touches, such as brass ceiling fans, fine toiletries, and hair dryers. Some rooms have mirrored walls and walk-in closets, and there's no extra charge for a balcony. There's a small, pleas-

ant bar and cafe with tables set up on the pool terrace. The
homemade biscuits, crêpes, and frittatas are especially
good. **Lafitte Guest House** (1003 Bourbon St. 504/581–
2678, 800/331–7971 $$–$$$) changed hands last year, but
all indications are that it's as charming as ever. A lavishly
restored 1849 mansion, it boasts a high Victorian parlor
and a grand staircase sweeping up a full three stories. The
rooms are decorated with a combination of antiques and
good reproductions, and one room is authentic Eastlake.
Complimentary continental breakfast is served in the
room or in a lush garden filled with statuary and flower-
ing plants. Come late afternoon, wine and hors d'oeuvres
are gratis in the parlor. The balconies and upper floors
offer great vistas of the Quarter and the city skyline.
Bourbon Orleans Hotel (717 Orleans St. 504/523–2222,
800/521–5338 $$$–$$$$) is conveniently located right
behind St. Louis Cathedral. The rooms are pretty standard,
although the public areas are nicely appointed with
columns, chandeliers, and furniture in the Queen Anne
style. Some people prefer rooms on the raucous Bourbon
Street side, but if you want peace and quiet, request to be
put somewhere else. There's a pool and restaurant. This is
another great place for people-watching during carnival,
as a number of fancy society balls are held upstairs.

One of the Quarter's most-photographed buildings is the
Cornstalk Hotel (915 Royal St. 504/523–1515 $$–$$$),
an 1816 white Victorian with its signature cast-iron fence
in the design of corn stalks, complete with ears of corn.
Legend says the owner built the fence to ease the home-
sickness of his Midwestern bride. The mood is set when
you enter a foyer with chandelier light multiplied by mir-

rors. There are 14 rooms, with sitting rooms, all different and furnished with such Victorian touches as marble-topped tables, oriental rugs, and four-poster beds. Some even have stained-glass windows.

Guests at the **Hotel de la Poste** (316 Chartres St. 504/581–1200, 800/448–4927 $–$$) enjoy something truly special—a dining room in the fine restaurant, **Bacco** [see **eating/coffee**]. There are 87 rooms and 13 suites in this centrally located hotel, many with balconies overlooking the street or an interior courtyard. You may want to request a ground-floor room with French doors opening directly onto the courtyard. A carriage house has four suites sharing a small sundeck.

The Rue Royale Inn (1006 Royal St. 504/524–3900 $–$$$) is a bargain, considering what you get. This 1830s building is nicely restored; the rooms, most with exposed-brick walls, are furnished in period reproductions. Most rooms have wet bars and kitchenettes, and a few have hot tubs for two. Some open onto the spacious galleries overlooking bustling Royal Street or the roomy courtyard with Jacuzzi. Elvis fans should know he wiggled and wailed on the adjacent gallery in the film King Creole. There's a complimentary continental breakfast. Built in 1848, the four-story **Hotel Villa Convento** (616 Ursulines St. 504/522–1793 $–$$$) takes its name from the nearby Ursuline Convent. The place was refurbished a couple of years ago, putting a nice gleam on an old gem. All 25 rooms are furnished with antique repros, some with chandeliers or ceiling fans, some with balconies—and check out the tapestry-padded elevator! A tropical courtyard is all yours for morning coffee and croissants or just relaxing. If you're still hungry, fresh-baked goodies are available at Croissant d'Or just across the street.

The Ursuline Guest House *(708 Ursulines St. 504/ 525–8509, 800/654–2351 $–$$)* occupies a late-18th-century Creole cottage that's been operating as a well-maintained inn for over 20 years. Thirteen modest rooms have private entrances, most opening onto a courtyard with palms, wrought-iron furniture, and a tiled, clothing-optional hot tub. A continental breakfast is included, and complimentary wine is served in the evenings. This is a real Quarter bargain, and very popular with gay and lesbian travelers. Another reasonable spot is **The Bourgoyne House** *(841 Bourbon St. 504/525–3983 $–$$$)*, a three-story manse dating from the 1830s. There are two suites in the big house and some budget rooms in the rear. Connecting them is a quiet courtyard perfect for reading, relaxing, or enjoying a glass of wine. The third-floor suite has a tiny balcony with dizzying views of Bourbon Street. No food available.

doing stuff

There is a French Quarter beyond boozing on Bourbon and antiquing on Royal. Once you've pigged out from one of the heavy-duty menus or maybe downed too many Jello shots, you'll need to work off some of that excess. Short of making an emergency gym run, walking is the best solution. Unless you're here between June and September, when you could float the steamboat Natchez down Canal Street on the humidity, the climate's ideal for strolling. There are plenty of relaxing sights and sounds to choose from, and even if you hated history in school, you should give it a chance in the French Quarter, mainly because it's nothing like what your teachers taught you. Ever see a Confederate submarine? Want to see the site of the notorious Quadroon Ballroom, where mixed-blood courtesans wooed potential white "protectors"? Or maybe you'd like a nighttime ghost tour? You can do all that, plus get face-to-face with an albino alligator, check out the latest IMAX release, or get your runes read. All without leaving the neighborhood.

The best place to start is where it all began, in 1718. Louisiana's most hallowed spot, the **Cabildo** (city hall) at Jackson Square, is where you can get a history lesson at your own pace. Built in the years 1791 to 1795, its roof burned in 1988, sparking a total renovation and the creation of a striking, state-of-the-art exhibition tracing the state's multicultural history. Unfortunately, there is much confusion and prickliness in the interpretation of a volatile past (the Confederate flag, for example, is no longer permitted to be flown from the pediment outside along with the French and Spanish flags), but the displays are still fascinating stuff. Don't miss Napoleon's death mask.

Even if churches aren't your thing, pop into **St. Louis Cathedral** next door. It's America's oldest cathedral still in use, has a truly moving austere beauty, and you can honestly feel a lingering Creole aura. The glorious fresco above the altar was recently restored after chomping termites literally brought down the house. Luckily it was in the wee hours, when nobody was hitting the rails. The neighboring **Presbytère**, a near twin of The Cabildo, has rotating exhibits which can be fun, and, yep, that's the Confederate submarine out front.

The park within the gates is the old **Place d'Armes**, used for military parades and public hangings in the French and Spanish days. The bronze statue of Andrew Jackson, erected in 1856 to commemorate the hero of the Battle of New Orleans, is unusual in that sculptor Clark Mills didn't cheat and use the horse's tail for support, a common 19th-century practice. The inscription on the statue's base, "The Union Must And Shall Be Preserved" was added by occupying Union General Benjamin Butler.

The Square before the Cathedral and the steps on the Decatur Street side are always lively with street musicians and performers, licensed by the city and obliged to rotate so everyone gets a chance to play. Some of them are truly amazing. It's always fun to get your tarot read and goof on the inevitable mimes. As you might expect, New Orleans has some creative mimes, including a black man in white face smothered with Mardi Gras beads and a robed, hooded angel complete with wings stationed directly in front of the cathedral. Toss 'em a buck and see what happens. Incidentally, most street musicians are legit and are an important part of New Orleans' heritage. If you stop to listen, please have the courtesy to tip. The same applies to performance artists and the black boys tap-dancing on street corners, a tradition dating back to slavery days. In the era of the ubiquitous sneaker, these innovative youngsters attach bottle caps to the bottoms of their sneaks and noisily tap-tap away. Some aren't so hot, but others, especially the groups of older kids, flaunt a synchronization that would make Gregory Hines proud.

Don't forget to inspect the local artwork hanging on the iron fences. Jackson Square has been called Montmartre-on-the-Mississippi, and you'd be surprised at some of the bargains, especially after a little friendly dickering. Some of the portraitists are amazingly adept, and yeah, they'll trim that double chin if you like. The caricature artists are not nearly as reverent, but lots more fun.

For a glimpse into the real Creole past, right on Jackson Square, step into the **1850 House** (525 St. Ann St. 504/ 568–6968). If this is a middle-class Creole apartment, the rich must have lived like kings. Check out the rosewood furniture with damask upholstery, velvet and scalloped-lace draperies, and elaborately carved Prudent Mallard tester bed with shimmering mosquito netting. Not to mention a sensational view of Jackson Square.

One of the few buildings to survive the Great Fire of 1794, **Madame John's Legacy** (632 Dumaine St.) was recently reopened to the public after years of closure due to a shortage of state funds. It was built in 1789 on the site of a house destroyed by the Great Fire of 1788, and remains a rare example of early Creole design. Madame John was a fictional character in George Washington Cable's story Tite Poulet. Instead of period furnishings, downstairs you'll find an exhibit on the house and upstairs a contemporary Louisiana folk art collection. The thing here is the architecture. The Cabildo, Presbytère, 1850 House, Madame John's Legacy, and Old U.S. Mint [see below] are all properties of the Louisiana State Museum (504/568–6968). Admission to each is $4 for adults.

Three other historic French Quarter homes are open to the public. **Beauregard-Keyes House** (1113 Chartres St. 504/

523–7257) was briefly the residence of Confederate General P.G.T. Beauregard—a Confederate factoid that spurred its restoration. It was also home to best-selling author Francis Parkinson Keyes; *Dinner at Antoine's* is her most famous book. Ms. Keyes' decanter collection, private chapel, and vast court-yard are highlights. The docents don't always reveal that the mansion subbed as a bordello in that potboiling paean to miscegenation, *Mandingo*. The Italianate **Gallier House** **(1118–1132 Royal St. 504/525–5661)** was home to one of New Orleans' most celebrated architects, James Gallier, Jr., and remains a showcase for his innovative talents. Built in 1857, this National Landmark boasts elaborate plaster cor-nices and moldings, gasoliers of bronzed gunmetal and French trompe l'oeil wallpaper. The ornate, heavily carved rosewood Belter furniture is mind-boggling. Gallier, inci-dentally, was originally Gallagher; newcomers often Frenchi-fied their names out of deference to the ruling Creole society.

The red-brick Georgian facade of the 1831 **Hermann-Grima House** **(820 St. Louis St. 504/525–5661)** comes as a real architectural jolt in the Creole Quarter. The grand inte-rior has Corinthian columns, carved friezes, and a Regency chandelier. The cypress doors are made to resemble mahogany, and one bedroom has wallpaper resembling drapery. Millionaire Felix Grima could certainly have sprung for the real thing, but in those days faking it was fashion-able. If you fancy grillwork, check out the 1838 **Mil-tenberger House** **(900–906 Royal St.)**. Alice Heine was born here in 1910 and became the first American princess of Monaco when she married Prince Louis (sorry, Grace). There's some spectacular black grillwork at **1035 Royal Street**, made all the more dramatic by the gigantic ferns.

Maspero's Exchange (*440 Chartres St.*) is infamous on two counts. In past incarnations it was a slave auction house and a coffeehouse where Andy Jackson allegedly planned strategy for the Battle of New Orleans. It's architecturally significant because of a rare entresol, or mezzanine, between floors. Today it's a restaurant.

A grand house with a grim past, the so-called "haunted house" at **1140 Royal Street** has been the focus of many books and documentaries. Onetime owner and demented, high-born Creole Delphine Lalaurie was accused of torturing her slaves, and was driven from the city by an angry mob when her dirty deeds were exposed. The moaning ghost of a slave girl who plunged from the roof rather than submit to further whipping supposedly still hangs out here. Some of the haunted house tours exaggerate shamelessly about this mansion—it's been totally rebuilt since those hideous events of 1833.

Another place with a macabre past is the **Gardette-Le Prêtre House** (*716 Dauphine St.*). Built in 1836, it has one of the highest galleries in the city, with mirrored windowpanes on the top floors giving an illusion of transparency when viewed from a block away. The brother of Turkish Prince Cousrouf was murdered on this site, along with his five child brides. Neighbors said the gore was so intense that the streets ran with blood, and the crimes were never solved.

Not as horrific but equally controversial is the **Civil Courts Building** (*900 Royal St.*). It's a magnificent marble structure to be sure, but it required the destruction of a full block of glorious Spanish Creole townhouses when it went up in 1908–09. It's since served as headquarters for the U.S. Department of Wildlife & Fisheries and as a television sound stage, and sat empty and decaying for years before being proposed for a casino. Happily, it's finally being restored as the Louisiana Supreme Court.

Also worth a peek is the **Musée Conti Wax Museum of Louisiana Legends** (*917 Conti St. 504/525–2605*) with exhibits on voodoo, jazz, and Mardi Gras depicting the region's colorful past. Although some of the wax figures are startlingly lifelike, they're probably of most interest to children. **The Historic New Orleans Collection** (*533 Royal St. 504/523–4662*) has constantly changing exhibits, most of them interesting and well mounted. Subjects of past displays have included Tennessee Williams, the sugarcane industry, and various jazz artists. Check out the window displays of antique pharmaceutical paraphernalia (is that a leech jar?) at **The New Orleans Pharmacy Museum** (*514 Chartres St. 504/565–8027*), and then step inside to the 1820s world of Louis J. Dufilho, the nation's first licensed pharmacist. Whether or not you're interested in medicine, it's hard not to be intrigued by this unique little museum. If nothing else, it will make you appreciate modern medicine.

Alas, the **Orleans Ballroom**, once the site of those glamorous Quadroon Balls, is now only a meeting room in **The Bourbon Orleans Hotel** (*717 Orleans St. 504/523–2222*) [see **sleeping**]. After the balls ended in the 1860s, Thomy Lafon, a free man of color, bought the place and gave it to the Negro Sisters of the Holy Family, an order of black nuns. That order, incidentally, had been founded in 1842 by the daughter of a Quadroon mistress, so there's an irony in there somewhere. For the record, a Quadroon is someone who is one-quarter black, three-quarters white; Octoroons were one-eighth black, seven-eighths white. New Orleans had, by far, the South's largest population of free blacks, who boasted a high culture.

The oldest building in the Mississippi Valley is the **Ursuline Convent** (*1114 Chartres St. 504/529–3040*), dating back to 1752. This enormous walled compound has been expertly restored and includes a beautiful parterre garden which can be glimpsed through the gates. Tours are available, as are research facilities. Next door is the former Chapel of the Archbishops (1845), now called **Our Lady of Victory**, a jewel-like house of worship still in use. Pop your head inside and take a look.

There's a fine Mardi Gras display at the aforementioned **Old U.S. Mint** (*400 Esplanade Ave. 504/568–6968*). Exhibits include a partial reconstruction of a Mardi Gras float and parade, lavish costumes, jewelry, and more. For music lovers, the Mint also has a fascinating jazz exhibit with, among other things, Satchmo's trumpet. On that note, time to move on up Esplanade Avenue, dividing the Quarter from the Faubourg Marigny downriver. Esplanade is one of the finest boulevards in the city, a place where wealthy Creoles promenaded in their carriages. Joggers and dog-walkers now enjoy the shade of magnificent live oaks dating from the 19th century. Granted, its grandeur has faded, and its onetime solid row of elegant mansions is broken by sagging fixer-uppers and modern architectural intrusions, but Esplanade still has plenty left from its glory days. The most notable example is the sprawling **Gauche Villa** at the corner of Royal Street, a splendid Italianate complex built in 1856. It was restored in 1938 by Matilda Gettings Gray and again in 1969 by her daughter, Matilda Gray Stream. The complex extends to Barracks Street, and is famous for its lavish ironwork. Tourists are fond of scrambling up the gates to get a better look at the lush courtyard with its beautiful cast-iron fountain.

Turn left on North Rampart Street, the lakeside border of the Quarter. This decaying commercial/residential strip is the current target of something called Renaissance on Rampart, and although progress is showing, the area remains risky at night, with **Louis Armstrong Park** being downright dangerous. You're pretty safe by day if you act like you know what you're doing. Rampart has an indelible place in the history of American music, and not just because of its namesake blues tune. Across the street in the Faubourg Tremé is Louis Armstrong Park, the site of **Congo Square**, where African slaves gave birth to jazz. A historical marker commemorates the spot and a statue of Satchmo commemorates New Orleans' most famous native son. The park also has the **Municipal Auditorium**, site of many Mardi Gras balls, and the **Mahalia Jackson Center for the Performing Arts** (504/565–7470), home to the **New Orleans Opera**. On nearby Basin Street, another famous blues street, is the site of Storyville, the infamous red-light district where young Louis played. A historical marker in the Basin Street neutral ground is all that's left of it; it's long since been replaced by the Iberville public housing project. Now, it's not safe to go there.

Composer Moreau Gottschalk lived on Rampart in the 1830s, between Bienville and Conti streets, and by the turn of the century Rampart was known as the Tango Belt, a sizzling strip of Latin cabarets. It didn't take long for jazz to jump over from Basin Street, spawning a number of happening joints. Funky Butt [see **music/clubs**] is a throwback to that fabulous era. Other musical memories are generated by **Hula Mae's Tropical Wash** at No. 838, formerly Cosimo Matassa's J&M Studios, where Little Richard, Fats Domino, and Smiley Lewis recorded back in the '50s.

At the corner of Conti is **Our Lady of Guadeloupe Chapel** (411 N. Rampart St.), built in 1826 and quickly pressed into service as a funerary chapel. Until mosquitoes were identified as the cause of malaria in 1900, swampy New Orleans was the site of terrible plagues. Thousands died in a single season, making it impossible for St. Louis Cathedral to handle all the funerals. The large St. Jude shrine is definitely worth a look. The historic chapel is also the occasional site for jazz concerts and rocking gospel, so ask around. It's an experience you shouldn't miss.

When you don't want any more history, head down Canal toward the Mississippi. Cross the streetcar tracks to the truly impressive **Aquarium of the Americas** (1 Canal St. 504/861–2537), rated one of the top five in the country, with a million gallons of fresh and salt water and over 6,000 species of fish, amphibians, reptiles, and birds. Highlights include the Gulf of Mexico exhibit's 400,000-gallon shark tank teeming with toothy denizens, the Caribbean Reef's underwater tunnel, a scaled-down Gulf oil rig, the world's largest exhibit of jellyfish, shark petting, and a mini-Amazon rainforest tucked into that towering half-dome. If that doesn't bring out the kid in you, check out the albino alligators, red-bellied piranhas, black-footed penguins, rare paddlefish, and truly bizarre batfish. Whimsical sculptures, including a gigantic shark fin, dot the plaza between the Aquarium and the river. This is where you can board the *Cotton Blossom* for a seven-mile cruise up to Audubon Zoo. Truth is, the view's pretty boring unless you're seriously into wharves or enjoy getting in-your-face with mammoth barges and tankers, but it's a pleasant-enough alternative to driving. Most people prefer to cruise one way and take the **St. Charles Streetcar** the other. Next door is the **Entergy IMAX Theater** (*1 Canal St. 504/ 581–4629*), with a regularly changing calendar of films.

Continue downriver to **Woldenberg Park**, a splendid green space with weeping willows shimmering in cool, riverine breezes. Some simply stretch out on the grass to study the awesome cloud formations sweeping off the Gulf of Mexico. If your timing's on-target, you'll be sere-naded by calliope music from the *Natchez*, the only bona fide 19th-century stern-wheeler calling New Orleans home. Hop aboard and get reborn on the bayou, or just enjoy a narrated harbor cruise. You can also take a jazz din-ner cruise with the famed Dukes of Dixieland. It can be fun, but be warned that the music, city lights and bygone ambience of the *Natchez* far outshine her food. For more info and sailing schedules on the *Natchez* and the *Cotton Blossom*, call **New Orleans Steamboat Company** (**504/586–8777, 800/233–2628**).

Past the *Natchez* is the wooden **Moon Walk**, with benches where you may get serenaded by a splendid sax player or panhandled by black-clad punks. While you're enjoying watching the ship traffic of one of the world's busiest ports, remember that you're on reclaimed land. In fact, that whole expanse you've just walked from the aquarium

is built on pilings pounded into the river. You're never far
from water in New Orleans.

spectating... Le Petit Théâtre du Vieux Carré (616
St. Peter St. 504/522–9958), known locally as Le Petit, is one
of the oldest theaters in America. Musicals are usually its
forte, and a recent staff shake-up suggests there has been a
definite improvement in quality. Le Petit also hosts a number of other events, including the Tennessee Williams/New
Orleans Literary Festival in the spring and the William
Faulkner celebration in the fall.

Royal Street after dark is a delightful counterpart to
the loud lunacy of Bourbon Street a block away. A stroll
between Bienville and St. Peters streets not only invites
window shopping but also introduces you to some truly
fine street singers. You may encounter a black quintet har-
monizing '50s standards, an opera singer belting arias, or
a mesmerizing dulcimer player. A carriage with a wedding
party may stop to be serenaded. Just another magical
moment in the Vieux Carré.

body

The French Quarter is far more celebrated for undoing the
body than redoing it, but there are a few good places for
honing and toning. The oldest and most famous is the
New Orleans Athletic Club (222 North Rampart St.
504/525–2375), a classy old structure whose age belies its
modern touches. There are the requisite workout facilities
and pool of course, but you can really kiss off too much

rich food and/or drink with a visit to **Le Salon** (504/
581–4999) in the club. A massage, manicure, pedicure,
facial, and peel works wonders for last night's self-abuse.
The full-body rub with a sea salt/oil paste will rejuvenate
you for almost anything. Guest memberships are available.

Earthsavers (*434 Chartres St.* 504/581–4999) is one of
five around town, a chain of holistic spas striving for that
ideal balance of body, mind, and spirit. They come damned
close, with their honey-almond-yogurt detox/rejuvena-
tion treatment and the seaweed facial guaranteed to revive
tired faces. They also offer shiatsu and Swedish massage.
You can unwind later in the second-floor relaxation room
or courtyard with soothing fountain. This is the place for
rejuvenation in the Quarter.

If you think **Headquarters** (*900 Dumaine St.* 504/
522–2666) is paying homage to Marilyn Monroe, you're
right. This friendly neighborhood haircutter has a jazzy
display of MM stuff, but that doesn't mean you'll come out
looking like a blonde bombshell (unless you request it).
These guys have been coiffing Quarterites for years, but
walk-ins are welcome.

With its trademark red windmill right by Mary's True
Value Hardware, **Moulin Rouge Beauty Salon** (*906 Bourbon St.* 504/568–0465) is hard to miss. So is owner George's
motorcycle, complete with faux-coffin sidecar, parked out
front when he's in residence. This place is a one-man time
trip for ladies and gentlemen who want a dose of local
gossip while getting coiffed, plus a healthy dash of pure
Quarter eccentricity. For an appointment, call and leave a
message.

You'll find some of the best styling and coloring at

Arthur's House of Glamour (533 Wilkinson St. 504/581–2464), locally known as the home of "big hair." This place also does excellent manicures. **Happiness Hair Salon** (907 Iberville St. 504/528–9185) offers a full range of cut and color options, as well as manicures, pedicures, and waxing. They also carry a selection of hair-care products.

Warlocks (733 St. Louis St. 504/581–5843) is popular with younger locals after trendier cuts. Rounding out the list are **Ivette Keller** (527 Dumaine St. 504/522–1688), **Guy Keefer Salons** (621 St. Louis St. 504/523–2545), the newly relocated **Eclipse Salon** (536 Bienville St. 504/522–3318) and **Fountain of Beauty** (815 Toulouse St. 504/586–9207). **Mr. Jack's Louisiana Haircutters** (111 Decatur St. 504/522–7762) draws customers from the CBD as well as the Quarter.

Ready for the tattoo plunge? Technically on the edge of the Quarter, **Aart Accent Tat-2 Cafe** (1041 N. Rampart St. 504/581–9812) is impossible to miss with those giant '60s-ish murals verging on day-glo. It's not as garish inside, although some of the tat pics on the walls are pretty out there. The staff is friendly enough and know what they're doing, but they've got an unnecessary touch of attitude. Nobody wants to go in knowing just what they want and then be talked out of it by an artist pushing his own designs. You're the one who has to live with it, right? They're also a bit overpriced, probably due to a tourist trade drawn by an outrageous storefront that wouldn't be permitted in the Quarter. You'd be better off at Orleans Ink in the Marigny [see **faubourg marigny** chapter].

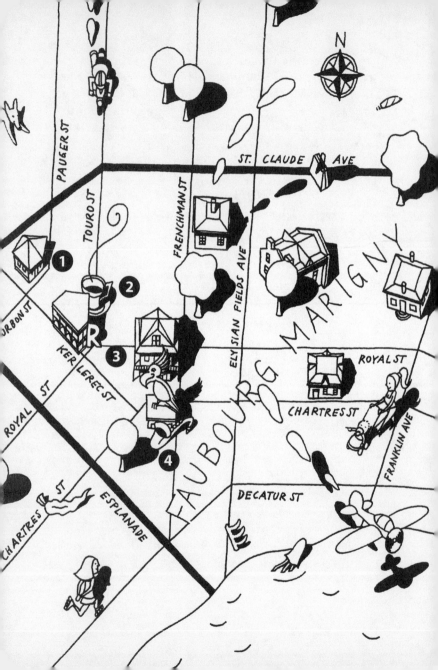

faubourg marigny

The Faubourg Marigny was named for Bernard Xavier Philippe de Marigny de Mandeville, who, upon his planter father's death in 1800, became the richest 15-year-old in America. While studying in Paris, Bernard got addicted to the dice game craps, which he brought to New Orleans, and by the age of 20, he was forced to carve up the family plantation to pay gambling debts. But Bernard retained a sense of humor, naming a street Rue de Craps, now Burgundy Street.

MONTEGUT ST

turn page for map key

Faubourg is French for "suburb." The Faubourg Marigny
was the second suburb outside the original town plan and
the first Creole suburb.

It was originally created for working-class people who
could not find living space in the congested Quarter.
When a huge wave of German immigrants washed ashore
in the mid-19th century, so many settled here among the
Creoles that the neighborhood was nicknamed Little
Saxony. Today the Faubourg Marigny Historic District is
bounded by Esplanade Avenue, St. Claude Avenue, Press
Street, and the Mississippi River. Locals call it simply "the
Marigny."

Adjacent to and immediately downriver from the French
Quarter, it has a charm all its own. Its architecture is almost
exclusively 19th century, with Creole cottages, gingerbread
shotgun houses and a couple of church spires dominating
the neighborhood. Many homes have been lovingly
restored by aficionados of the period, while others lan-
guish in the debilitating heat, paint peeling and walls dis-
tressed, abandoned like cast-off lovers. Still others are
burned out and boarded up, fate unknown. No one seems
to mind that all this sits cheek by jowl. In fact, it's that
delightful mix of fine and funky that sets the Marigny apart.

Marigny residents also benefit from a serious drop in
real estate prices occurring the moment you cross
Esplanade Avenue and leave the Quarter. They're proud of

map key

1 Dolliole-Davis Cottage   3 Snug Harbor
2 Cafe Marigny   4 Cafe Brasil

their clever choice and swear they wouldn't live anywhere else. In addition to lower rents, they enjoy quiet, tree-lined streets and their own village green, Washington Square, facing Elysian Fields. It's a refuge for joggers, moms with carriages, gays, street kids, the occasional derelict, and other assorted locals. Their easy mix says everything about this eclectic neighborhood.

The unofficial main drag is Frenchmen Street, named for the French patriots who threw out the Spanish in 1768 in America's first colonial rebellion against a European power. They were executed in Jackson Square for their efforts, but New Orleans has not forgotten their courage. It's serendipitous that the street named for these martyrs should now be home to some of the most happening clubs in town. It also has some super restaurant bargains. Beyond that, it's a pretty quiet neighborhood.

eating/coffee

Food venues in the Marigny are limited but varied and surprisingly good. Remember that although the neighborhood is safely walkable by day, at night, unless you're in a well-lit, highly trafficked area like Frenchmen or Esplanade, you'd better grab a cab.

Cost Range per entree
$/under 10 dollars
$$/10–15 dollars
$$$/15–20 dollars
$$$$/20+ dollars

coffee... **P.J.'s Coffee & Tea Cafe** (634 Frenchmen St. 504/949–2292 **$**) is part of the popular chain. P.J.'s has three freshly roasted and brewed hot coffees with a selection changing daily, plus cold-brewed iced coffees. There are the usual macchiatos, cappuccinos, and lattes, but for something a little different try the espresso dolce, which is brewed with pressurized water to extract the essence of the coffee. The white-chocolate cappuccino and honey-cream dessert coffees are a rich indulgence. Both hot and iced tea are available, along with hot and iced chai.

creole/cajun... Deep in the Marigny, **Feelings** (2600 Chartres St. 504/945–2222 **$$–$$$$**) is a charming architectural oddity combining a 19th-century store with 18th-century slave quarters from the long-vanished D'Aunoy plantation. Peeling brick walls and ancient masonry team with shutters and overhead fans for a quintessential New Orleans ambience. To the left as you enter is a pleasant dining room with paintings of tropical flora. To the right is a bar and the controlled jungle of a courtyard teeming with banana trees and elephant ears. You can dine indoors or out. Always a favorite, the medallions of veal D'Aunoy are sautéed with herb lemon butter and topped with sliced mushrooms and hollandaise sauce. The beef tournedos and barbecued shrimp are also delicious, as are the zesty crab cakes. If you can, save room for the diet-bashing peanut-butter pie.

Intimate **Snug Harbor** (626 Frenchmen St. 504/949–0696 **$–$$$**) offers a good range of local fare, including the standard crawfish étouffée, shrimp Creole, barbecued shrimp, and fried oysters, but also Southern fried chicken, steaks, and sandwiches. Their juicy burgers are some of the best in town. This is the place for goofy tropical drinks like Neptune's Monsoon and the Huma Huma, which serves two, along with Goombay Punch and the Snug Harbor, a Polynesian grog. The food and drink are pretty good, but you definitely come here for the music, not the munch [see **bars/music/clubs**].

eclectic...
The **Cafe Marigny** (1913 *Royal St.* 504/945–4472 $–$$$) was a simple but popular coffee-house before they added (recently) multicultural cuisine. Breakfast highlights are tangy black-bean cakes with fried eggs, and spicy andouille hash with potatoes and fresh sage. Salads and creative sandwiches take over at lunchtime with breads made in-house—the focaccia and pita are super. Dinner appetizers include a silky, garlicky hummus and tempura shrimp in a wasabi sauce with ginger-peach chutney. Popular entrees are the grilled Asian pork chop served with stir-fried veggies and noodles, or grilled tuna on a bed of artichoke hearts, Roma tomatoes, and green lentils, sauced with a reduction of balsamic vinegar and white wine. The chocolate-pecan praline tart makes a fine finale. You can eat indoors or enjoy one of the outdoor tables where the passing parade of quirky faubourg humanity always entertains. Bring your own spirits.

Dream Palace Reality Grill (534 *Frenchmen St.* 504/945–2040 $$), located above the hard-rockin' Dream Palace, is scarcely a place you'd purposely choose for dinner. But as long as you're there, grab a table outside on the balcony and consider the grilled salmon and tuna steaks, or maybe the crawfish ya-ya, a pasta dish drenched with an inspired amalgam of crawfish tails, mushrooms, and a tasso-laced cream sauce. The food is fine, but what this place really has going for it is the music and the views: French doors open onto a balcony that is the unquestioned hot spot for checking out the weekend action on Frenchmen Street.

cafes/diners... If you're on a budget or want to hang with the locals, beat feet to **Buffa's** (1001 *Esplanade Ave.* 504/945–9373 **$**). It's dark and decidedly on the dingy side, but what do you expect at these prices? The friendly bartender sometimes doubles as waiter and will hustle out your order unless he needs to chat with his regulars. There are daily specials like Southern-fried veal cutlet, spaghetti & meatballs, smothered pork chops, lasagna, and more, all at rock-bottom prices. The cook has obviously never heard of cholesterol—if you like it on the lighter side, grab the garlic bread and wring out some of the butter. Fun, cheap, and always a kick. The restrooms are such a hike you almost need a passport.

La Péniche (1940 *Dauphine St.* 504/943–1460 **$**) is extremely popular with the gay set as well as Marigny locals. This onetime corner grocery store may remind you of a small-town '50s cafe with its paneled walls and plants. It does a brisk business right into the wee hours, when people stagger home from a night of carousing in the Quarter. For breakfast, try the crawfish or crab omelettes and check out the daily specials. Lunchtime, your best bet for taming a ferocious appetite is the enormous Katherine burger, which comes with a variety of trimmings, and the fried-seafood dishes make a hearty dinner. The crowd is usually festive, though the waiters usually aren't.

soul food/southern... An instant hit, **The Praline Connection** (542 Frenchmen St. 504/943–3934 $) has soul food and down-home cookin' so good it'll make you wanna holler. Your taste buds start acting up as soon as you walk in the place, where a dapper young African-American staff in black fedoras and crisp white shirts waits to take your order. The baked chicken and fried chicken are true taste thrills, as are the homemade meat-loaf, stuffed bell peppers, and barbecued ribs. Enjoy them with the comfy flavors of mustard, collard, or cabbage greens; red, white, or lima beans; crowder peas with okra, macaroni and cheese, or potato salad. It all comes with smokin' cornbread and is best washed down with iced tea. Now surely you have room for the bread pudding with praline sauce? On your way out, stop in the bake shop for some fab pralines to go. Purists may carp, but the choco-late ones are divine. It's not hard to understand why this place has opened four branches and operates a concession stand at the airport!

southwest... **Santa Fe** (801 Frenchmen St. 504/944–6854 $$) is in an old house overlooking Washington Square. Although it's been adapted for restaurant use, you still get the feeling that you're dining in someone's home. That's due in part to the amiable staff, big wicker chairs so com-fortable you never want to get up (and after too many mar-garitas you may not be able to!), and a hospitable cuisine best described as Southwest with a New Orleans accent.

You can start with the traditional margarita or opt for a glass of sangria to accompany the zesty ceviche or portabello mushroom soup. Main courses swing from such heavy fare as a chicken breast rolled with pumpkin seeds and cheese to an airy crabmeat/veggie plate splashed with spicy sauce. The *puerco con manzanas* is another fave.

thai... In an area swarming with outstanding Creole and Cajun fare, **Siam Cafe** *(435 Esplanade Ave. 504/949–1750 $)* is the exotic and welcome alternative, not only bringing popular Thai cuisine to the nabe but doing it with sass. Standards like the inevitable pad thai and spring rolls are good and the chicken curry—a velvety blend of chicken and veggies in a golden coconut-milk—is superb. The lighting can be on the dark side, a sort of Asian funk that's totally appropriate for this part of the Marigny. For a real cross-cultural journey, head upstairs and check out the live music in the Dragon's Den.

bars/music/clubs

The Faubourg Marigny has a handful of hip clubs that constantly lure Quarterites across Esplanade. Tourists should follow suit if they love music—they'll find some of the most happening sounds, here or anywhere. The undisputed heart of the action, and maybe the hippest two blocks in town, is Frenchmen Street between Royal and Chartres. You can't help ogling the gnarly socioeconomic gumbo packing the clubs and hanging on the streets. Students, Gen-Xers, bohos, alternaqueers, aging hippies, pierced punkers, and slumming uptown types—the lost and the found and the still-looking. Most of these savage and not-so-savage beasts with that primordial need to be soothed are bound together by sound. Heads are even occasionally turned here—surprising for a city where they've seen and done it all.

The granddaddy of them all is **Snug Harbor** (*626 Frenchmen St. 504/949–0696*) where you can munch a juicy burger [see **eating/coffee**] and stick around for some intense jamming. It's one of the best places in town for rhythm & blues and local jazz, the home away from home for such pros as the Ellis Marsalis Trio, Charmaine Neville, and Lil' Queen. It won't be long before the fantastic sounds in this intimate room swoop down and take you somewhere mystic. The name for this cozy joint is deliciously appropriate. **Cafe Brasil** (*2100 Chartres St. 504/ 949–0851*) is a loose-leafed combo of club, bar, and coffeehouse. Again, the crowd is a mishmash of cocktailers and caffeine-heads, and you'd have to be Little Nell from the Country to believe all these folks are on a natural high. Underground no more, Brasil offers gigs to anyone and everything. One night the place is jazz-jumping with old-timers showing the kids where it came from, or there might be a band from Latin America or a group so new they're still arguing over the name. Spontaneity is often the game, and if the sound doesn't suit you, move on. Cafe Brasil is also fun for special events, such as their Sunday-night tango lessons complete with Argentine band. Hours may vary and sometimes no one answers the phone. You did see the movie *Brazil*, didn't you?

Another musical grab bag is **The Dream Palace** (*534

Frenchmen St. 504/945–2040) (briefly known as Cafe
Istanbul) where the ever-popular Radiators held forth for
years. That alone guarantees the place a giant silhouette on
the local music landscape. The sound is live, and the young
crowd livelier, lounging in comfy chairs or swooping
across the huge dance floor to the beat-of-the-moment.
You can end up working it to a salsa or other Latin beat,
jiving to some hard-core New Orleans jazz, or getting in
the mood with some down-home, heartbreaking blues,
not to mention reggae. You just may hit one of the occasional underground parties, when the place is packed with
perennial hipsters in their funerary duds and not a few
pierced princes and princesses grooving on the cool '70s
ceiling murals.

As bars go, **Buffa's** (1001 *Esplanade Ave.* 504/945–9373),
a dimly lit, narrow joint, is about as neighborhoody as
you can get, walls plastered with yellowing photos of
locally famous folks and long-forgotten things (check out
the snake). The cheer comes from the colorful, usually
friendly locals, happily shooting the bull while tossing
down the booze and brew. This is a great spot for taking
the city's pulse on everything from the mayor's most
recent ego trip to the latest casino crisis. It's like riding
with a chatty cabbie. The **Apple Barrell Bar** (609
Frenchmen St. 504/949–9399) is almost literally a hole in
the wall, a dark, paneled watering spot that's been slaking
local thirsts for years. Things can get pretty lively on the
weekends and during Mardi Gras, and if you like privacy
or are claustrophobic, this isn't your spot.

Last but definitely not least is **Vaughan's** (800 *Lesseps St.*
504/947–5562), a red-hot spot deep in the Bywater, the

Marigny's mostly seedy downriver neighbor. Don't be put off by the honky-tonk exterior. Embrace it and you'll be rewarded by the sweet, sultry sounds of Kermit Ruffin, who may be New Orleans' most famous young jazz trumpeter. During breaks, Kermit's loyal fans eat red beans and rice, as if they needed a reason to stay for another set. The depressed neighborhood's downright scary, but a cab will get you in and out just fine.

buying stuff

Because it never really deviated from its original purpose as a residential area, shopping is simply not the Marigny's strong suit. Locals have never shown much interest in being shopkeepers, no doubt because of the wealth of goods available in the retail behemoth across Esplanade Avenue. Still, there are a few spots worth a look.

books... The **Faubourg Marigny Bookstore** (600 Frenchmen 504/943–9875) is the South's oldest gay, lesbian, and feminist bookstore, in operation since 1977. It stocks best-sellers as well as classic titles and hard-to-find items. Owner Alan Robinson also carries a small line of greeting cards, posters, CDs, and other gift items of special interest to gay shoppers. Everyone is welcome.

collectibles... It seems like every inch of space is occupied at **Judy's Collage** (2102 Chartres St. 504/945–0252), a veritable catacomb of collectibles that would take you hours to inspect closely. You'll find everything from jewelry to dishes, tin signs to lamps, and funky souvenirs from years gone by. The store has been featured in numerous music and commercial videos, as evidenced by the collection of 30 or so photos on the walls. Judy herself collects palm trees, which means you're wasting your time coveting the unusual metal palms near the front door. They're left over from the 1984 Louisiana World's Fair, and they ain't for sale. If you're staying in the Quarter and enjoy junking, this place is definitely worth a stroll across Esplanade.

sleeping

The Marigny is largely a bedroom community, but because of its proximity to the French Quarter it offers a surprising number and range of accommodations. Visitors who assume they'll find more reasonable rates here are right, although there are a couple of high-end places that compete vigorously with those in the Quarter.

Cost Range for double occupancy per night on a weeknight. Call to verify prices.

$/under 100 dollars
$$/100–150 dollars
$$$/150–200 dollars
$$$$/200+ dollars

The **Melrose Mansion Hotel** (937 *Esplanade Ave.* 504/944–2255 $$$$) is a grand 1884 Victorian manse facing the leafy boulevard of Esplanade. It has four rooms and four suites with hot tubs, one with private patio. All have high ceilings and hardwood floors and are handsomely appointed with 19th-century Louisiana antiques. You can have breakfast in the formal dining room, alfresco by the pool, or in your four-poster bed. Cocktails are served nightly in the posh drawing room, and a stretch limo provides airport transportation. An exercise room helps work off those excess New Orleans calories.

Its deluxe neighbor a few doors down is the **Hotel de la Monnaie** (405 *Esplanade Ave.* 504/947–0009 $$$), with suites for guests as well as condos. The formidable gray stone exterior with its panoply of flags and chandelier gleaming within gives the impression that a grand lobby will greet you. Not. There's only a small reception area with a desk to the right and a sitting library to the left, but everything is nicely appointed and maintained. All suites have kitchenettes, whirlpool tubs, and sofa beds. There are two courtyards with fountain and pool, indoor parking, and a concierge. Incidentally, the name means "currency" in French.

The **Claiborne Mansion** (2111 *Dauphine St.* 504/949–7327 $-$$) is another period manse. Once the home of Louisiana Governor Claiborne, this 1855 beauty is unquestionably one of the city's grandest B&Bs. The five suites are exquisitely appointed, with hand-painted carpets, enormous marble baths, fireplaces with original mantles, and queen-sized beds handsomely executed in mahogany or iron. The smaller quarters in the former service wing in the rear are no less luxurious and look into an enormous landscaped courtyard with great live oaks, cabana, arbor, and a swimming pool complete with water-

a revel without a cause

In the August torpor of 1971, in a French Quarter dive called the Golden Lantern, a handful of bored drag queens decided that it had been too long since there was a parade. It didn't matter that the city had, by far, more festivals than any other in America or that Mardi Gras alone counted more than 60 parades. Common sense should've warned anyone to chill during the anaesthetizing summer, but logic has always been in notoriously short supply below sea level. Besides, drag queens are famed for determination as well as attitude. Sewing machines hummed, glue guns were hauled out from carnivals past, and in the twinkling of an overly mascaraed eye, a gaggle of dragsters appeared at the Golden Lantern ready for their sequined take on a Labor Day parade.

Southern Decadence Day had arrived. Dubbed "Decadence" and nicknamed "gay Mardi Gras," it was an instant smash. Word quickly spread to gay communities throughout the South, and over the next few years, the parade ranks steadily swelled with out-of-towners wanting in on the fun. Since there were no rules on who could participate—or on anything else for that matter—it wasn't long before the leather boys got into the guise-and-dolls act. They were eventually joined by still more revelers in costumes of every description and persuasion, stirring cocktails and naughty mischief along the way.

The parade soon spawned associated activities, turning

Decadence into a four-day event. Aside from the Sunday parade, there's kick-off Thursday's Big Wig Show with prizes, Friday's Wig-Out, and Saturday's Mr. Louisiana Leather contest at the State Palace Theater. There are a dozen or so other events, but the Sunday parade remains the key event, mincing off at 2 p.m. at the Golden Lantern. These days the route is lined by thousands of spectators cheering the imaginative costumes, or lack thereof, and towering hairdos shaped like teddy bears, flamingoes, and tornados, and made of everything from aluminum foil to Spanish moss. The action keeps going until dawn, and by Labor Day, many welcome the traditional "Hung Over and Broke Party" at the Parade disco.

With no official sponsors, the growth and success of Decadence is driven only by the considerable energy of its participants. In 1997, hotel owners finally acknowledged the huge influx during the doldrums of late summer when bookings are at a traditional low. They started offering special deals for Decadence visitors. There is no official estimate of the crowd, but 10,000 seems a conservative guess for those attending the 1998 celebration. Most gay bars reach a saturation level seen only during Mardi Gras or Halloween, with several intersections virtually impassable due to crowds overflowing onto the streets. City fathers, as they often do, look the other way from yet another bit of French Quarter bawdiness. Besides, it's obviously good for business.

spouting lion's heads. Delightfully, the fruits and vegetables in the complimentary breakfast come from a garden next door. If your stay at the Mansion isn't memorable, it's not because the staff doesn't try.

Across the park is the **Parkview Marigny B&B** (726 Frenchmen St. 504/945–7876 $–$$). The nicely renovated one-story yellow house has 14-foot ceilings, hardwood floors, and a brick patio. Every room has ceiling fans, private bath, cable TV, and a four-poster plantation, canopy, or Victorian bed. Continental breakfast is served in the dining room. Just two blocks from the French Quarter, this one's a bargain. Two 1850s townhouses have been joined to create **The Frenchmen** (417 Frenchmen St. 504/948–2166, 800/831–1781 $$–$$$), a small 25-room hotel that looks far more atmospheric from the outside. Unfortunately, the 19th century pretty much vanishes once you step onto the two-toned pile carpeting and find yourself amidst other jarringly modern touches. The dining room, with its reproduction antiques, is only a reminder of how much heritage has been lost, and the nondescript rooms confirm it. The swimming pool and Jacuzzi in the lush courtyard definitely add a pleasing touch, but the rooftop sundeck is a cement wasteland, hardly inviting during the fierce New Orleans heat. Pluses include proximity to the Quarter, reasonable rates, and balconies off some rooms.

doing stuff

The Marigny can't compare with the endless attractions of its world-famous neighbor, nor does it want to. That doesn't mean there aren't a few things worth exploring in a neighborhood whose charm lies in quietness and an abundance of historic architecture. When the Quarter gets to be too much, cross Esplanade and wander the streets of the Marigny. Stop for a cappuccino at the Cafe Marigny and enjoy the rejuvenating leafy quiet of Washington Square.

The fun of the Marigny is exploring, but there are several outstanding early- and mid-19th-century structures worth seeking out. One of the oldest is the **Nathan-Lewis-Cizek House** (926–28 Kerlerec St.), built in 1806, remodeled 30 years later, and again in 1976. Also called Sun Oak cottage, it's a rare example of a Greek revival galleried Creole cottage and boasts a rusticated facade and dogtrot. It's the home of restoration architect Eugene Cizek and artist Lloyd Sensat, Jr., both major forces in the Faubourg Marigny Improvement Association. Open by appointment only as a gallery and, occasionally, as an inn.

The **Dolliole-Davis Cottage** (1436 Pauger St.) dates from 1820. It would be considered a standard Creole cottage, except that it has five sides. The odd but charming shape was dictated by a lot conforming to existing streets and a bend in the nearby river. The original builder, Jean-Louis Dolliole, was a free man of color who constructed several Creole cottages. Nearby is the 1830 **Flettrich House** (1445 Pauger St.), a fine example of a one-and-a-half-story Creole cottage. The detailing is superb, including Ionic pilasters in the facade and a plain classic door frame.

The three-story residence at **501 Frenchmen Street** is a perfect example of a Creole townhouse with a wrap-around gallery. The ironwork is original to the 1840s building which, typically, had a commercial ground floor with apartments on the upper levels. Facing Washington Square is the grand but understated **Claiborne Mansion (2111 Dauphine St.)**. An exemplary two-story Greek revival house built for Louisiana Governor W.C.C. Claiborne, it remained in the family until 1919. The mansion has been beautifully restored and endures as an elegant B&B [see **sleeping**].

Incidentally, if you decide to go calling at the home of Stanley and Stella Kowalski at 632 Elysian Fields, an address immortalized in Tennessee Williams' *A Streetcar Named Desire*, you'll be disappointed . . . just like Blanche. It's a barber shop. Obviously Tennessee was taking his usual poetic liberties.

Just across the railroad tracks from the Marigny (some say on the wrong side!) is a neighborhood called the Bywater, where residents close to the river claim their houses tremble when a freighter rounds the bend. No one knows for sure why it's called that, since most every place in New Orleans is by some kind of water. The most popular, and certainly the funniest, explanation is that the name came about when telephone exchanges were being assigned and Ma Bell meted out BYwater for these folks. The exchanges are long gone, but the rather romantic name lingers on. The area is speckled with historic architecture but is largely unsafe for walking, even in the daytime.

body

Ever had a hankering to have your body safely invaded by
metal or ink? Visit **Orleans Ink Tattoos and Body
Piercing** (610 Frenchmen St. 504/947–2300). If cleanliness
is next to godliness, these people are offering a divine service indeed. Forget all the comic-book images of tattooers
dressed in undershirts and smoking smelly cigars. The staff
here is throughly professional and gives excellent guid-
ance whether you want a tiny rose on your shoulder, a
post through your tongue, or a gold hoop someplace très
intime. They'll even send a limo for you. Tattoo parlors have
come a long way, baby.

garden districts

6

This is New Orleans at its best and worst, a surreal combination of grandeur and decay, majestic mansions and lethal public-housing projects. You'd best pay attention if you don't want to wind up in the wrong neighborhood. The Lower Garden District stretches roughly from above Lee Circle to Jackson Avenue, between Prytania and Chipewa streets. It's a mixed bag architecturally, ethnically, and socioeconomically, and is on the brink of a major comeback. Directly upriver is the Garden

turn page for map key

District, a 14-block area defined by St. Charles Avenue, Jackson and Louisiana avenues, and Magazine Street. This is New Orleans' undisputed architectural glamour-puss, with one outrageous mansion after another. The homes were built largely by career-conscious Yankees who quickly became Southernized and raised elegant living to an art form. A leisurely stroll through this area shows you just how much moonlight-and-magnolia grandeur could be purchased in the days before income taxes and the Emancipation Proclamation.

St. Charles Avenue is one of the great and certainly one of the most beautiful of America's urban thoroughfares, a throwback to an era when people took Sunday drives to see the sights. There are plenty of eye-popping vistas, from gloriously sprawling live oaks and clanging streetcars to monstrous stone manses, the grand spread of Audubon Park and even a reproduction of Hollywood's Tara. Better see it now before the Formosan termites start bringing down those awesome oaks.

eating/coffee

The fringe of the Garden District has it all, from garlic restaurants and single's pickup joints to smart cafes and haute cuisine. Many places offer indoor or outdoor dining

map key		
	1 Lafayette Cemetery No. 1	4 The Red Room
	2 Commander's Palace	5 Gernon-Edwards-St. Martin House
	3 Anne Rice's House	6 Lee Circle

with views of historic St. Charles Avenue with its canopy of oaks and its noisy streetcars. In the heart of the District itself is world-famous Commander's Palace, the preferred dining destination of knowledgeable visitors.

Cost Range per entree
$/under 10 dollars
$$/10–15 dollars
$$$/15–20 dollars
$$$$/20+ dollars

cafes/diners... Delightfully frozen in time, the **Bluebird Cafe** (3625 *Prytania* St. 504/895–7166 $) is real rather than retro, from the menu to the basic decor. Oh, it's got a few '90s touches, like grilled vegetables, yogurt with fresh fruit, and a healthy mixture of eggs, tamari, cheese, and nutritional yeast, but that's hardly what keeps the efficient wait staff hopping. Most people hit the Bluebird for fried-egg sandwiches, tomatoes stuffed with chicken salad, gigantic pancakes filled with fruit, burgers, and a corned-beef hash that may be the best in Louisiana. This nostalgia-laden joint, with bustling waitresses balancing awesome plate-loads amid the smells of home cooking, is as comfy as an old shoe.

creole... Unless you've been in a galaxy far, far away, you've heard of **Commander's Palace** (1403 *Washington* St. 504/899–8221 $$$–$$$$), the undisputed grande dame of uptown eateries, a longtime tradition, living legend, and home of the original jazz brunch. Chef Jamie Shannon is running the show these days, and he's added

architecture

New Orleans' spectacular architecture was born in France, Spain, and the West Indies, and molded by the steamy, sub-tropical climate. What eventually emerged was the Creole cottage, a single-story wooden structure with a steeply pitched side-gabled roof. The discovery of clay, scarce on the Mississippi river delta, introduced bricks, although of such poor quality they had to be reinforced with posts. A superb example is **Lafitte's Blacksmith**, 941 Bourbon Street, built in 1772. A much grander version of the Creole cottage is **Madame John's Legacy**, 632 Dumaine Street, built in 1789. Much of the old Vieux Carré looked like this before major fires almost erased the town in 1788 and 1794.

The Spanish arrived in 1768, and 20 years later rebuilt the burned city with elegant Creole town houses, two to four stories high, with intricate wrought- and cast-iron fancies, and steep side-gabled roofs often with several dormers. The vista of Royal Street from Governor Nicholls Street toward Canal reveals a concentration of these unique structures—popular until the 1850s—with spacious galleries extending as far as the street (they are never called balconies, which are smaller and uncovered). On Jackson Square, **St. Louis Cathedral** is Spanish Gothic, while the **Cabildo** and **Presbytère** are pure Spanish Baroque.

The **Pitot House**, 1440 Moss Street in Bayou St. John, is a superb example of the West Indian raised plantation house from the Spanish period. It has distinctively stout lower columns and slender wood-turned upper columns called colonnettes. The Americans introduced the raised center hall cottage, usually a story and a half raised two to eight feet off the ground. These are scattered throughout the Garden District and Uptown areas.

By the 1820s the Americans had also introduced their town houses, narrow three-story brick structures with balconies usually on the second floor. The finest surviving examples are in the 600 block of Julia Street, called **Julia Row**, and date from 1832. There are more in the Lower Garden District.

The popular "shotgun" house arrived in the 1840s—a string of connected rooms with no central hallway, often embellished with ornamental brackets, galleries, bays, and pillars. Hundreds are scattered throughout the Faubourg Marigny, Esplanade Ridge, and the Irish Channel. They're easily recognizable by the narrow fronts and deep sides.

Greek revival grandeur peaked in the uptown Garden District from the 1830s–1860s. Secreted in leafy glades are gorgeous antebellum mansions: Second Empire beauties, Victorian gingerbread, Prairie, Regency, even American Georgian. A stroll through this purely residential area (no buses allowed!) is an architecture lesson unto itself.

some personal (and welcome) flourishes to the estab-
lished menu. Commander's is celebrated for turtle soup,
eggs Sardou, and bread pudding, just to name a few. These
are deservedly beloved, but check out Chef Shannon's
adventurous shrimp and tasso with five-pepper jelly. If
you're feeling courageous before dinner, try the chef's
New Orleans Weather Forecast, a cautious concoction of
local rum (yes, they're making it here again) and ginger
beer delivered in a highball glass with a slice of sugarcane.
There's patio dining, but if you can get a seat in the glorious garden room embraced by ancient live oaks, it's like
dining in a tree house. You can even walk through the
kitchen to see the site of these culinary miracles. Visiting
New Orleans without dining at Commander's is virtually
a breach of local etiquette.

Much local hoopla surrounded the 1998 opening of
Emeril Lagasse's third New Orleans restaurant, **Delmonico
(1300 St. Charles Ave. 504/523–9307 $$$)**. Everyone had
heard about the lavish 16-month renovation of the 1890
building, which housed a Creole restaurant from 1895 to
1997. The dining rooms are exquisitely appointed, with
chandeliers resembling bouquets in the Rose Room and a
view of the wine cellar from the Crystal Room. The focal
point of the ground floor is *Foodscape*, an oil painting by
Amy Weisskopf that is a handsome paean to Creole food.
Speaking of the food, there have been complaints that pre-
sentation gets preference over taste, that some portions are
minuscule for the price, that cookaholic Emeril has overex-
tended himself this time. Judge for yourself, starting with
the sherry-laced turtle soup or barbecued shrimp served
with garlic bread. The Caesar salad is prepared tableside,

but consider the fried green tomatoes and lump crabmeat drizzled with remoulade. Among the rather classic entrees are the individual beef Wellington with mushroom foie gras duxelles in puff pastry and a Perigourdin sauce, and the crabmeat Imperial. The epicurean razzle-dazzle is all there, but is it worth the price?

The Chef's Table (2100 St Charles Ave. 504/525–2328 **$$$**) offers a delicious collision of Continental and local cuisines. Favored dishes include the fried green tomatoes with crawfish remoulade, lobster and wild mushroom bisque, Asian fire shrimp, and filet mignon stuffed with Boursin, but by all means try the crabmeat ravigote with poached asparagus. For the finale, there's crème brûlée and a jazzy banana-white-chocolate-mousse pie. The Chef's Table is a laboratory for the fledgling New Orleans Culinary Institute, which trains chefs and dining-room personnel and gives cooking classes too. Don't worry. The food and the person bringing it to your table are both pros.

The Caribbean Room in the Pontchartrain Hotel (2031 St. Charles Ave. 504/524–0581 **$$$**) should be a delightful throwback to the days of elegant hotel dining, since it was once the best hotel dining room in town. However, these days the dowager is tired, and has been drastically downsized by remodeling and change of ownership. The food has suffered accordingly, so that seafood mainstays like turtle soup, pompano Pontchartrain, and trout Eugene are only wan reminders. The famous Mile-High Ice Cream Pie survives by a thread.

Tucked in an old house just a couple of blocks off St. Charles Avenue and oozing charm is **Cafe Atchafalaya** (901 Louisiana Ave. 504/891–5271 **$$**), which may make you think you're somewhere on the Gulf coast. This is because the menu combines down-home Dixie with chic Creole fare, an unbeatable combo. With choices like that, you can have a crab cake to whet your appetite for "rather Southern specialities" like chicken and dumplings or country-fried steak. Or maybe you want stuffed eggplant in Creole sauce before the grilled lamb chops? You get the feeling the super-friendly staff would really be happier if they could share your table rather than wait on it. If you've got a large party, it's fun to commandeer the upstairs dining room facing St. Charles. The cafe's name, by the way, comes from that ferocious river just to the west of town that almost captured the Mississippi during the Great Flood of '73.

eclectic... The place made the six o'clock news when local writer Anne Rice took out full-page newspaper ads trashing restaurateur and Popeye's Chicken founder Al Copeland for profaning elegant St. Charles Avenue with excessive neon. Her target was **Straya (2001 St. Charles Ave. 504/593–9955 $$)**, his latest in a chain of local restaurants. A compromise was finally struck, but not until after the local press had a field day with the high-profile squabblers. The star- and ribbon-wrapped salmon-y exterior and eye-popping interior is definitely much more L.A. than LA, but it's really a lot of fun when you're inside looking out at the 19th-century Zion Lutheran Church across the avenue. The food is a wild and crazy fusion of Creole and Southwest. Check out the pizza topped with oysters Rockefeller and the amberjack almondine. Or maybe you're in the mood for a huge hickory-grilled chipotle pork chop crowned with an ancho chili demiglace and served with sautéed garlic spinach. You can always opt for one of the outsized salads, one of the best bargains on the menu.

An intense study in scarlet, **The Red Room** (*2040 St. Charles Ave. 504/528–9759 $$$–$$$$*) is housed, believe it or not, in a chunk of the Eiffel Tower disassembled in Paris and shipped over only to become a series of failed venues. If crowds are any indication, it will hit the mark this time as an inspired combo of restaurant and dance club [see **bars/music/clubs**]. The architectural design is adventurous, but it can sure sap heat out of the food between kitchen and table. Yet, Chef Guia's tuna pastrami with fried lotus fruit is engaging, as are the nut-crusted sweetbreads and expertly executed foie gras. The whole speckled trout with a sauce meunière hits the mark, while the leathery boar chops miss. The music magically morphs from a small combo in early evening to a larger, much louder band by 9:30 or so. The crowd changes too, and the staff of tuxedo-clad waiters is replaced by cocktail waitresses and a roving cigarette girl. If the food seems overpriced, remember that the live music is included.

Bouchon (*4900 Prytania St. 504/895–9463 $$*) is also known as the Wine Bistro. It remains one of the hottest spots on this stretch of Prytania, a gathering place for lemmings who like to be on display along with the food. While sipping your choice of cab, chab, or chard, try an international cheese or one of the homemade pâtés, duck with green peppercorns perhaps, or the delectable rabbit with tarragon. Follow that with their fine onion soup, continue with fillet of beef with gratin dauphinois and finish with a silky crème brûlée and coffee.

Neighborhood joints are scattered all up and down the avenue, but this one really welcomes strangers. The utterly unpretentious, no-frills **Avenue Pub** (1732 *St. Charles Ave.* 504/586–9342 $) has all the standard goodies for a local hangout, including hamburgers (really good!), buffalo wings, chili-cheese fries, and cheese sticks. The po' boys are the only real clue that you're not in Anywhere, U.S.A. That, plus the fact that the regulars seem so intent on having a good time. Cheap and fun.

St. Charles Tavern (1433 *St. Charles Ave.* 504/523–9823 $$) stays busy almost all day, and is popular with locals and tourists as well. If you're in a pig-out mood, try the belly-busting trolley platter stacked with fried catfish, oysters, and shrimp, plus stuffed shrimp, hush-puppies, onion rings and french fries. Less daunting fare includes sandwiches, shrimp Caesar salad, and catfish Lafayette. The weekend special is prime rib.

Samuel's Avenue Pub (1628 *St. Charles Ave.* 504/ 581–3777 $$) is thronged with a younger set more interested in posing and preening than dining. There's no other explanation for the popularity of this place, which has interesting menu choices that don't quite deliver. The grilled tuna salad, burgers, black tie pasta, and crab cakes are okay, no more, and the service can be s-l-o-w. You'd be wise to sit outside on the deck, order a brew, and enjoy historic St. Charles Avenue before going elsewhere to dine.

international... Mike's on the Avenue (628 *St. Charles Ave.* 504/523–1709 $$$) took the city by storm a few years ago when chef Mike Fennelly arrived from Santa Fe with a fascinating blend of Southwest and Louisiana tastes—

and that's not all the fusion going on in this place. Along with chef Scott Serpas, he's also drawn from Asia, France, and Italy. For starters, try fab smoked salmon and crawfish remoulade, box sushi with sweet-onion confetti and ponzu, or lobster nacho with smoked cheddar cheese, grilled peppers, onions, and black bean coulis. Move on to New Orleans barbecued oysters, pasilla crab cakes with roasted-pepper salsa, and five-spiced cured crispy duck with house-made hoisin sauce. All this is served up in a strikingly airy, minimalist space with tall windows commanding spacious views of the avenue.

italian... One of the jewels in the revitalization of the Lower Garden District is **Bravo** (*1711 St. Charles Ave.* *504/525–5515 $$$*), the latest link in a Midwestern restaurant chain. Recycled from an abandoned car dealership, it's a sort of Roman fantasy bordering on caricature, but nice nonetheless. The focus is northern Italian, and most of it is right on the mark. Both the crusty Tuscan bread and focaccia are house-baked and fresh. The fried calamari, almost enough for two, makes a good appetizer, as does the wood-grilled portabello mushroom with sautéed spinach and creamy aioli mix. Entrees like the lasagna and grilled fish, all delivered in copious portions, are delicious, as is the ravioli brio, packed with cheese, spinach, and a creamy butter sauce, served with asiago cheese, mushrooms, and fresh asparagus. A young staff is knowledgeable without pandering, and even the parking valets seem eager to please.

Igor's Garlic Clove Restaurant (*2135 St. Charles Ave.* *504/522–6602 $$*) is housed in a funky red house with an awning proclaiming Giant Burgers, Pizza, Laundromat,

tennessee williams

In 1938, at age 24, Thomas Lanier Williams, better known as Tennessee, fled a sheltered, stifling home life in St. Louis for the French Quarter, then a slum attracting artists and writers with its cheap rents. Tom was no doubt shocked by the free-wheeling bohemian lifestyle and confessed 40 years later that his new environs triggered "a certain flexible quality in his sexual nature," at last liberating him to embrace his homo-sexuality.

He initially stayed with friends behind what's now Preserva-tion Hall, soon moving to a boarding house at 722 Toulouse Street, now part of the Historic New Orleans Collection. In 1977, the house's curved staircase was immortalized in his play *Vieux Carré*. Nearby, at 523 Royal Street, was the long-since-vanished Musée Mechanique, which found its way into *Eccentricities of a Nightingale*.

Williams rambled from California to New York before return-ing to New Orleans in 1941 after his play, *Battle of Angels*, flopped off-Broadway. He said his greatest need was free-dom. "I find that in New Orleans," he said, "and it certainly was a great impetus to me as a writer." In 1941, he was a house-guest at the 1860 Bultman House, 1521 Louisiana Avenue, in the Garden District. The two-story conservatory, clearly visible from the street, supposedly inspired him to write *Suddenly Last Summer*. He stayed briefly at the Pontchartrain Hotel but soon heeded the seductive siren of the Quarter, living precariously before finally finding success with *The Glass Menagerie* in 1945. He took an apartment at 710 Orleans Street behind the cathedral, where he worked on *Camino Real*, then moved to the third floor at 632 St. Peter Street, just above a rattle-trap streetcar route. There he continued work on *Summer and Smoke* and something that eventually became *A Streetcar Named Desire*, which earned him world-wide fame in 1947 and his first Pulitzer Prize. A second came for *Cat on a Hot Tin Roof* (1955), set in his native Mississippi.

Williams was a rootless citizen of the world during the '60s, but occasionally returned to New Orleans, where he stayed in Room 9 at the luxurious Maison deVille, 727 Toulouse Street. Ironically it's almost directly across the street from that pathetic garret he first called home in the Quarter. He stayed for a while in an apartment at 909 St. Louis Street, and in 1969 finally became a New Orleans homeowner. His house was at 1014 Dumaine Street, where he occupied Apartment B upstairs. He was relatively content, at least for one with a fundamentally tormented soul, and just before his 1983 death he referred to his brass bed as the place where "fourteen of my happiest nights were spent" and the spot where he wanted to die. Sadly, he expired in a New York City hotel and was buried in St. Louis, a city he loathed. His adopted hometown salutes the playwright and his legacy in the annual spring Tennessee Williams/New Orleans Literary Festival.

Game Room and more (don't confuse it with Igor's Lounge & Game Room next door, with its wonderfully greasy burgers, wildly eclectic interior, and outrageous waiters). There's a storefront/dining area open to the street, providing ventilation for garlic breath. Igor found an obvious gimmick and is making it work beautifully—unless you're the vampire Lestat. Standard local dishes such as jambalaya, shrimp Orleans, and red beans and rice get a garlicky twist, as does the shrimp pasta. This is a comfortable, laid-back joint where your secret passion for garlic is indulged.

mexican... At **Vaquero's (4938 Prytania St. 504/891–6441 $$),** the Mexican food comes with a decided Southwest/Native American twist. Earth tones, low-key lighting and tropical greenery provide a chicly rustic backdrop for some thrilling dishes. Try some quesadillas with fried rock shrimp or go wild over smoked shrimp with asadero, cheddar, and goat cheeses, and anaheim and cascabel peppers under a smoked tomato cream sauce. Also check out the ancho-glazed shrimp, New Mexico dry-rub venison or Navajo fillet. Corn and flour tortillas are made fresh at the tortilla bar. Happy hour is one of the hottest in town, no doubt due to their top-shelf margaritas.

bars/music/clubs

The largely residential Garden District is definitely not the place for club action, although there's one must-try exception. Throwing both youngsters and thirtysomethings into the mix is **The Red Room** (*2040 St. Charles Ave. 504/*

528–9759), the area's newest musical oasis, luring dance-crazed patrons with groups like Johnny Angel & the Swinging Demons and Freddy Omar's Latin Dance Band. You may want to call Arthur Murray after seeing the dance floor on Wednesday's Jazz Latin night. Cocktail waitresses and cigarette girls add to the retro ambience, and a full dinner menu is available [see **eating/coffee**]. By ten or so the focus invariably shifts from food to fun.

sleeping

Since they are largely residential areas, the Garden Districts have only a handful of accommodations, most of them strung along St. Charles Avenue. There are a few compelling B&Bs, however, some of which emanate the real ambience of this special part of New Orleans.

Cost Range for double occupancy per night on a weeknight. Call to verify prices.
$/under 100 dollars
$$/100–150 dollars
$$$/150–200 dollars
$$$$/200+ dollars

Since 1927, **The Pontchartrain Hotel** (2031 *St. Charles Ave.* 504/524–0581, 800/777–6193 $$–$$$) has attracted such notables as Rita Hayworth, Orson Welles, and Tennessee Williams with a quiet, European ambience and grand suites (small rooms are also available). It still works hard but is unfortunately showing its age. There are a concierge and business services, but few of the amenities of the newer hotels.

Ramada Plaza Hotel-St. Charles (2203 *St. Charles Ave.* 504/566–1200 $$) is more like a fine European hotel than the routine roadside Ramada. The well-appointed rooms are hardly what you'd expect from a chain, and the matching service makes for one of the best lodging bargains in town. There's no dining room, but both Igor's locations are right down the block.

Josephine Guest House (1450 *Josephine St.* 504/524–6361, 800/779–6361 $$–$$$) is a striking Italianate building dating from 1870. It's richly appointed with antiques and oriental carpets and has rooms in the main house and the original garçonnière (bachelor's quarters) in the rear. Rooms are comfortably large, all with spacious baths and phones. A complimentary Creole breakfast is elegantly served in your room or on the patio.

The **Quality Inn Maison St. Charles** (1319 *St. Charles Ave.* 504/522–0187, 800/831–1783 $–$$) is unlike any Quality Inn you've ever seen, a well-executed combination of six historic buildings surrounding small courtyards. Amenities include pool, hot tub, health club/spa, bar, complimentary shuttle to the Convention Center, and round-the-clock security.

The **St. Charles Guest House B&B** (1748 *Prytania St.* 504/523–6556 $–$$) calls itself low-tech, and with good reason. There are no phones, faxes, or TVs, but that opens up more time for the banana-tree-shaded patio, pool, and extensive library. There are comfy rooms with antiques, queen-size beds and private baths as well as small backpacker rooms with a shared bath. A good budget buy.

doing stuff

The Lower Garden District was carved from the Delord-Sarpy plantations in 1806. As designed by Barthélémy Lafon, it was to be a wildly ambitious Greek revival faubourg with streets named after the Greek gods and muses, a circular park called the Place du Tivoli, a huge coliseum, and a cathedral. The street names endure and the grand Place evolved into Lee Circle, but the rest never got off the drafting table. Most of the homes were built before the Civil War, meaning there's an abundance of two-storied, galleried Greek revival and Italianate town houses and a scattering of Creole cottages, shotgun houses, and stunning raised villas. The areas along Prytania and Coliseum streets are easily and safely walked in the daytime. However, pay attention to your surroundings; they can change in an unhappy flash.

You'll find several grand examples of Anglo-American mansions from **2000–2200 Prytania Street**. A fascinating merger of Greek revival and Italianate is the **Gernon-Edwards-St. Martin House** (1514 Prytania St.). Built in 1860, it boasts a graceful double gallery with both square and round columns crowned with Corinthian capitals. Next door is the almost identical **Fairchild Guesthouse**. Both repose behind notably ornate iron fences. The four-story **St. Anna's Asylum** (1823 Prytania St.) dates from 1857 and is a superb example of Greek revival. **The mansion at 1531 Camp Street** dates from the 1850s.

The "center hall villa," a style of home with generous galleries where indoor furniture could be dragged out-

doors on stifling evenings, became chic in the 1840s.
Dramatic ceilings rose as much as 16 feet to contain the
hot air, a practical design that remained popular into the
1880s. A number of these fine homes remain, notably at
1007 Jackson Avenue, **1431 Josephine Street**, and
2127 Prytania Street. The 1830s **Stanley House** (*1729
Coliseum St.*), the home of merchant Henry Stanley, was
moved to the current location in 1981 from 904 Orange
Street. Stanley's name became world-famous when taken
by his adopted Welsh son, John Rowlands, who, in 1871,
uttered the words, "Dr. Livingstone, I presume." Young
John's signature is etched into a windowpane of his small
room off the kitchen.

It's hard to say who was more stunned by the 1803
Louisiana Purchase: the xenophobic Creoles who suddenly
found themselves with a most unwanted landlord, or the
Americans who couldn't get a foothold in the old French
city. Snubbed by local society, the wealthy newcomers retaliated with a neighborhood of big houses on bigger lots, an
American sneer at the urban, tightly packed Quarter. They
set out to teach the haughty French the meaning of the
word "grand" and scored big-time with something appropriately called the Garden District, a luxuriant oasis in one
of the greenest cities in America. The camellias of winter
give way to the azaleas of spring. The long summer brings
a profusion of bougainvillea, crape myrtle, oleander, jasmine, sweet olive, splashes of purple, magenta, pink, laven-
der, and gold which stretch into camellia season without
so much as a pause. This is the ever-bloomin' South of
which poets have written so effusively. What they don't
glorify is the fact that much of this fragrant foliage was

originally planted to mask the potent stink of nearby slaughterhouses, mercifully razed years ago.

The Garden District was hewn from the Livaudais plantation in the mid-1820s and incorporated as the City of Lafayette in 1833. Its glory days were golden but fleeting— not even enduring to the turn of the century—but the serene and aloof area leaves an undeniable impression. Walking tours are available, but there's a strict ban on tourist buses. Except for the occasional local tour and Anne Rice's house, Garden District homes remain steadfastly closed to the public. It is, after all, a neighborhood rather than a museum zone. (Remember, very few of the present occupants are descended from the original families, hence the hyphens in so many historic house names.)

The Garden District is best explored by picking up a map and hopping on the streetcar for a leisurely ride out glorious, tree-lined St. Charles Avenue. Inaugurated in 1833, the **St. Charles Streetcar** is the oldest continually operating line in the world and was designated a National Historic Landmark in 1973 (fare is $1, exact change required; dollar bills accepted). There are some interesting sights before you get to the Garden District. Just above Lee Circle is the **1916 Jerusalem Temple, No. 1137**, with a striking mosaic facade. At No. 2040 is the Red Room [see **bars/music/clubs**], a onetime chunk of the Eiffel Tower, now a happening club. The Garden District begins at Jackson Street. On the left at No. 2336 is the 1850 **Hackett House**, a hint of what's to come. The next block is First Street, where you'll get off and start wandering amid the amazing assortment of Greek revival, Italianate, West Indian, and Moorish mansions. You'll see Italian villas drenched with wrought iron, Gothic revival homes, and architectural details like octagonal turrets, fences resembling iron corn stalks (there's also one in the Quarter), and rooms with 18-foot ceilings. Prytania Street is an especially rich stroll.

Despite so much competitive glamour, a few homes manage to stand out for one reason or another. The oldest is the 1838 **Toby-Westfeldt House** (2340 Prytania St.), a fine example of West Indian architecture with raised front porch, brick supports below, and square Doric columns above. The 1872 **Bradish Johnson House** (2342 Prytania St.) is full-blown Second Empire with all the details—and then some—of the style created by Napoleon III's Paris architects. It's been the McGehee School for Girls since 1929. In the 2300 block of Coliseum Street is a row of handsome cottages nicknamed the **Seven Sisters**.

The city's most famous novelist and horror-meister, Anne Rice, lives at **1239 First Street**, the Victorian inspiration for her book *The Witching Hour*. This house and her other Garden District home at **2524 St. Charles Avenue** are open to the public **(504/899–6450)**. The 1849 Greek revival **Payne-Strachan House** (1134 First St.) is that strange combination of private home and historical site. The Confederacy's first and only president, Jefferson Davis, expired here in 1889, and is commemorated by a sidewalk marker.

The Musson House (1331 Third St.) is an Italian villa built in 1850 by the president of the Cotton Exchange, Michael Musson, uncle of French Impressionist Edgar Degas. The stunning cast-iron galleries were added in the 1880s. The largest home in the Garden District is the 1865

Robinson-Jordan House (1415 Third St.), built by a Virginia tobacco merchant. This Italianate/Greek revival confection supposedly cost $80,000—a kingly sum in the last year of the Civil War. The ceilings are 16 feet high! You'll find that unusual cornstalk fence at **Colonel Short's Villa (1448 Fourth St.)**. The 1859 house has double parlors measuring 43 by 26 feet.

Your wandering should bring you to the walled 1833 **Lafayette Cemetery No.1** (entrance on Washington Street between Prytania St. and Coliseum St.). A Protestant burial ground, with aboveground vaults like its downtown Catholic counterparts, it boasts lavish sepulchers and appropriately haunting funerary statuary. It was originally needed as a resting place for yellow-fever victims, and is a repeat performer in Ms. Rice's Vampire Chronicles.

Return to St. Charles Avenue and catch the streetcar again. On the right, at No. 2919, is **Christ Church Cathedral**, built in 1887. This paean to Victorian exuberance is the diocesan headquarters of the Episcopal Church. Four more blocks on the left is the stately **Bultman Funeral Home** at No. 3338. In the '30s, three 19th-century wooden houses were cleverly combined to create this columned manse, the city's most prestigious funeral home. Directly next door is the 1860 **Bultman House** (1521 Louisiana Ave.), a superb example of a raised American villa. The American Library Association designated the house a Literary Landmark in 1988 [see **Tennessee Williams** sidebar]. The streetcar ride continues into uptown [see **uptown** chapter].

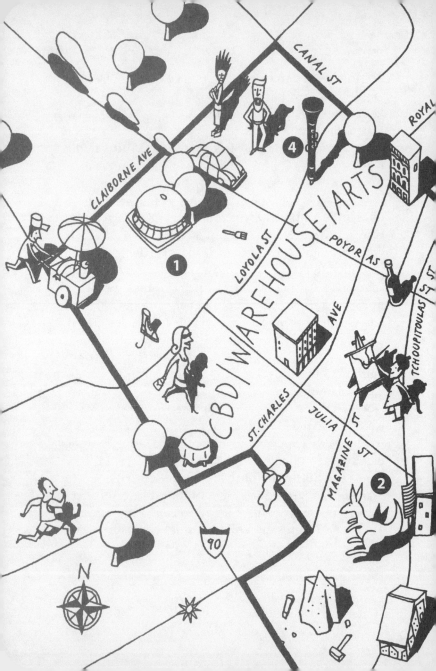

cbd/warehouse/ arts district

Except for the happy reawakening of Lee Circle, and a scattering of 19th-century structures, some handsomely restored, others sadly neglected, the CBD or Central Business District looks like any other urban American center, with high-rises, plazas, fountains, and an occasional piece of good sculpture. Canal Street, the main commercial drag, is distinguished for being one of the widest thoroughfares in the world. Its 171 feet accommodate six lanes of

turn page for map key

traffic, plus two bus/streetcar lanes and rows of trees (look closely at them and you'll see dangling beads left over from bygone Mardi Gras parades). Although Canal has some glorious fin-de-siècle and belle epoque buildings, its lingering grandeur is somewhat lost in a forgettable amalgam of good hotels intermingled with the ubiquitous fast-food joints, drugstores, and mundane shops selling sneakers, wigs, clothing, electronics, and, of course, tacky souvenirs.

The recent closings of Woolworth's, Krauss Department Store, and Maison Blanche on Canal were alarming, but fortunately plans are in place to recycle the empty buildings. Maison Blanche is currently being reinvented as the Ritz-Carlton New Orleans, which will no doubt give a much-needed shot of adrenaline to that humdrum stretch of Canal. Hopes for further rejuvenation are also pinned on the great, unfinished hulk that is the future home of Harrah's Casino, an enterprise that's been in and out of the courts almost since it began construction a few years back. Suits and countersuits among the city, the state, developers, and private citizens' groups reached comic-opera proportions, and the real story is doubtless Byzantine beyond comprehension. What's been dubbed the "Titanic sunk on Canal" is so far only a monstrous monument to greed. A much-scaled-down casino is scheduled to open before the turn of the century, but stay tuned. New Orleans has heard this time and again.

map key

1 Louisiana Superdome	4 Holiday Inn Downtown-
2 Vic's Kangaroo Cafe	Superdome
3 Spanish Plaza	

The other commercial boulevard is Poydras Street, leading from the river to the behemoth Louisiana Superdome [see **doing stuff**]. Both Canal and Poydras have their share of skyscrapers, many of which were built during the '80s, when the region was flush with an oil boom. Unfortunately, none of the new buildings is architecturally distinctive, but the city somehow managed to wind up with an impressive skyline. Viewed from Interstate 10 as it soars high over the Industrial Canal, it's a near-perfect triangle, dominated by 1 Shell Square, at 51 stories the city's tallest building. The prominence of hotels among the towers tells much about the city's tourist-driven economy. Hilton, Sheraton, Inter-Continental, Meridien, Hyatt, Doubletree, Holiday Inn, Westin, and Marriott are all here, with more on the way.

Dominating the lakeside of the CBD is the Louisiana Superdome. Resembling a gigantic flying saucer, this, the world's largest room, is home to the popular but perpetually beleaguered New Orleans Saints. The Dome, as locals call it, is currently getting a new neighbor, a stadium to house the New Orleans Brass ice-hockey team. The sports complex is connected to New Orleans Centre, a vast urban shopping mall, which competes for retail dollars with two more gigantic CBD retail complexes, Canal Place and Riverwalk. Like most urban cores, the CBD is deserted at night except for hotels and a handful of restaurants, and it is not especially safe.

Just upriver from the CBD, between the Lafayette Square District and the monstrous Convention Center, is the Warehouse/Arts District, New Orleans' answer to New York's SoHo. Rejuvenated by the 1984 World's Fair, it

good eats

Locals are fond of saying, "There are two times of day in Louisiana: mealtime and in between." Indeed, favorite topics of discussion at lunch are what you had for breakfast and where you're going for dinner. New Orleans food is a genuine original, arguably the only true American cuisine. It was created by African and Creole cooks who worked miracles with the abundant local ingredients [see **the dish on dishes** sidebar]. The emergence of nouvelle cuisine in the '70s undermined the traditional fare that had made New Orleans famous, as cream sauces and fried foods were dismissed as passé and unhealthy. But by the late '80s, haute Creole cuisine had returned with a vengeance, refining an epicurean faith whose holy trinity is celery, onions, and peppers. Chef Paul Prudhomme put Cajun cooking on the map, while Susan Spicer, Horst Pfeiffer, and others tailored old Creole dishes for modern palates without sacrificing respect. The city's most famous chef of the moment is, of course, Emeril Lagasse, who not only has three local restaurants and one in Las Vegas, but is also the darling of the Food Network. The celebrated Brennan family of restaurateurs continues to hold a place of honor, with the original Brennan's, Mr. B's Bistro, Bacco's, Ralph Brennan's Redfish Grill, Palace Café, Dickie Brennan's Steak House, and their fabulous Garden District flagship, Commander's Palace, presided over by Ella Brennan herself. New Orleans cuisine is again at the forefront, right where it belongs.

teems with art galleries, loft apartments, luxury condos, trendy bars, coffee shops, and fine restaurants. For some, it's most famous as the birthplace of the restaurant Emeril's. For others, it's a snappy urban neighborhood unlike any other in town.

eating/coffee

The CBD/Warehouse/Arts District is second only to the French Quarter in variety of cuisines and venues serving them. Not many cities can offer the unbridled down-home glory of Mother's just a few blocks from the Grill Room at the Windsor Court, regarded by many as the finest restaurant in the world. You can dine memorably while rotating in the sky or watching Cajun dancers, amid overwhelming opulence or in a flophouse known to have housed murderers. The choices and extremes are yours, and they're oh-so-New Orleans.

> **Cost Range** per entree
> $/under 10 dollars
> $$/10–15 dollars
> $$$/15–20 dollars
> $$$$/20+ dollars

cafes... One of the most beautiful of the many Warehouse District renovations, the **Red Bike Bakery & Cafe** (*746 Tchoupitoulas St. 504/529–2453 $-$$*) manages to be trendy without being offensive. It has absolutely delectable designer sandwiches made with all-natural house-baked bread, decent wines by the glass, and some creative gourmet dishes. Try the chipotle-rubbed chicken breast on a plate with tequila-creamed corn and roasted potatoes. If you're a pasta maven, check out the shrimp and crawfish linguine and roasted-red-pepper ravioli.

Ernst Cafe (*600 S. Peters St. 504/525–8544 $*) has been feeding locals for nearly a century, but some years back, when the sprawling Convention Center expanded yet again, the place was remodeled and reborn. During happy hour, it swarms with yuppies. After that, it's fairly popular with other locals and conventioneers. The food is nothing to write home about, but the po' boys, gumbos, and chicken salads are pretty safe bets. This has been a family-owned place from the beginning, and they do try to make you feel at home.

You're almost guaranteed a good time at **Vic's Kangaroo Cafe** (*636 Tchoupitoulas St. 504/524–4329 $*). If the name doesn't suggest Australia enough, the menu will. The baby back ribs are fresh off the barbie, and the baked brie with mango chutney lends the place an unexpected touch of class. Unless it's sweltering outside, chow down on the super shepherd's pie: ground beef simmered in red wine, broth, and a bit of Guinness stout, and topped with mashed potatoes, veggies, and cheddar cheese. The well-stocked bar offers a big choice of Australian wines and beers. As if all this isn't enough down-under fun, there's live music, too.

cajun... Mulate's (*201 Julia St. 504/522–1492 $$*) comes as a surprise, not so much for the food (clearly Cajun food is not uncommon in this town) as for the music and dancing. The original restaurant still rocks over in Breaux Bridge, but this city version is pretty damned authentic. The seafood platters and the blackened ribeye are killers, and the catfish Mulate—so famous, it's on the menu at EuroDisney—is a broiled fillet doused with craw-fish étouffée and served with jambalaya, cole slaw, and potatoes. Unless you eat so much you can't move, those fiddles may entice you to the constantly lively dance floor.

Living proof that appearances are deceiving is **Uglesich's** (1238 *Baronne St.* 504/523–8571 $), a sagging, hopelessly faded shack stuck in a crummy area. The inside doesn't fare much better, but who cares when you're about to wolf down some of the most mouth-watering Louisiana food. The seafood is so fresh, you'd expect it to jump off your plate, and if you're lucky you'll be here when the soft-shell crabs come in. The appetizers are all delicious, but you've just got to taste the fried green toma-toes topped with shrimp remoulade, a lowly dish made celestial here. The portions aren't always enormous, but the taste and quality are.

Michaul's on St. Charles (840 *St. Charles Ave.* 504/ 522–5517 $$-$$$$) is a triple Cajun threat: food, music, and free dance lessons; it's the reason why something's always going on in this Warehouse District joint. If you're tired of blackened redfish, this is the place to try its milder bronzed cousin. There's also a dandy crawfish étouffée and a signature salmon dish topped with crabmeat in a creamy lemon sauce.

coffee... The hottest coffeehouse in the area is **True Brew** (200 *Julia St.* 504/524–8441), which is just as much

the dish on dishes

Andouille (ahn-DOO-wee) A fat Cajun pork sausage spiced with lots of garlic.

Barbecue Shrimp Shrimp cooked in a peppery butter sauce and served in the shells, usually in gumbo bowls.

Chicory A plant whose roots are dried, roasted, and ground before lending New Orleans coffee its distinctive taste.

Court Bouillon (koo-bo-YON) The local version of bouillabaise in an aggressive red sauce.

Crawfish A small, edible crustacean and multipurpose ingredient.

Creole Mustard Uses the spicier, darker seeds which are marinated before preparation. A definite and distinctive kick.

Dirty Rice A tangy dish made with liver and spices which give it a mottled or "dirty" look.

Etouffée (AY-too-FAY) Literally "smothered," it's a Cajun technique wherein something is covered with vegetables and slow-cooked in a tightly covered pot.

Filé (FEE-lay) A powder made from wild sassafrass, most commonly as a thickening agent tossed into gumbo at the last minute. A gift of Louisiana Native Americans.

Grillades (gree-ODDS) Thin slices of veal or beef served in a gravy made from tomato-based roux. A breakfast favorite.

Gumbo A hearty soup with a roux base, containing any combination of chicken, shellfish, sausage, or okra and spiced at the whim of the cook.

Jambalaya A dense Spanish and Cajun dish of rice cooked with chicken, ham, sausage, and shellfish.

Maque Choux (mock shoe) An Indian-style dish with stewed corn and tomatoes.

Mirliton (meer-lee-TONE) A pale green cucumber cousin resembling a pear and tasting like a squash. Usually stuffed with a mixture of bread crumbs and crawfish or shrimp.

Muffaletta (muff-a-LAH-ta) Literally a plate-sized sandwich packed with Italian meats and cheeses and drenched in olive salad. A true New Orleans original.

Pain Perdu (pan-pair-DU) Literally "lost bread," it's a local version of French toast made with marinated French bread.

Po' Boy Local slang for "poor boy," a generous sandwich made with French bread and packed with everything from fried oysters to ham. "Dressed" means the addition of lettuce, tomato, and mayo.

Pralines (praw-LEENZ) Candy made with sugar and pecans and guaranteed to give you a serious sugar rush.

Roux (roo) A sauce made with slowly cooked flour and butter that's the base for gumbo and many other local dishes.

Remoulade Sauce (RUM-uh-lahd) Tangy Creole seafood cocktail sauce with a mustard base.

Sauce Piquante (PEE-cont) Spicy red gravy.

Tasso A spicy, red-peppered ham.

Z'herbes A Creole contraction meaning "with herbs."

fun for live theater [see **doing stuff**] as it is for food and coffee. Here's the spot to see denizens of the Warehouse District and not a few artists popping in from nearby galleries and studios to re-energize for that next masterpiece. At lunchtime, the big counter bustles with folks hungry for yummy pastries, quiches, and designer sandwiches like chicken Parmesan and turkey avocado. The hottest-ticket items are the flour tortilla wraps. Try the hot-pepper cheese with greens, cucumbers, sun-dried tomatoes, and Monterey Jack doused with guacamole and the tangy house vinaigrette. This place does such a turnover, the coffee's always fresh, and there's a good variety too.

continental/creole... Sazerac, in the Fairmont Hotel **(123 Baronne St. 504/529–4733 $$$)**, is a throwback to days of elegant hotel dining, both in decor and menu. There's a quiet, lush charm about this attractive room with its dark, inviting upholstery, period portraits, gleaming gasoliers, and enormous flower arrangements. Although the service can be uneven, the food is straightforward and untouched by trendiness. Choose from offerings like steak Diane, filet mignon, grilled veal chops, or lemon-pepper breast of duck. About the only really daring move is the marinated Anchiote chicken served with corn salsa and polenta fries with a Creole sauce. The trademark oysters Sazerac owe their enduring popularity to a combination of oysters Rockefeller, Bienville, and Pierre. There's pleasant live piano music in the evenings.

creole/southern... Veranda, in the Hotel Inter-Continental **(444 St. Charles Ave. 504/525–5566 $$$–$$$$)**,

is the brainchild of chef Willy Coln, who's made magic in this glass-enveloped, lushly landscaped hotel atrium. Dinners are a memorable experience, especially if you're a fan of beef au poivre, rack of lamb, Creole bouillabaisse, or Louisiana crab cakes. Another winner is the veal-and-shrimp Barataria, sautéed veal marinated with fresh shrimp in an oyster-mushroom sauce and served with herbed rice. Chef Coln's genius really takes wing, however, during the fabled Sunday jazz buffet with the bottomless champagne glass. Not only is the variety of this feast staggering, so is the presentation. You'll keep going back to see if you've missed something.

Bizou (*701 St. Charles Ave.* 504/524–4114 $$-$$$) is the brainchild of chef Daniel Bonnot, who gives French Creole dishes a nouvelle twist, with emphasis on meat. Try the rabbit terrine, lamb loin with mint sauce, or filet mignon with oyster dressing, but don't ignore the crawfish cakes served with baby greens dressed with Creole mustard, a tangy Tabasco beurre blanc, and vinegar chips. Be sure and try something with Chef Brunot's own remoulade made with julienne celery and Dijon mustard.

Palace Café (*605 Canal St.* 504/523–1661 $$-$$$$) is a smart brasserie operated by the famed Brennan family of restaurateurs, who obviously know what they're doing. This splendid structure was recycled from the venerable Werlein's Music building. The grand staircase leading to the mezzanine and the dark, clubby bar are only a couple of the touches making this a special space on lower Canal Street. For starters, try the crabmeat batôns, then progress to the sinful Creole crabmeat cheesecake, seafood boil, or veal shank. Regulars wouldn't think of exiting without some white-chocolate bread pudding under their belts. Did you notice the handsome jazz murals?

cuban... **Liborio** (322 *Magazine* St. 504/581–9680 $) has been a favorite CBD lunch spot for years. The spotlight is on Cuban food, from classic picadillo and ropa vieja to roast pork with black beans and rice. There are also daily specials, as well as stewed rabbit, grilled pork loin, Cuban beef hash, and grilled calf tenderloin covered with a bleu cheese gravy and served with sweet plaintains. If you get a hankering for Cuban or just want to save a couple of bucks, this is definitely the place.

Owned by the same family, and with a scaled-down menu, **Cubanacan Restaurant** (530 *Natchez* St. 504/ 581–9688 $) is really a combination of deli and coffeehouse. Office workers looking for a quick lunch pop in for the fat Cuban sandwiches, made with pork, ham, cheese, and pickles, and enjoy them in a courtyard loaded with charm. Plenty more regulars come just for the rich Cuban coffee made from espresso and medium-roast Colombian blends. The mood may be Cuban, but honest-to-goodness American breakfasts are available too.

down-home... Both locations of the **New City Diner** (828 *Gravier* St. 504/522–8198, 1340 *Poydras* St. 504/561–0061 $) are '50s style joints with '90s sensibilities. The old Southern standards, including chicken-fried steak, beef brisket, and banana pancakes, are here, but there's also fancier, trendier fare such as eggplant lasagna, fried catfish with roasted pecans and a lemon meunière sauce, and cranberry-pecan muffins. This place is strictly breakfast and lunch, and a big stop for downtown working stiffs, suits to coveralls. Good and cheap.

Mother's Restaurant *(401 Poydras St. 504/523–9656 $-$$)* is Cholesterol Central, and the lines out front indicate its popularity. This unpretentious place is a local institution patronized mostly by downtown workers, although there's no shortage of folks driving in from the burbs. Veterans wanting black ham on a biscuit arrive early, knowing the crisp, succulent outside meat will be gone by lunch. A genuine local creation is the roast beef "debris" sandwich made with chunks of meat and the oh-so-flavorful scrapings from the bottom of the pan. You can get it alone or in a combo po' boy with baked ham, slaw, mayo, and Creole mustard. The richly seasoned red beans and rice is also a knockout.

Downstairs from the Hummingbird Hotel, one of the city's legendary fleabags, is the equally legendary **Hummingbird Grill** *(804 St. Charles Ave. 504/523–9165 $)*. You know you're in for something special when you see a sign warning hotel guests not to take anyone to their rooms (twice-convicted murderer and Norman Mailer protégé Jack Henry Abbott of *In the Belly of the Beast* fame was arguably the most celebrated guest). It's always an adventure dining here, and, hell, even cops love the place. This is honest, real, down-home diner grub, and it's all tasty, from the homemade biscuits to the juicy burgers. There's no need to list the choices: every greasy-spoon dish you've ever had is here, and then some. The place is always a trip, more so when you're winding up a night of pub-crawling. The Hummer is a New Orleans tradition.

eclectic... Family-owned **O'Henry's Foods & Spirits** (*301 Baronne St. 504/522–5242 $-$$*) has four enduring restaurants around town. They've been keeping customers happy with frequent menu improvements and changing gimmicks such as free appetizers and free Sunday eats for the kids, who love being encouraged to throw peanut shells on the floor. The fare is on the hearty side, from the generous burgers topped with the famous house hickory sauce and served with steak fries, to the cheese fries loaded with melted Swiss and cheddar cheeses, bacon, green onions, diced tomatoes, and sour cream, served with ranch dressing. Whew! On the saner side, there's Cajun grilled tuna steak, tangy Southwest chicken with black beans, and garlic shrimp pasta.

One of the hottest young watering holes in town—and the name says it all—is **Lucy's Retired Surfer's Bar & Restaurant** (*701 Tchoupitoulas St. 504/523–8995 $$*). It has all the trappings of a California hang-out/get-loose palace, including a sandpile with volleyball net, a hopping happy hour, and two-for-one drinks on Wednesday's Big Wave Night. All margaritas are made with Cuervo Gold—or maybe you wanna try the heart-stopping Shark Attack. If you want food, there's some fine Cal-Mex fare like zesty shrimp spring rolls, or go whole-hog via the Dinner with Elvis at Hussongs, a concoction of chicken and cheese enchiladas, beef burrito, fajita sauce, and salsa verde, glopped with fresh salsa and sour cream, dished up with Spanish rice and refried beans. You'll either love it or it'll turn your belly into a hunka, hunka burnin'... whatever.

Up 42 stories, **Riverview** (*555 Canal St. 504/581–1504 ext. 4530 $$$-$$$$*) offers one of the glitziest looks at the city. Unfortunately the food is nowhere near as exciting, supporting that old adage that the higher the restaurant, the lower the quality of the food. The Marriott chefs aren't bad, just mediocre in a city where they should be better. The lobster omelette tries, as does the dinner veal chop, but . . . well, they ain't up to that awesome view.

french... **La Gauloise Bistro**, in Le Meridien Hotel (**614 Canal St. 504/527–6712 $$$-$$$$**), should hardly come as a surprise: It's a French bistro in a French-owned hotel in an old French city. The decor in this roomy space is brasserie-style, with tile floors, comfy banquettes, lots of mirrors and shiny brass, and two walls of windows. Try to get a seat overlooking Canal Street. Start with the duck breast salad with poached pears or the pecan crab cakes, and move on to the frogs' legs persillade, mixed grill, or Gulf shrimp à la Provençale, lightly sautéed in olive oil with garlic, parsley, tomato, thyme, and basil. Then maybe you can indulge in chocolate profiteroles.

Another hotel venue with a French accent is **Metro Bistro** in the Pelham Hotel (**200 Magazine St. 504/529–1900 $$$$**). Formerly the notoriously noisy Graham's, the cavernous space has been softened, hushed, and imaginatively lit. Chef Christopher Brown stirs up such interesting fare as crêpes filled with oysters Rockefeller, shrimp with risotto doused with coriander vinaigrette, and a double pork chop buried beneath a mound of ratatouille. There are some 40 well-chosen wines, most of them available by the glass. For the finale, the Metro chocolate mousse cherry bombe will make a sweet explosion in your mouth.

international... **The Grill Room**, in the Windsor
Court Hotel (*300 Gravier St. 504/522–1992 $$$$*), has won
almost every important culinary award and then some.
Modeled after the Grill in London's Savoy Hotel, it's
regarded by many as the finest restaurant in New Orleans,
and fairly reeks of luxe, from the Lalique chandeliers to
the absolute fortune in artworks gracing its walls. Now
presided over by chef René Bajeux, the service is flawless,
with a bevy of attentive waiters and an extremely knowledgeable sommelier. The menu is a challenge simply
because everything looks so good. Seafood fans will be in
gustatory heaven with the pound-and-a-half Chinese ginger-
smoked lobster served with stir-fried veggies on a bed of
fried spinach, or the grilled tuna Rossini. The pine-nut-
crusted rack of lamb is an experience in succulence. Many
diners feel there's no place to go but down after they've
experienced The Grill Room. C'est magnifique!

Pork fat rules! **Emeril's** (*800 Tchoupitoulas St. 504/528–
9393 $$$-$$$$*) is where it all began, and thanks to chef
and Food Network darling Emeril Lagasse's much-publi-
cized over-the-top television stardom, this place should go
on forever. Carved from an old pharmacy warehouse, and
a major player in the Warehouse District's amazing come-
back, Emeril's has exposed-brick and glass walls lightly
accented by local artworks and a curved food bar where a
fortunate handful of diners may actually get to watch
Emeril at work. (The energy level back there can be awe-
some!) Many foodie fans come prepared to order their
favorites, but for the uninitiated there are some must-trys,
such as the New Wave barbecued shrimp and the smoked
mushrooms and angel-hair pasta tossed in a house-cured

tasso cream sauce. Emeril is also famed for his andouille-crusted redfish and his tasting menus with choices from his award-winning wine list. The noise level can be intrusive at times, but diners don't seem to mind. An experience for sure.

Seafood sparkles at **The Sugar House** (315 Julia St. 504/525–1993 $$-$$$$), where dishes are turned out with an innovative touch. The menu teems with local shrimp, crab, crawfish, and a variety of Gulf fish, including tuna from Louisiana's Grand Isle that's grilled to perfection. The jerk-spiced chicken is delivered with grilled plantains and an exotic pineapple salsa, and the baked crab-stuffed shrimp bathed in a light curried coconut oil, topped with toasted, shredded coconut and served with confetti rice and veggies is scrumptious.

japanese...
The city's first sake bar, **Rock-N-Sake** (823 Fulton St. 504/581–7253, $$-$$$$), is a true blend of East and West. Traditional sakes are available, along with fine sushi, sashimi, and cooked Japanese classics like tempura and teriyaki, but there are also some innovative sake drinks, in a happening Warehouse District space with wooden beams, exposed brick, contemporary art, and music, all working in concert. To start, there are 25 premium sakes to choose from. You can sip them solo or have a sake margarita, or a Sake Melon Ball Purple Haze (a Japanese cocktail made with sake and plum wine). Sushi aficionados will adore the tuna, the whitefish, and the damned good California roll. If you want to share, try the Rock-N-Sake bouquet for two, sashimi sculpted into flowers, with assorted rolls and sushi. The staff is effervescent and eager to please.

pizza... **Warehouse District Pizza** (325 *Howard Ave.*
504/529–1466 $-$$) claims to make "the biggest pie in
town," and you may agree when you get a look at their cul-
vert-sized 20-inch monsters. Choices can be overwhelming when you have to decide between sauces, toppings,
and cheeses. Their other claim to fame is a tasty collision of
Italy and Louisiana: try their pizzas topped with crawfish
étouffée.

seafood... **Kabby's Restaurant & Sports Edition**, in
the Hilton Hotel (2 *Poydras Pl.* 504/584–3880 $$$) is a kick-
back kinda place commanding a terrific view of the river.
It serves a reliable range of seafood favorites, including a
Cajun seafood pot-au-feu, snapper Barataria, seafood
boudin, and shrimp Creole. If you've brought a big
appetite, dive into the grilled seafood platter heaped with
Gulf shrimp, crab cakes, and a spicy grilled crawfish cake.
The pasta verdura and peppered duck breast with andouille
sausage dressing are a couple of the alternatives to seafood.
This place is always crowded for Sunday brunch.
   Anthony's Seafood House, located in the Riverwalk
shopping center (1 *Poydras St.* 504/524–1243 $$), is New
Orleans' only seafood steamery and one of the best lobster
houses in these parts. Check out the tanks as you walk by
and ask Anthony to blacken one of those babies for you.
He'll boil it with garlic butter and spices and then grill it
with olive oil, more butter, and blackening spices.
Definitely not purist stuff—but tasty.

steaks... New Orleans has never been famed as a beef
town, but if you get a hankering for a red-meat fix, zip up

to **Top of the Dome** in the Hyatt Regency Hotel (500 *Poydras Plaza* 504/561–1234 $$$-$$$$). This is the only revolving restaurant act in town, and corny as it seems, there's really an awesome urban spectacle unfolding outside the window. There's a complete range of beef cuts, including tender prime rib and hearth-blackened New York strip, but don't overlook the seafood. This place seems to make a special effort to get the freshest fish possible, and serves it in a variety of innovative ways.

bars/music/clubs

The most sophisticated cocktail lounge in town is **The Sazerac Bar** in the Fairmont Hotel (123 *Baronne St.* 504/529–7111). A graceful journey back in time, the mood is unrushed and the room is swank. The past surges at you through glorious murals of the old New Orleans marketplace and waterfront, reminiscent of those powerful WPA works of the '30s. Try the signature Sazerac cocktail, a native blend of whiskey, sugar, bitters, and anise flavoring.

The Mermaid Lounge (1100 *Constance St.* 504/524–4747), on the cusp of the Warehouse District, is definitely geared toward the young crowd, but plenty of over-30s pack the tiny space. In addition to blues and progressive rock groups, surf and klezmer bands crowd into a corner and let enthusiastic patrons fight it out for room. Those who can't fit hang outside, where impromptu street parties sometimes blossom. *Offbeat Magazine* says Sunday nights at the Mermaid are the "best pickup jazz jam in town."

Recently converted from bistro to bar, **Fleur de Lee**

(1032 St. Charles Ave. 504/588–2616 $$) is an intimate spot on the riverside of Lee Circle and attracts a happy, happening younger crowd. The revamped space has a living-room feel provided by comfy couches and art-covered walls, and is frequently energized by live music or DJs.

buying stuff

With the exception of galleries, CBD shopping is organized by site rather than by category. This is because all the stores of interest, with few exceptions, are confined to Riverwalk, Canal Place, and New Orleans Centre: urban malls making New Orleans one of the few large American cities with a healthy retail core downtown. This monstrous concentration of literally hundreds of stores makes downtown shopping a snap.

canal place... At the foot of Canal Street is **Canal Place** (333 *Canal St.*), a slick urban retail center with three stories of upscale tenants like Saks Fifth Avenue, Gucci, Williams-Sonoma, and more. With the usual transparent, mirrored elevators, marble floors and benches, fountains, and a handsome landscaped atrium, it's a quiet, unrushed place to shop (except for holidays and some weekends) and a great way to escape the heat.

On the first floor you'll find **Mignon Faget** (504/865–7361), a local jeweler whose clever creations have garnered her a worldwide clientele. Her architecturally inspired designs are especially smart, but you'd be amazed at what she can do with streetcars, crawfish, and red beans!

Rhino Contemporary Crafts Co. (504/523–7945) is a nonprofit artists' cooperative exhibiting the works of over 80 local talents. You'll find paintings and photography as well as hand-woven clothing, ceramics, furniture, jewelry, and more.

On the second floor is a kiosk operated by **Donna Browne** (504/523–4816) displaying high-fashion jewelry made by local and national designers. Emphasis is on glass works and fine sterling-silver pieces. **The Custom Shop** (504/523–3004) specializes in custom-made shirts, but they also make suits, ties, dresses, blouses, and jewelry.

canal street... Canal Street was once one of the nation's grand shopping streets. Although it's lost major department stores to the burbs and to mergers, two fine shops still linger from the glory days. **Adler's** (*722 Canal St.* 504/523–5292) carries a top-shelf selection of jewelry, watches, china, crystal, and silver. It's been calming the nerves of New Orleans brides and their moms for decades. Just off Canal is **Rubenstein Bros.** (*102 St. Charles Ave.* 504/581–6666) which has been fitting proper young New Orleans gentlemen for their first tuxedoes since 1924. The store also has designer clothing and accessories for both ladies and gentlemen, with attentive service that's a real trip back in time. Superchef Susan Spicer of Bayona helps New Orleanians spice their food (not that they need help!) with **Spice, Inc.** (*1051 Annunciation St.* 504/558–9993). She's collected spices from all over the world for this fun shop with its crazily shaped shelves, which also offers gift baskets, catering, and a cooking school.

galleries... The bulk of galleries in the Arts District are clustered on Julia Street, with a few on Camp and Poydras streets. New facilities open all the time; besides, the area is made for casual exploring. The following is a sampling.

Ariodante Contemporary Craft Gallery (535 Julia St. 504/524–3233) focuses on ceramics, jewelry, glass, and decorative objects. Exhibitors are both local and national. **Arthur Roger Gallery** (432 Julia St. 504/522–1999) is one of the most prestigious in the district. Local and national artists show here in media ranging from painting and sculpture to photography and works on paper. **The Contemporary Arts Center (C.A.C.)** (900 Camp St. 504/523– 1216), is another complex carved from a historic building, includes innovative exhibition space for some of the area's most avant-garde artists.

D.O.C.S. (709 Camp St. 504/524–3936) is the spot for more artworks in a contemporary vein, including paintings, pastels, pen and ink, pencil drawings, photography, and sculpture. **Lemieux Galleries** (332 Julia St. 504/522–5988) shows works in all major media, with emphasis on jewelry, ceramics, folk art, and "Third Coast Art" focusing on south Louisiana. **Marceline Bonorden Gallery** (1400 Poydras St. Suite 394 504/587–7900) represents almost 50 artists from all over the country. They carry an enormous selection of paintings and sculpture as well as kaleidoscopes and other unusual items.

One of the most prestigious galleries in the district is **Marguerite Oestreicher Fine Art** (626 Julia St. 504/581–9253). This is the one to visit for master drawings from the 17th, 18th, and 19th centuries, as well as contemporary paintings, sculpture, drawings, and prints by

Louisiana artists. **Still-Zinsel** (328 Julia St. 504/588–9999) has an unusual collection of regional, national, and international artists working on paper, plus contemporary paintings, photographs, and sculptures. **Wyndy Morehead Fine Arts** (603 Julia St. 504/568–9754) focuses on a different artist every month. The gallery represents over 75 contemporary artists from all over the U.S.

new orleans centre...
New Orleans Centre (1400 Poydras St. 504/568–0000) is tucked between the Superdome and the Hyatt Regency. It's anchored by **Macy's** and **Lord & Taylor**, with every chain store imaginable in between. Except for crawfish gumbo in the food court and the occasional spectacular views of the Dome, you could be in Anycity, U.S.A.

riverwalk...
Rising phoenix-like from the debris of the 1984 World's Fair, **Riverwalk** (1 Poydras St.) stretches along the Mississippi for half a mile, with three levels and 140 stores, pushcarts and eateries. The main entrances are behind the Hilton Hotel and off Convention Boulevard. What's fun about shopping here is the ever-present Mississippi River, the outdoor walkways for viewing river traffic, Caribbean cruise ships docked so close you can almost touch them, and the informative historical markers.

Riverwalk had a really unwelcome visitor a few Decembers ago when an out-of-control freighter, Bright Field, plowed into the complex, destroying shops before stopping just a few feet short of a gambling boat whose captain (sensibly) sounded, "Abandon ship!" The damage was extensive, as some of the stores collapsed into the

Mississippi, prompting locals to call it a Christmas miracle that no one was killed. There's a small exhibit on the ground floor, with photos of the disaster.

Though many of Riverwalk's tenants are shops you probably have at home, there are some local shops too, some tasteful, some trashy, all fun. For souvenirs and leisure wear, try **Bayou Trading Co.** (504/529–1283). **Pierre Crawdeaux** (504/529–7747) has more of the same plus leather handbags, belts, and shirts with a Louisiana theme. The gimmick at **Voo Doo New Orleans** (504/566–1100) is nothing but T-shirts and caps with the word "voodoo" imprinted on them (yawn).

Bayou Bangles (504/522–0146) has plastique items like crawfish brooches and other New Orleans–type baubles, with more at **Jazzin' on the River** (504/529–2941). **Rine Chapeaux** (504/523–7463) has a super selection of hats for men and women, ranging from the frivolous to the fine. **Greek Designs** (504/524–5246) carries Greek-style clothing for women and fishermen's caps for men. They also have some souvenir plates and a few pieces of sculpture.

Artworks of Louisiana (504/523–4430) carries pretty standard works, framed and unframed, of Louisiana subjects. Lotsa the usual plantation stuff, if that's your pleasure. **DeVille Books & Prints** (504/595–8916) has a good selection of local cookbooks, history and art books on New Orleans, and books by Louisiana and Southern authors. There are also some interesting New Orleans gift items. **Street Scene Gallery** (504/595–8865), carries woodgraphs, an artform created by artists Bob and Sylvia Yike in 1980. Depicting New Orleans scenes, they're a mixed-media print of the carved wood, hand-painted by the artists. Very jazzy stuff.

With its glitzy visual assault of gold, purple, and green and oversized costumed carnival mannequins, it's impossible to miss **Mardi Gras Madness (504/568–9504)**, on the upper level near the food court. It's owned by Accent Annex and is a super place to buy carnival souvenirs. There are more baubles, bangles, and beads at **Masks and Make-Believe (504/522–6473)**, which has wondrous masks for parties or balls, or for hanging on your wall at home.

If you're after food items, check out **Tabasco Country Store (504/522–2888)**, on the second level by the escalator; it has every imaginable item connected with Louisiana's world-famous hot sauce. There are potholders, aprons, spoon rests, cookbooks, you name it. Popular are the fancy metal and ceramic containers for folks too grand to put a bottle right on the table. **Creole Delicacies Gourmet Shop (504/523–6425)** has three locations in the city carrying a good choice of cookbooks, spices, local comestibles, hot sauces from everywhere, and other local cooking things. There's a cooking school in the rear. There's always a crowd gathered at **The Fudgery (504/522–8030)**, where young, enthusiastic candy makers show how to create fudge with passion and panache. The fudge is as irresistible as the show producing it.

sleeping

As you'd expect, overnight accommodations in the CBD cater primarily to conventions and businesspeople, but there are some small places offering both luxury and budget beds. For garden-variety tourists and the occasional sightseer, those behemoths along Canal Street are conveniently close to the French Quarter.

Cost Range for double occupancy per night on a weeknight. Call to verify prices.
$/under 100 dollars
$$/100–150 dollars
$$$/150–200 dollars
$$$$/200+ dollars

In a class by itself is the celebrated **Windsor Court** (300 *Gravier St.* 504/523–6504, 800/262–2662 $$$$), ranked by *Condé Nast Traveler* as the best hotel in the world. Describing it truly saps the superlatives. It's the sort of exquisite environment you can't really appreciate unless you're there. With the exception of an always grandiose flower arrangement in the lobby, understatement rules. Eventually you notice the millions of dollars' worth of art gracing the walls, in both public and private rooms and suites, and the ultra-tasteful **Le Salon** where guests can take high tea every afternoon. Upstairs in the world-class **Grill Room** [see **eating/coffee**], diners feast beneath Lalique chandeliers and more priceless artworks. There are four times as many suites as rooms, all exceptionally large and nicely appointed, with canopy or four-poster beds, marble vanities, and well-stocked wet bars. With 58 rooms, 264 suites, and two penthouses—each with twin terraces offering commanding views—there's simply every amenity imaginable. Flawless.

The Fairmont Hotel (*123 Baronne St.* 504/529–7111, 800/527–4727 **$$$$**) is the former Roosevelt, once one of America's grand hotels. Built in 1908, it was extensively spruced up and tweaked a couple of years ago, and efforts to upgrade continue. The block-long Victorian lobby stretches from Baronne Street to University Place, and evokes bygone grandeur with its marble floors and chandeliers. More nostalgic touches are found in the art deco Sazerac Bar [see **bars/music/clubs**] and Sazerac Restaurant [see **eating/coffee**] with live piano music. The 685 rooms and 50 suites all have down pillows, electric shoe buffers, and bathroom scales. There are the expected big-hotel amenities, plus two tennis courts.

Connected to the Superdome and New Orleans Centre shopping complex, the gigantic **Hyatt Regency New Orleans** (*500 Poydras Plaza* 504/561–1234, 800/233–1234 **$$$–$$$$**) is perfect for fans of sports and shopping. The bright lobby is a touch of razzle-dazzle, with fountains and some monstrous chandeliers, and the sensible rooms thankfully pale by comparison. If you want a view, ask for a corner room with two walls of windows. Special, slightly larger accommodations with makeup mirrors and hair dryers are also available. Private balconies or patios are available too. With 1,084 rooms and 100 suites, there are plenty of choices. All amenities are available, including a beauty salon, game rooms, laundry service, and a revolving restaurant, Top of the Dome [see **eating/coffee**].

Another giant is the **Hotel Inter-Continental** (*444 St. Charles Ave.* 504/525–5566, 800/445–6563 **$$$–$$$$**), with 481 rooms and 30 suites in the heart of the financial district. The building is a rosy granite monolith with a charming second-floor lobby teeming with potted palms and modern art, and there's a swimming pool on the 15th floor. The rooms are spacious, if rather unimaginatively decorated, and have baths with mini-televisions and hair dryers. The Inter-Continental is big with conventioneers and businesspeople who may request two-line phones and TV teleconferencing. In addition to a bar, pool, exercise room, VIP lounge, and more, there's also Veranda, a first-class Creole/Southern restaurant [see **eating/coffee**].

Practically hanging over the Mississippi, with views to prove it, the **Westin Canal Place** (*100 Iberville St. 504/566–7006, 800/228–3504 $$$$*) has some spectacular surprises, including a vast rose marble lobby on the 11th floor with enormous arched windows inviting the French Quarter and river right inside. The 397 rooms and 41 suites are nicely appointed in soothing, muted colors, and most have sensational views. The VIP lounge serves the usual complimentary continental breakfast and afternoon appetizers. There are all the extras, plus room service from Le Jardin restaurant and a rooftop pool 30 stories up. Do a few laps and then gawk at the magnificent bend in the Mississippi far below. Upscale shoppers can run amok in Canal Place [see **buying stuff**] right next door.

Le Meridien New Orleans (*614 Canal St. 504/525–6500, 800/543–4300 $$–$$$$*) is part of a French-owned international chain, which explains its European ambience. Understated elegance engulfs visitors walking through the marble lobby frequently punctuated by grand floral arrangements. A jazz pianist plays daily, with a Dixieland band taking over on weekends. There are 494 rooms and seven suites with the usual amenities, plus an outdoor heated pool and sauna, and aerobics classes.

At first approach, **Le Pavillon Hotel** (833 *Poydras St.* **504/581–3111,800/535–9095 $$-$$$$**) looks like it drew inspiration from Versailles' Hall of Mirrors. The original hotel was built in 1905; it's been completely refurbished with a decidedly Continental feel. An especially nice touch is the marble railing in the Gallery Lounge, which supposedly came from the Grand Hotel in Paris. The place is especially popular with businesspeople and attorneys. There are 220 rooms and seven suites, all roomy, with old-style high ceilings and traditional decor. Amenities include turn-down service, terrycloth robes, business services, hot tub, pool, health club/spa, and more.

The Queen & Crescent Hotel (344 *Camp St.* **504/587–9700, 800/975–6652 $-$$$**) is one of the popular new European-style small hotels. The 129 rooms are not large but are nicely decorated and include mini-bars, safes, plush robes, and in-room fax and modem capabilities. Rates include complimentary continental breakfast and other amenities. Even smaller is the four-story **Pelham Hotel** (444 *Commons St.* **504/522–4444, 800/ 659–5621 $$-$$$$**) which is, with only 60 rooms, a pleasant alternative for guests tired of huge, impersonal hotels. Part of the admirable push to recycle historic office buildings, the Pelham is a smart hotel whose inviting lobby features rich green marble floors and striking flower arrangements. All rooms have marble baths with hair dryers, fluffy robes, and English soaps, but the rooms are small and those in the core of the hotel are windowless. Amenities include concierge, twice-daily room service, and access to the pool and fitness center at the nearby Sheraton. The biggest plus is ordering room service from the menu of the fabulous Metro Bistro [see **eating/ coffee**] right downstairs.

At 47 stories, **The Sheraton New Orleans** (*500 Canal St.* **504/525–2500, 800/325–3535 $$–$$$$**) is the city's tallest and second-largest hotel. It's also "convention city," complete with a gigantic lobby humming with activity. The 1,100 rooms and 72 suites are comfortable if undistinguished, with more perks available as you go higher in the building. The service is usually brisk and efficient despite the size of the operation. The Gazebo Lounge in the lobby offers live jazz nightly.

The New Orleans Marriott Hotel (*555 Canal St.* **504/581–1504, 800/228–9290 $$–$$$$**) is the city's largest, with 1,236 rooms and 54 suites: another haven for conventioneers. The rooms are nothing special, but the service is friendly and the location terrific. Rooms facing downriver have fantastic views of the French Quarter. The usual Marriott amenities.

The **Holiday Inn Downtown-Superdome** (*330 Loyola Ave.* **504/581–1600, 800/535–7830 $$–$$$**) is fairly unremarkable—standard amenities, clean and servicable rooms, jazz in the lounge—but its 150-foot *trompe l'oeil* clarinet is definitely worth seeing.

doing stuff

Some real architectural treasures lurk within the CBD, and with a little prowling you can uncover them. For the

record, there are four locally designated historic districts—
Canal Street, Lafayette Square, Warehouse, and Picayune
Place. Canal Street was rather grandly named for something
that was never more than a ditch. It was the original "neutral ground" dividing the French and American sectors, a
term used by modern New Orleanians instead of "median."
Notice that downriver streets still bear French names,
while the upriver thoroughfares are English. Once an
unusual coexistence of business and residential properties,
Canal Street eventually went totally commercial, with only
one fashionable home remaining. Tucked away on Canal is
an 1844 mansion designed by James Gallier, Sr. for William
Newton Mercer. Today it's the exclusive, strictly men-only
Boston Club (*824 Canal St.*). On lower Canal, across from
the casino eternally-in-progress, is the massive **U.S. Customs House**, occupying an entire city block between
Decatur and North Peters streets. Designed in Egyptian
revival style, it was begun in 1847 but not finished until
the 1880s due to the intervening Civil War. The great marble hall, 84 by 128 feet, is both an engineering and an
aesthetic marvel, rising almost six stories to a plateglass
ceiling. Plans are underway to use part of the space as an
Insectarium, the first in the United States and a compan-
ion facility to the nearby aquarium. The rather undistinguished facade of the **Saenger Theater** (*Canal St. at N.
Rampart St., 504/524–2490*), conceals a splendiferous
interior mercifully saved from the wrecker's ball. It's host
to concerts and Broadway road shows. The **Orpheum
Theater** (*129 University Place, 504/ 524–3285*) is another
beauty from bygone days and home to the Louisiana Philharmonic Orchestra and New Orleans Ballet.

At the intersection of St. Charles and Howard avenues is the recently refurbished **Lee Circle**, a handsomely landscaped mound with a 60-foot marble Doric column crowned by a bronze statue of Confederate General Robert E. Lee. It was dedicated in 1884, in time for the World's Industrial and Cotton Centennial Exposition uptown. Quarterites joke that Lee's posture, arms folded, back turned, suggests that he's blithely ignoring uptown, but then they also insist that the nearby Y.M.C.A. sign stands for Yankees Might Come Again!

The white precast concrete office building facing the circle is the **Hancock Building**, the second of four New Orleans buildings designed by the prestigious architectural firm of Skidmore, Owens, and Merrill. The solid but airy structure helps anchor a site almost destroyed by the elevated interstate highway only a few feet away. The plaza is filled with art and, most notably, **a fountain by Isamu Noguchi**, who respectfully acknowledges General Lee's statue with an upturned crescent-shaped stone atop a sculpted version of a fluted Doric column. Currently under construction is the **Ogden Museum of Southern Art**, which will house what is arguably the largest and most comprehensive collection of Southern American art, with over 1,100 works. A property of the University of New Orleans, the Ogden is slated to open in 2004. Other future components include the Louisiana Artists' Guild, which will occupy a seven-story building across Howard Avenue, and other facilities yet to be announced.

At the rear of the Ogden is the **Confederate Museum (929 Camp St. 504/523–4522)**. Built in 1891, this old stone building is the oldest museum in Louisiana, and houses all sorts of Southern Civil War memorabilia. Buffs will be enthralled, while others may appreciate the extensive collection of battle flags, uniforms, weapons, and portraits. The museum also houses a portion of General Robert E. Lee's silver camp service and a suit of evening clothes belonging to Jefferson Davis, the only President of the Confederacy. Across the street is the **Contemporary Arts Center** (900 Camp St. 504/528–3800) which stages art exhibits and multimedia events as well as plays by local and nationally famous playwrights. At **St. Patrick's Church** (724 Camp St. 504/525–4413), built in 1838 and modeled after England's Yorkminster cathedral, the sermons were in English—the Americans' response to St. Louis Cathedral, whose services were only in French.

With their Eastern seaboard quality, the splendid row townhouses of **Julia Row** (600 block of Julia St.) come as a total surprise in this Latin city. Dating from 1832 and called the Thirteen Sisters, they were proof to the Creoles that the neighborhood was becoming Americanized. By 1976, they were the core of skid row and on the verge of physical collapse, when one unit was restored to become headquarters for the **Preservation Resources Center** (604 Julia St. 504/581–7032). The PRC works to rejuvenate, renovate, and restore the city's abundance of historic structures. Their arrival triggered a flurry of restorations in the derelict area. A turn-of-the-century warehouse became **Julia Place Apartments** (330 Julia St.). **Gallery Row**, a mixed-use building, merged 1830s stores with a 1912 building, and the Magazine Place luxury apartments were created from the 1910 Swift Foods Wholesale Market building. Julia Street is also the heartbeat of the Arts

District. Don't miss the concentration of galleries here, as well as Camp and Poydras streets [see **buying stuff**].

Built in 1845, **Gallier Hall** (*545 St. Charles Ave.*) is considered by many to be the finest example of Greek revival architecture in New Orleans, with its magnificent Ionic columns and marble portico. It was built in response to and in defiance of the Creoles' insistence on governing the French Quarter from the Cabildo. This grand structure was City Hall until it was replaced in 1957 by a new, utterly mundane box in the Civic Center on Poydras Street. On Fat Tuesday, the mayor toasts the krewes of Rex and Zulu from the grand steps. Across St. Charles Avenue is **Lafayette Park**, the American answer to Jackson Square. Its ancient trees offer relief in this urban core, and the park is a favorite lunch spot for office workers. The statue on the granite pedestal is of John McDonogh, a rich planter who freed and educated his slaves. At his death in 1850, he willed half his $3 million estate to schools for the poor in New Orleans and Baltimore. The bronze statue is of U.S. Senator Henry Clay. This is a great place to rest your feet.

The unique and innovative **Piazza d'Italia** (*Poydras St. near Commerce St.*) has a strange, sad history, with a final chapter yet to be written. The result of a 1974 design competition won by famed artist Charles W. Moore, it honors the wave of Italian and Sicilian immigrants that came to New Orleans at the turn of the century. The inspired combination of water, stone, and neon delineates a map of Italy while saluting its classical architecture. It's a source of much embarrassment that the city and sizable Italian community have allowed the structure to deteriorate, with plans to restore it apparently deteriorating too. Ironically, a corpse was found floating in the once-beautiful Piazza in the opening scenes of the film *The Big Easy*.

There's more ethnic celebrating at the foot of the **World Trade Center** (2 *Canal St.*), built in 1966 to house offices of diplomats and consulates, now slated to become a hotel in part. The gilded equestrian statue of Joan of Arc was a gift to the city from the people of Orleans, France. Casino construction has made a mess of the Place de France where the Maid of Orleans should be straddling her horse in peace. An imposing statue of Winston Churchill holds forth at British Park Place near the entrance to the Hilton, while Bernardo de Galvez, a governor of Spanish Louisiana, marks the entrance to Spanish Plaza with its dazzling 50-foot fountain. A gift from Spain in the '70s, it acknowledges that nation's influence on the city and region. The once-beautiful tiles representing Spanish provinces have begun to show wear and tear, but the fountain is still spectacular. If you visit during the sizzling summers, don't be surprised to see someone dangling their feet in the refreshing waters. There are glorious views of the busy river traffic and the twin spans of the Crescent City Connection. The entrance to Riverwalk is to the right.

Riverwalk [see **buying stuff**] is home port to two ships: the *Cajun Queen* riverboat and *Creole Queen* paddlewheeler (504/529–4567), docked near the Hilton; they are available for harbor and battlefield cruises, respectively. Night cruises, including a dinner buffet, are also available. As with most dinner cruises, the view's much better than the eats.

spectating... True Brew (200 *Julia St.* 504/524–8441) is a combination theater and coffeehouse that's a

colorful throwback to the Greenwich Village of bohemian days [see **eating/coffee**]. It's mostly locals by day, but when the theater's got something going, the crowd will be from all over. True Brew stages some of the most innovative local productions in town, usually comedic satires, and is a favorite of playwright Ricky Graham and his often leading lady Becky Allen. Graham's *...And the Ball and All* was a side-splitting send-up of a blue-collar female carnival krewe that enjoyed an extended run largely due to repeat customers. The fun was so fast and furious no one wanted to miss anything. Another recent hit was *Ruthless*, a kicky musical that could be described as *All About Eve* meets *The Bad Seed*. If it's cutting-edge theatrical lunacy, you'll find it at True Brew.

The **C.A.C.** stages several plays a year in their small but state-of-the-art facility. Recent productions have included such diverse works as *Dancing at Lughnasa* and *Jeffrey*. The center was prestigious enough to lure Edward Albee as playwright-in-residence a few years back, as he was completing his latest work, the ill-fated *Fragments*. The C.A.C. also has a pleasant, rather trendy Cyber Cafe and a concierge named Isabella whom visitors will find both friendly and very knowledgeable.

The Southern Repertory Theater Company (*Canal Place, second level 504/861–8163*) offers a variety of plays annually. They often present productions associated with the Tennessee Williams/New Orleans Literary Festival and participate in the annual New Orleans Film Festival.

In August, several blocks of Julia Street are closed to traffic and turned into one big cocktail party as the Warehouse District Arts Association holds White Linen, its

annual benefit for local galleries. The attire is strictly
white, making for a lovely tropical spectacle as serious art
lovers wander the galleries while uptown dilettantes
socialize, schmooze, and air-kiss. Another aesthetic fête is
Art for Art's Sake, which usually blooms the first Saturday
in October. The art season is officially launched as galleries
on Royal, Julia, and Magazine streets open their new
exhibits and serve abundant wine and cheese. The evening
culminates in a bash at the C.A.C. complete with more
food, drink, and late-night dancing. This one has grown so
big that people have begun to wear costumes for the occa-
sion, mobbing Julia Street like it's Bourbon on Fat Tuesday.

For spectating on a grand scale, no place in the world can
top the **Louisiana Superdome** *(1500 block of Poydras St.
504/587–3663)*. The "Windowless Wonder" is the biggest
room in the world, built in 1975 at a cost of $180 million.
Tall as a 27-story skyscraper, it covers over 13 acres, seats
76,504 fans, and has a computerized climate-control system, requiring over 9,504 tons of equipment! The Dome is
built on land so low that if ships could sail in from the Mississippi they'd float overhead like balloons. It's home turf
to the New Orleans Saints of course, but has also hosted
Superbowls, entire Mardi Gras parades, the Disney world
premiere of *Hunchback of Notre Dame*, and even Bette Midler.
This modern marvel was an instant tourist attraction and
tours are available.

Surely few people come to New Orleans for the movies,
but there are five theaters in the **Canal Place Cinema**
(Canal Place, third level 504/581-5400) if you've just got to
see the latest release.

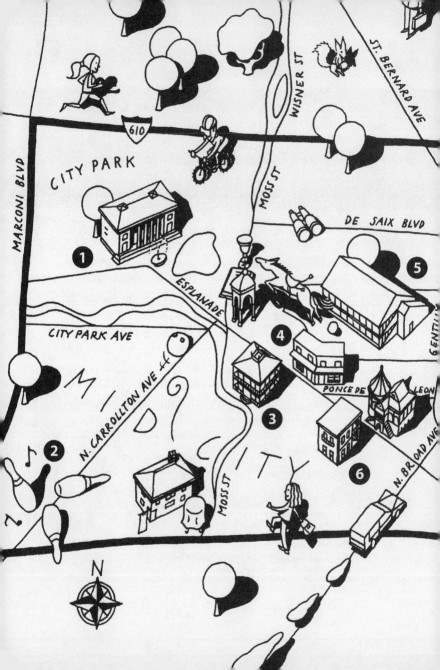

mid-city/ bayou st. john

Mid-City is a crazy quilt of neighborhoods sprawling above the French
Quarter somewhere between
Pontchartrain Expressway, City Park,
and the Fair Grounds (site of the
internationally famous Jazzfest and
the nation's oldest racetrack). From
the house that Edgar Degas stayed in,
to the wild live music at Mid-City
Lanes, the area's attractions are varied
and scattered. For purposes of simpli-
fying, the separate neighborhood of
Bayou St. John will be included here,

ESPLANADE

turn page for map key

along with Esplanade Ridge and City Park. As usual, the character of neighborhoods can change abruptly, so keep your wits about you if you feel a sudden urge to go exploring.

New Orleans is notoriously flat, but slight fingers of land rise here and there, the legacy of receding Mississippi floodwaters aeons ago. All but indiscernible to the naked eye, they're usually noticed when heavy rains turn them into fortunate islands. One such rise is Esplanade Ridge, which is the route of Esplanade Avenue, running three miles from the French Quarter to City Park and Bayou St. John. The thoroughfare became a prestige address for 19th-century Creoles and later Americans, who built an astonishing conglomeration of glorious homes along its often muddy wake. Some 190 remain today as a reminder of that glamorous era of gaslights, carriages, and liveried coachmen.

At the far end of Esplanade is City Park, the third-largest urban park in America, with 1,500 acres of botanical gardens, golf courses, tennis courts, lagoons, hiking trails, picnic areas, boating, fishing, a wonderful children's playland, two sports stadiums, and the impressive New Orleans Museum of Art. The park is a subtropical oasis so vast it seems deserted on weekdays, but is always busy with families on weekends. The nearby Fair Grounds boasts a racetrack dating to antebellum days.

map key		
1 New Orleans Museum of Art	4 Whole Foods Market
2 Mid-City Lanes	5 Fair Grounds
3 Pitot House	6 Degas House

eating/coffee

Because this area is almost strictly residential, you won't find many famed or hyped eateries. All the better for mixing with the locals and learning firsthand why this city has some of the best people-watching in the world and, surprisingly, some of the best ethnic eating too.

Cost Range per entree
$/under 10 dollars
$$/10–15 dollars
$$$/15–20 dollars
$$$$/20+ dollars

cafes/diners... For years, **Michael's Mid-City Grill** (4139 *Canal St.* 504/486–8200 $-$$) has packed in the locals as the home of the "Big Bucks Burger." It's also known for homemade soups and gigantic salads. Michael recently decided to add seafood to the menu, and the shrimp remoulade and fried shrimp sandwich are more than respectable.

If you're hankering for a quick, hearty breakfast or simple but tasty lunch, head for **Robin's On Canal** (2501 *Canal St.* 504/821–9800 $), a strictly local joint that's a bit of a trip back in time. Most of the waitresses have been here a while, and they make an effort to get your food out in a hurry. They serve all the standard breakfast fare, including a variety of fluffy pancakes and omelettes as well as steak and eggs, and a good choice of down-home-cooking plates for lunch.

You can get lunch and dinner at **Trolley Stop Cafe** (614 *S. Carrollton Ave. 504/866–9301 $*), but breakfast is the really big deal. The silver-dollar pancakes and the omelettes, especially the ham and cheese and Western models, are stellar, and the buttery biscuits are so fluffy you think they're gonna float right off your plate. Belgian waffles are appropriately crisp and come riddled with bananas and nuts or sinful chocolate chips. For lunch and dinner, try the mushroom burgers, country steak, or a variety of seafood platters, all brought by a staff that's an amazing combo of fast and cheerful.

chinese... **Five Happiness** (3605 *S. Carrollton Ave. 504/482–3935 $$-$$$$*) has a menu that could take you an entire carnival season to peruse, but once you've decided, sit back and let the staff serve the happiness. This enormous, bustling place with its quintessential Chinese-restaurant decor has been frying egg rolls and slinging egg drop soup for years. A few of the premier picks include moo shu pork, Mandarin minced chicken, and baked duck. The chef also does a nice number with the local shrimp, either tossed with pecans or sautéed with veggies in his own special sauce.

coffee/dessert... New Orleanians love to call places landmarks, but there's no doubt the label applies to **Angelo Brocato's** (214 *N. Carrollton Ave. 504/486–1465 $*). Once located in the French Quarter when that neighborhood was heavily Italian, Brocato's relocated home will remind you of an old-timey ice cream parlor. There are even overhead fans turning at a snail's pace and apothecary jars gaudy

with candies. If you care anything about Italian sweets, you'll lose your mind for the homemade cannolis, crisp cones filled with ricotta cheese and a sweet pudding that mixes chocolate and vanilla. There are fruity Italian ices for calorie counters, but few can resist the *torroncino*, spumoni, and *cassata*.

cajun/creole... Gabrielle (3210 *Esplanade Ave.* 504/ 948–6233 $$$) is an intimate spot near the Fair Grounds. Chef Greg Sonnier and his wife Mary are sticklers for freshness, meaning the creative goodies rolling out of their kitchen have something special. The Oysters Gabie are not to be missed, carefully baked and garnished with roasted garlic and artichokes and delivered au gratin. The chef's skills with game are apparent in the succulent slow-roasted duck and the rabbit tenderloin wrapped in prosciutto. You might want to wrap things up with a rich coffee and Peppermint Patti: brownie cake served with peppermint ice cream drizzled with a warm chocolate sauce.

There's no sane reason for venturing into this raunchy part of town unless you're heading to **Dooky Chase** (2301 *Orleans Ave.* 504/821–0600 $$$). Once you're under the spell of this place, which has been here for decades, you won't think about anything except what's steaming in front of you. The venerable and charming Leah Chase's food is about as pure New Orleans as you can get: sure-handed recreations of such old Creole dishes as shrimp Clemenceau, panéed veal, sausage jambalaya, stuffed shrimp, silky greens, and a filé gumbo rich with okra, shrimp, and crawfish. There are even heart-healthy dishes for those concerned about cholesterol. The room is comfortable and unpretentious, with some fine paintings by black artists. At Dooky's you're in for a no-nonsense celebration of one of the world's great cuisines. And how can you not love that name?

With all due respect, when was the last time you were served anything but communion in church? For another sort of religious experience, try **Christian's (3835 Iberville St. 504/482–4924 $$$-$$$$)**, housed in a handsomely restored 1904 Lutheran church. The reverential ambience lingers, with arched windows admitting a golden glow and conical hanging lights echoing those graceful curves. Dark paneling, banquettes, and chairs and snowy tablecloths showcase colorful food like shrimp Marigny sautéed with pearl onions, mushrooms, sun-dried tomatoes, and garlic flamed in brandy with a Dijon butter sauce. There are also specialty acts like the Avery Island duckling, half a fried, deboned domestic duck delivered with a Tabasco-and-orange demiglace and sweet-potato chips; and Filet Farci Bayou la Loutre, a filet stuffed with an oyster and garnished with more oysters in a demiglace sauce. If only the cramped seating was as heavenly.

Liuzza's By The Tracks (1518 N. Lopez St. 504/943– 8667 $) is an institution masquerading as a hole-in-the-wall. As the name suggests, it's close to the New Orleans racetrack, a point driven home by the vintage photos of horses, jockeys, and so forth, interspersed with Mardi Gras decorations that stay up year-round. Don't be fooled by these modest surroundings. There's a terrific chef in the kitchen, whipping up crispy soft-shelled crab, crab cakes, divine garlic oysters, and truly some of the best gumbo in the city. The oyster-artichoke soup is also a knockout. For meat lovers, there are corned beef, pork chops, juicy burgers, and all sorts of daily specials. The ever-effervescent waitresses will explain it all for you.

down-home... Talk about a blast from the past! **Ye Old College Inn** (3016 S. Carrollton Ave. 504/866–3683 $) is left over from the Eisenhower years—with a menu to prove it. This family-owned neighborhood hangout specializes in meat-with-two-vegetables fare, fried seafood, and sandwiches, but unless you tend to make up your mind fast, the huge menu with the tiny type may complicate any decision-making. The Southern-fried chicken is a popular mainstay, along with the vegetable soup, red beans and rice, gumbo, and the fried seafood platter. The po' boys are all delicious, and if you're really feeling indulgent, order the chicken-fried steak on a bun with lettuce, tomatoes, and mayo.

eclectic... Not to be confused with their sister restaurant by the tracks [see **cajun/creole**], **Liuzza's** (3636 Bienville St. 504/482–9120 $-$$) is another neighborhood emporium bustling with area locals and other New Orleanians who know a good thing when they eat it. Try their Italian eggplant po' boy or the popular Frenchuletta, which must be tasted to be believed. There's also a delish catfish beurre blanc and an artichoke pasta tossed with shrimp. It's all washed down with huge glasses of iced tea or frosty mugs of beer. Liuzza's fare is so good you wouldn't mind paying double the price, and she's been dishing it out for half a century.

french... Café Degas (*3127 Esplanade Ave. 504/945–5635 $$-$$$*), named for a nearby house once visited by painter Edgar Degas, is a little piece of Paris bistro tucked away among the leafy bowers of Esplanade Avenue. The menu is familiar French fare, served with some panache, indoors or out. The rather basic appetizers include onion soup, salmon, and pâtés; the salads are equally predictable. Things perk up with such entrees as Cornish hen roasted with rosemary and served with black-currant sauce, and rabbit cooked with mushrooms in hard cider. You might also consider the lamb rack and the veal T-bone, both of which are prepared according to the chef's whim du jour. Lunch fare includes a variety of omelettes, led by the Chamberry omelette with bacon, leeks, potatoes, and cheddar cheese. If you're lucky, one of the city's brief afternoon rainstorms will make music on the tin roof.

italian... Mandina's (*3800 Canal St. 504/482–9179 $-$$$*) is so unimposing that you could drive right past this corner clapboard building without noticing it. It's pretty plain inside too, just a couple of packed, noisy rooms, one with a bar, walls lined with fading newspaper clippings, tables laminated. The mundane evaporates the minute the veteran waiters hustle out bowls of the famous, gloriously rich turtle soup. Mandina's remains enormously popular with locals who love the happy marriage of Italian and Creole foods, such as the stuffed bell peppers with shrimp and meat filling, dished up with limas and killer baked macaroni. When you see the dimensions of the half-loaf seafood po' boys, you'll wonder who could eat a whole one. A Saints linebacker maybe?

The enduring popularity of **Venezia** (134 N. Carrollton Ave. 504/488–7991 $–$$) is one of the great mysteries in a city famed for culinary excellence. The chef seems to delight in slathering overly sweet Sicilian red sauce over everything, overwhelming whatever natural tastes might lurk underneath. Examples are the breaded veal, meatballs, and braciola. The crawfish pasta tossed with mushrooms, green onions, and heavy cream is one escape route.

jamaican-creole...

New Orleans' only Jamaican-Creole restaurant, **Palmer's** (135 N. Carrollton Ave. 504/482–3658 $$) is the culinary playground for Jamaican chef Cecil Palmer. His skills with his spicy native cuisine are flawless, from jerk meats and escaveche to curries. His ceviche is excellent, as is the Bahamian seafood chowder. The classic Jamaican chicken is marinated in hot peppers and onions, then sauteed and served with a rich sauce made from the marinade. Shrimp Betty is served in a tangy sauce over fettuccine, and the West Indian goat comes with rice and peas. The Caribbean pork with apples and potatoes is also good. The decor is surprisingly spare, considering the brightly painted palm trees on the outside. This place is fun, different, very reasonable, and an exotic celebration for your mouth.

korean...

Genghis Khan (4053 Tulane Ave. 504/482–4044 $$$) has music as good as its food. For those unfamiliar with Korean cuisine, try the chongol hot pot (beef and shrimp in broth), the signature shrimp Genghis Khan, or charcoal-grilled marinated beef. Most first-timers enjoy the whole fish that's marinated in sake and spices and deep-fried without becoming greasy. The traditional kimchee is decidedly an acquired taste, and some of the dishes are pretty spicy, so ask the helpful wait staff questions before ordering. After they've answered your questions and brought your food, they'll entertain you with classical music complete with violins, pianos, and maybe a mezzo aria or two. If you're lucky, owner/classical violinist Henry Lee will perform. For a place with such a ferocious name, it's deliciously genteel.

natural-foods/takeout...

There's a chain of these stretching all the way to California, but still, you've missed something if you haven't experienced **Whole Foods Market** (*3135 Esplanade Ave. 504/934–1626 $*). Nature rules here, and so do shoppers in Birkenstocks and ponytails. There's a huge selection of organic produce, home-made soups, hot plates like red beans and rice, and fresh baked breads, desserts, and muffins. The deli counter is a wow with curried turkey salads, falafels, veggie tamales, and an inspired combination of shrimp, hearts of palm, and green onions in a Creole mustardy/mayo sauce. Head for the tables outside where you can enjoy the trees and people-watching of Esplanade Avenue. The prices for lunch are manageable, but regular shopping in this place would send your grocery bill into orbit.

spanish...

Despite its history as a Spanish colony, New Orleans has virtually no real Spanish restaurants. **Lola's** (*3312 Esplanade Ave. 504/488–6946 $*) tries hard to fill the gap with a tiny cafe, and the long lines say it's working. The gazpacho is fine and the traditional paella can be ordered with meat, seafood, or vegetables. There is also a good garlic chicken and a paprika-marinated roast pork loin. This place is a real bargain, but the wine list is nonexistent. B.Y.O.B.

steak... You'd hardly expect New Orleans to launch one of the most successful chains of steakhouses in the country, but this is the original **Ruth's Chris Steakhouse** (711 *Broad St.* 504/486–0810 $$$–$$$$). When Ruth took over Chris' Steakhouse back when, who knew she'd become an empire? Her secret is the best steak money can buy, cooked to absolute perfection and served sizzling. You won't find a better fillet anywhere in town, but if you want variety, consider the mixed grill, which includes beef, chicken, and andouille. Savor the meats with nicely turned asparagus with hollandaise and one of Ruth's eight potato dishes, including a luscious au gratin, julienne, shoestring, and a Lyonnaise variety not found at her other venues. The decor is more clubby than posh, and draws everyone from designer suits and self-important local politicos flaunting cell phones to down-home dudes in duck-hunting duds. Ruth's is also very popular for celebrating birthdays, anniversaries, promotions, and shady business deals. Super people-watching!

Serving up sizzlers since 1933, **Crescent City Steakhouse** (1001 *N. Broad St.* 504/821–3271 $$-$$$) is the godfather of all New Orleans steak houses. It looks it too, but don't be fooled, because they still have a way with beef. The fillet is definitely a preferred cut, but you can't go wrong with the strip sirloin, porterhouse, or ribeye either. For side dishes, try the broccoli au gratin and brabant potatoes, but steer clear of the salads and onion rings. If the big dining room is humming and you really want privacy, sequester yourself in a booth and draw the curtains.

thai... **Bangkok Cuisine** (*4137 S. Carrollton Ave. 504/482–3606 $$*) is a welcome Asian break for Mid-City diners. The food seems unusually fresh, well-prepared, and perfectly spiced by the Semiesuke family who, incidentally, introduced most of New Orleans to Thai cooking. If you like fish, the Siam whole fish with ginger is good, as is the tilapia fillet, lightly fried and embellished with a sauce flavored with garlic, basil, shrimp, onions, mushrooms, and corn. The more adventurous can try the stuffed giant squid. If you want to really wake up your palate, order the calamari doused with a blazing chili sauce. There's also narai beef, peppermint-leaf chicken with bamboo shoots, and green curry with chicken and eggplant. The exotic ambience is enhanced by attractive, amiable waitresses in traditional dress.

vietnamese... One of the most recent additions to the New Orleans ethnic tapestry is the Vietnamese. Lucky for us, they brought their culinary skills with them, and the tasty results are places like **Lemon Grass Cafe** (*3605 S. Carrollton Ave. 504/482–3935 $$*), probably the best Vietnamese restaurant in the city. Chef Minh Bui works culinary miracles combining his native skills and Louisiana native bounty. His talents crest with a sinfully rich bouillabaisse made with angel-hair noodles and served with cilantro garlic bread (talk about an explosion of flavors!). There's also the boned lacquer duck served with sticky rice and sweet baby bok choy, pan-sautéed marinated pork loin with lemon-grass rice and veggies, and broiled stuffed Dungeness crab that's one of the messiest pleasures around, but worth it. Don't overlook the crab, tuna, and shrimp dumplings.

bars/music/clubs

Mid-City's entertainment is found mostly in its handsome, tree-lined streets, New Orleans' last bayou, and glorious City Park. There are only a couple of clubs worth checking out, but one is a real knockout—or is that knock-down?

Unquestionably one of the most bizarre and irresistible music venues in the world, **Mid-City Lanes** (*4133 S. Carrollton Ave. 504/482–3133*) is a recycled bowling alley known locally as Rock 'N' Bowl, where you can listen to top-notch live music while playing a few frames. This is the spot to hear living legends like zydeco maestro Boozoo Chavis and blind blues guitarist Snooks Eaglin, as well as extremely popular acts like the Iguanas and George Porter. There's also **Bowl Me Under**, a downstairs addition with more music and a dance space where energetic young swingsters take to the floor in '30s and '40s retro drag. On weekends, the joint is really jumping! If you need to get re-energized, grab some fried shrimp, mozzarella cheese fries, pizza, alligator, or oysters. Who cares about calories? You'll dance it off! When you finally take a breather, ask a local to explain the superb New Orleans murals.

The **Canal Bus Stop Bar & Grill** (*2828 Canal St. 504/822–2011*) is an absolute trip and defies categorization and, almost, description. The place always seems to be rocking with something, whether it's the daily beer specials, ladies' nights, unusual drink specials, or just the blaring big-screen TV. Some nights there's even a live DJ. The food is plentiful, good, and falls smack dab in the

fire on the bayou: jazzfest

You are standing in a field at sunset, surrounded by hundreds of thousands of people with huge smiles on their faces. You're tired and sunburned, but still you find the strength to move your body to a funky rhythm. This is the ecstatic exhaustion that is the final hour of Jazzfest, the collective harmony that sets this festival apart from any other. For two weeks out of the year, the music that forms the undercurrent of New Orleans life takes over the town completely, as thousands of musicians from around the world descend upon the New Orleans Fair Grounds to play for a crowd that in 1998 reached half a million people. What began in 1967 as a showcase of local music created to ease everyone into the summer heat has grown into a ten-day extravaganza that draws music lovers from far and wide to fest and feast on the bayou.

The first International Jazz Festival was held in 1968, but even luminaries like Louis Armstrong, Dave Brubeck, and Woody Herman failed to draw crowds. George Wein, who master-minded the Newport Jazz Festival, was brought in, and comfort genre, with spaghetti and meatballs, pork chops, stuffed bell peppers, chicken, and an assortment of tasty po' boys. The sandwiches are enormous, a foot long or so, and are packed to the max with all sorts of meats and vegetables. The buses don't really stop here, but the fun does.

promptly proposed a dual celebration—an outdoor fair of music, food, and local handicrafts, and evening concerts with guest stars. Everything finally came together in 1970, when Congo Square bloomed with four stages, a gospel tent, and a scattering of arts and crafts booths. Native daughter Mahalia Jackson blew the roof off along with trumpeter Punch Miller and the legendary Duke Ellington. As the festival began to make a profit, the Jazz & Heritage Foundation administered the monies in grants to various local cultural groups and artists. These grants, now exceeding half a million dollars, help maintain the city's extraordinary musical legacy.

Over the past three decades, Jazzfest has metamorphosed into something beyond its creators' dreams: a celebration of much more than music and food. The event is an inspiring mingling of races and classes, of straights and gays, of young and old, celebrating together the magic of New Orleans. For a few beautiful days, festival goers can actually experience Louis Armstrong's "Wonderful World."

sleeping

Keep in mind that staying in a hotel or B&B in this part of
town means you're away from most of the action. For visitors who want to come home and relax after a busy day
of shopping and sightseeing, that's fine, because most of
these places have an abundance of historic New Orleans
ambience, and their proprietors appreciate guests who
take the time to enjoy it. Those who are mostly interested
in clubbing and carousing will find this splendid isolation
an inconvenience. The choice is yours.

Cost Range for double occupancy per night on a
weeknight. Call to verify prices.
$/under 100 dollars
$$/100–150 dollars
$$$/150–200 dollars
$$$$/200+ dollars

If anything, the exquisitely restored **Degas House**
(*2306 Esplanade Ave.* *504/821–5009, 800/755–6730*
$$–$$$$), boasting its own historical marker, languishes
beneath a surfeit of destiny and charm. A classic 1852
double-galleried Greek revival home, it was built by the
Musson family, who entertained their famous relative,
French painter Edgar Degas, here [see **doing stuff**]. The
rich hand of the past is felt from the moment you enter
the foyer and see reproductions of Degas' works on two
parlor walls. The six rooms and one suite have period fur-
nishings, private baths, cable TV, and names like Estelle's

Suite and Garrett Room, after members of Degas' American family. Some have 14-foot ceilings, balconies, and king- and queen-sized rice beds, and original fireplaces. Complimentary extended continental breakfast is taken in the breakfast room, and a tour is included. This place is a real gem.

Esplanade Villa (2216 *Esplanade Ave.* 504/525–9760, 800/308–7040 **$$**) is in an 1880 Italianate town house. It has all the expected charm, with high ceilings, some fine antiques, bathrooms with claw-foot tubs, and a patio with fountain. Breakfasts are tasty and hearty. There are five two-room suites, all with private baths. The drawback is the neighborhood, which is definitely iffy at night and not within walking distance to any cafes or clubs. Pleasant enough, but a bit high-priced for its location.

Lamothe House Hotel (621 *Esplanade Ave.* 504/ 947–1161, 800/367–5858 **$$–$$$$**) occupies a columned, antebellum double town house only a block from the Quarter. The feel of the house is high Victorian, complete with bronze and crystal chandeliers, period paintings, some glorious antiques, and oriental carpets gracing highly polished floors. Complimentary breakfast is enjoyed in a formal dining room, and afternoon sherry may be taken in a tropical courtyard filled with palms and banana trees. There are 11 rooms and nine suites, all with private bath. Amenities include 24-hour concierge and free on-site parking.

Maison Esplanade Guest House (1244 *Esplanade Ave.* 504/523–8080 **$$–$$$**) is a restored 1864 home two and a half blocks from the Quarter. All rooms and two-bedroom suites have phones, private baths, ceiling fans, four-poster beds, and hardwood floors. Unfortunately, it backs onto the dangerous Faubourg Tremé, meaning you'd better cab it at night.

The House on Bayou Road (2275 Bayou Rd. 504/ 945–0992, 800/882–2968 $$–$$$) occupies a 1798 indigo plantation built in the West Indies style by Canary Islander Domigo Fleitas. It's tucked away on two landscaped, mostly subtropical acres with ponds and patios to explore and enjoy.

music music music

Louis Moreau Gottschalk, America's first world-famous composer, lived in New Orleans in the 1830s, about the same time slaves were jamming to jazz's roots in Congo Square. Black "social aid and pleasure clubs" were formed in the 1880s, each with its own brass band, and jazz funerals were born as musicians buried one of their own. Achingly slow dirges set the mood until the deceased was laid to rest, at which point the brass bands exploded with jubilant song and the mourners behind danced in a "second line," often joined by passers by caught up in the moment.

By the turn of the century, jazz was full-blown in Storyville, the infamous red-light district just across Basin Street from the Quarter where Louis Armstrong's star rose from those ashes. Piano men in elegant brothels and plain whorehouses became known as professors. Dance clubs bloomed in Storyville, the Faubourg Tremé and the Seventh Ward, crashing

There are four rooms and four suites, some in the big house, some in separate cottages. One cottage suite has a skylight over the bed, a whirlpool bath, and a small kitchenette. All quarters are furnished with Louisiana antiques, including four-poster beds. Umbrella tables cluster around a swimming pool where a full gourmet breakfast is served. On Saturdays and Sundays there's a champagne brunch.

with the stock market in '29. The Swing era dampened jazz's popularity, and by the '40s its marriage to bebop, funk, and blues gave birth to rhythm and blues.

A very partial roll call of local musicians (by birth or by spirit) is astounding: Mahalia Jackson, Buddy Bolden, Jelly Roll Morton, Pete Fountain, Al Hirt, Professor Longhair, Clifton Chenier, Fats Domino (who lives in the Ninth Ward), Dr. John, Allen Toussaint, Dukes of Dixieland, the Storyville Stompers, the Funky Meters, the Neville Brothers and sister Charmaine, Bradford, Ellis, and Wynton Marsalis, the Radiators, and Harry Connick, Jr. But New Orleans has never been one to rest on its laurels. Today's music scene throbs with everything from Dixieland and Cajun to alternative, ska, and pure New Orleans funk. If you plan it just right, you can knock off three or four clubs in one night and live to brag about it. Or you can head on down for Jazzfest, the biggest musical bash of them all.

This B&B is a favorite of film stars seeking anonymity while working in town.

doing stuff

Esplanade Avenue is named for the parade grounds, or esplanade, at Fort St. Charles, which once stood at the river. It was born when the French Quarter suffered from overcrowding and a loss of status among Creoles who decided to take their snobbery elsewhere. Esplanade is an architectural treasure trove, unfairly overshadowed by the French Quarter and Garden District and therefore usually missed by visitors. The styles of houses run the gamut from Greek revival and Italianate to Victorian and Spanish. The Esplanade Ridge District is one of the largest in the city, covering 250 blocks from the Quarter to Bayou St. John and including the once-beautiful, badly deteriorated Faubourg Tremé. Grand Esplanade is much too long to be explored on foot, but the Esplanade bus runs right to City Park, offering good views of the many mansions along the way. You might also consider hiring a cab for a half day, taking things at your own pace and stopping wherever you're intrigued.

The undisputed but tragic queen of Esplanade and one of the most architecturally significant houses in the city is the **Dufour-Baldwin House** (*1700 Esplanade Ave.*). It was built in 1859, on the eve of the Civil War, at the then-staggering sum of $40,000. Designed by architects Howard and Diettel, it is a stunning example of the late Classic style, with a richness that absolutely glows. Unfortunately its future is uncertain, as ongoing restoration has been interrupted and the house is now for sale.

The **1852 Degas House** (2306 *Esplanade Ave.* 504/821–5009, 800/755–6730), now a choice B&B [see **sleeping**], was originally home to the Musson family, whose most famous member, Edgar Degas, came calling in 1872. Degas had an eye disorder exacerbated by the intense sub-tropical Louisiana light, but he still managed to produce over a dozen works here. The most famous is *The Cotton Office in New Orleans*, his first to be bought by a museum. *Portrait of Estelle*, a painting of his blind cousin arranging flowers by touch and scent, hangs in the **New Orleans Museum of Art** (504/488–2631) in nearby City Park. The original connecting parlors now serve as a gallery for fine reproductions of Degas' works. Reproductions were settled on for insurance purposes and the impossibility of maintaining proper climate control in an old Creole house.

First-timers seeing the house at **2326 Esplanade Avenue** often think it's under renovation. Wrong. The ungainly metal conglomeration clogging the front yard is the "archisculpture" of occupant/artist Bob Tannen. It's anyone's guess what it all represents, although neighbors and passersby concur that "eyesore" is a fair interpretation. If you must, check out the metal fish hanging nose-down in a tree, and the duct-taped tires on the front porch. Yikes!

The colossal **Luling Mansion** once fronted on Esplanade, but its lawn is now occupied by lesser structures. You can get a side view from 1438 Leda Court, and even from this perspective the house casts a magnificent image. To see it, turn right off Esplanade onto Verna Street, left at Marie

Court and left again at Leda. It's definitely worth the detour.
Built in the Italianate style and grandly situated atop an elevated terrace, it rises an impressive three and a half stories
and is wrapped in a masonry confection of graceful galleries and balconies. The intact appearance is unfortunately
misleading, as it's been divided into apartments.

Close to the end of Esplanade, near Bayou St. John, is **St.
Louis Cemetery No. III**. Also known as the Bayou
Cemetery, it was created in 1833 on a site once occupied
by the town's leper colony. It's available for tours [see
cemeteries sidebar].

Not technically part of Mid-City, Bayou St. John is the
city's last bayou, the others long ago having been filled up
or covered over. The bayou stretches five miles or so along
the border of City Park before emptying into Lake
Pontchartrain. There are important historic homes here,
many conveniently located on Moss Street. Most significant is the simple white **Pitot House (1440 Moss St.
504/482–0312)**, which would be equally at home in the
Caribbean. Built in 1799 by James Francis Pitot, New
Orleans' first mayor, it's a classic example of architecture
designed to withstand vicious summers and lashing rains,
with a steeply pitched roof and galleries shading and protecting the house itself. Cooling breezes were courted by
tall shuttered windows and French doors. Threatened with
demolition in 1964, the Pitot House was moved about
200 feet, restored by the Louisiana Historical Society, and
exquisitely furnished with period antiques. The porch
ceilings are painted grand rouge, a color popular with
Creoles and made by mixing brick dust and buttermilk!
Open for tours.

The **Musgrove-Wilkinson House** (1454 Moss St.) is a big if plain Greek revival home built in the 1850s. Originally a Bayou St. John plantation house, the **Evariste Blanc House**, or Holy Rosary Rectory (1342 Moss St.), dates from 1834. The slim colonnettes and round arched doors happily survived later efforts to "modernize" when Greek revival was all the rage.

Nearby is the so-called **Spanish Custom House** (1300 Moss St.), built in 1784, and another of the neighborhood's assortment of West Indian styles. The first level is masonry, topped by a graceful wooden upper story, and the floor plan facilitates much-needed cross ventilation. Its origins are unknown, but it was possibly built for Don Santiago Lloreins when the area was part of his plantation. No one knows where the strange nickname comes from, since there is no evidence the house served in any official capacity.

The **Blanc House** (924 Moss St.) was built in 1798. Once the plantation home of Louis Antonio Blanc, it features more of the West Indian thick lower columns supporting slender colonnettes. The steeply pitched roof, French windows, and striking jalousies are especially fine representations of this style, but there are Anglo-American touches in the center-hall floor plan and Federal-style woodwork.

At the end of Esplanade is a traffic circle with a statue of General P.G.T. Beauregard, the Creole Confederate general. It's the work of sculptor Alexander Doyle, who also created the statue of that other Confederate general at Lee Circle. The statue marks the entrance to **City Park** (504/482-4888), an enormous green area carved from the Allard Plan-

tation and given to the city by philanthropist John
McDonogh. First-time visitors are understandably awed by
the centuries-old live oaks, draped in Spanish moss, some
reaching limbs right to the ground. There is also a profusion of exotic natural flora.

The park entrance behind Beauregard's statue leads
dead-on into the **New Orleans Museum of Art** (City Park
504/488–2631), aka NOMA. Founded in 1910, it has a first-
class assortment of more than 35,000 artworks valued at
over $200 million. The collection is particularly celebrated
for fine American and French art, with emphasis also on
African and pre-Colombian art, and has one of the few
Fabergé collections in the world. A recent and much-needed
expansion greatly increased its exhibition space.

A half-circle behind the museum curves to the right and
crosses a bridge. To the left is Victory Avenue leading past
the **Pavilion of Two Sisters**, which looks like an
orangerie, to the **Botanical Gardens** (**504/483-9386**),
which has a conservatory, sculpture, rose gardens, parterre
gardens, and more. Just past the gardens is **Storyland**, an
old-fashioned theme park for kids. A favorite of New
Orleans children for generations, it has Mother Goose char-
acters that should make everyone smile. A ride on the genuinely fabulous vintage carousel, with wooden "flying
horses," zebras, and giraffes, is something your child will
never forget.

Victory Avenue leads past tennis courts, where you turn
left and left again onto Dreyfous Avenue. **The Peristyle** with
its graceful columns, guardian lions and serene lagoon
beyond is a symbol of the park and popular with photographers, picnickers, and lovers. At Christmas and Hanukkah,

this area sparkles with millions of lights as City Park enjoys Celebration in the Oaks. Over a narrow bridge and to the left are the famous **Dueling Oaks**, where many a hotheaded Creole lost his life to a well-aimed bullet or sword thrust. Although never legal, dueling continued until at least 1889, when newspapers reported that two duelists were arrested for disturbing the peace after shooting three times and still missing. Could bourbon possibly have been involved?

spectating... The **Fair Grounds** (504/944-5515) occupies the site of the old Union Race Course. Dating from 1852, it is the oldest racetrack in America still in operation. During the Civil War, the grounds were leased by infamous riverboat gambler George Devol, who staged boxing matches, baseball games, and bull-and-bear fights that would've given apoplexy to animal-rights activists. The Victorian-style grandstand entertained gamblers until it was destroyed by a seven-alarm fire in 1993. Old-timers say they're still not used to the sleek $27 million replacement, an enormous structure with blue-green tinted windows that seem to magnify action on the track. The season runs from Thanksgiving until the end of March, with a 12:30 p.m. post time. There are usually ten races a day and no night racing, because of insufficient lighting. During Jazzfest, the track is a multicolored tableau of humanity swarming to the sounds of music.

uptown

Upriver from the Garden Districts,
Uptown was sparsely settled with
Creole cottages and a handful of large
houses when growth arrived in the
late 1880s. Audubon Place, an
exercise in beaux arts chic,
was built in 1895 and remains one
of the city's most exclusive
and utterly inaccessible addresses.
St. Charles Avenue was eventually
lined with grand mansions, but
development toward the lake
was impossible because the land was
dangerously low-lying.

turn page for map key

By the 1920s, the areas had been reclaimed from the swamp and growth was volcanic. Today, Uptown—our biggest designated area, sprawling roughly from Louisiana Avenue to Carrollton Avenue between Tchoupitoulas Street and Claiborne Avenue—includes widely diverse neighborhoods and the university districts of Tulane, Loyola, and Sophie Newcomb as well as Audubon Park, home of the world-class Audubon Zoo.

Where St. Charles dead-ends into Carrollton Avenue is an area huddled against a curve of the Mississippi that's aptly called Riverbend. It's a warm, friendly amalgam of shotgun houses and cottages and the occasional big house. One chunk is a sort of mini-Magazine Street, lined with locally owned galleries, boutiques, restaurants, and specialty stores, refreshingly free of Gaps and Banana Republics. This is quiet, small-town New Orleans with an easygoing ambience all its own, and it's downright charming. Stop in for a cup of café au lait, put your feet up, and set a spell.

eating/coffee

Uptown eating is eclectic, quirky, funky, and most of all, fun. It can also be elegant and romantic. You can dine in a Victorian cottage, an 1870s town house, an authentic

map key		
	1 Mat & Naddie's Cafe	5 St. Charles Streetcar
	2 Camellia Grill	6 Tipitina's
	3 Brightsen's	7 Columns Hotel
	4 Audubon Zoological Gardens	

shotgun house, or even a recycled gas station. This is an almost tourist-free zone, yours to enjoy—with all that entails.

Cost Range per entree
$/under 10 dollars
$$/10–15 dollars
$$$/15–20 dollars
$$$$/20+ dollars

cafes... Mat & Naddie's Cafe (937 Leonidas St. 504/861–9600 $$–$$$) is secreted away in a modest River Road cottage hard by the train tracks. You can't help falling under its offbeat spell, nor will you be disappointed by the fusion-fueled eats. Try a seaweed salad, Vietnamese spring rolls, oysters Bienville in phyllo, coconut-lemon-grass shrimp, or the roasted double-cut pork chop with a green mole served with black-eyed peas. The chocolate truffle cake may send you into orbit.

Jacques-Imo (8324 Oak St. 504/861–0886 $$–$$$) is another quirky neighborhood joint you're gonna love. You can eat in the cozy front dining room or the enclosed courtyard out back. The list of goodies includes alligator sausage cheesecake, fried oysters with a tangy garlic sauce, and a grilled swordfish glazed with satsuma, sugar cane, and chili powder, topped with a zesty crabmeat salsa relish. The fried chicken is superb in a city not famous for it. Chef Jacques Leonard just may wander over to introduce himself and ask if you want something special. If that happens, carpe diem!

cajun/creole... **Brightsen's** (*723 Dante St. 504/ 861–7610 $$–$$$$*) occupies a smallish Victorian cottage in the Carrollton area and is regarded by some as the (gasp!) best restaurant in New Orleans. Indeed, chef Frank Brightsen has won numerous accolades, both local and national, and produces wonders in his small kitchen. Antiques, lace curtains, a floral carpet, and artworks by friends and customers lend the small dining rooms a warm, homey ambience, making you feel as if you're dining in a private home. The menu changes daily, the specials made more so because of Frank's insistence on the freshest-possible ingredients. He's helped by Louisiana's long growing season, which provides almost year-round summer produce. The butternut shrimp bisque is an excellent starter. The gratin of oysters with spinach, Italian sausage, and Romano cheese is absolutely wonderful, as is the rabbit with Louisiana cheese wrapped in phyllo with a roasted-garlic sauce. Frank's roast duck with cornbread stuffing and pecan gravy is the stuff game-lovers' dreams are made of. The grilled foie gras with sweet-potato purée is also a must-try.

The romantic **Columns Hotel** (*3811 St. Charles Ave. 504/899–9308 $–$$*) is almost as celebrated for its appearance as for its food, explaining why it's the site of so many wedding receptions, but it's also just a great place to rendezvous with someone special. There are some imaginative twists to familiar favorites, like eggs Benedict served over catfish instead of ham, or Caesar salad spiced with chunks of alligator. The less adventurous can stick to a rich seafood chowder brimming with fresh crab, scallops, and oysters.

chinese... **Kung's Dynasty** (*1912 St. Charles Ave. 504/ 525–6669 $–$$*) looks like a generic Chinese restaurant, but the mostly Hunan-style food puts emphasis on freshness and execution. Uptowners have packed the place for years, many choosing it for special occasions or watching the passing carnival parades. The food mostly overshadows the blasé service. Try the Peking duck (as either appetizer or entree); imperial beef, stir-fried in a spicy garlic and orange sauce; oysters Szechuan; or the signature crispy Kung's chicken in plum sauce.

coffee... **P.J.'s Coffee and Tea Company** (*7624 Maple St. 504/866–7031 $*) is a popular chain. P.J.'s has three freshly roasted and brewed hot coffees with a selection changing daily, plus cold-brewed daily iced coffees. There are the usual macchiatos, cappuccinos, and lattes, and also espresso dolce. Try the ultra-rich white-chocolate cappuccino or honey-cream dessert coffees. Both hot and iced tea are available, along with hot and iced chai.

creole... Upscaling a neighborhood hangout doesn't always work, but **Clancy's** (*6100 Annunciation St. 504/ 895–1111 $$–$$$$*) is a true success story. One of the city's first nouvelle Creole bistros, its focus is firmly on seafood. Recommendations include smoked shrimp with ginger, crabmeat ravigote, divine grilled baby drum with smoked salmon, and fried oysters with brie that should be renamed fried oysters with brio. Regulars often go for the panéed veal Annunciation which—ahem—comes close to being a religious experience.

Café Volage (*720 Dublin St.* 504/861–4227 $$–$$$) is part of the Riverbend renaissance, one of a series of revamped Victorian shotguns, and a real bargain. The side decks, which sparkle with pinpoint lights after dark, are nicely done with pots of red geraniums and weeping fig. The rear has a large deck that's tree-shaded with a touch of latticework. The interior glows with comfortable pastels, lace curtains, and bentwood chairs. You're greeted with a basket of French-bread strips brushed with tomato sauce, herbs, and Parmesan, as well as battered and fried okra strips. Affable Chef Felix Gallerani is adept at fusing classic Creole with Italian and French dishes, and the results are scrumptious. His signature quail à la Felix has a memorable rosemary sauce. The cold crawfish Volage is also good, delivered in a lemon-peppery marinade, and so is the soft-shell crab à la Gregory, sautéed in butter and white wine before being served atop ratatouille veggies. The grilled salmon is perfectly done with a caper and lemon butter sauce. The bread pudding, brimming with raisins, makes a nice finish.

Zachary's Restaurant (*8400 Oak St.* 504/865–1559 $$$) is retro '70s, a neighborhood hangout cooking up the kind of food New Orleanians grew up with—and lots of it! The fried-seafood platters are wonderful, but there's also a good beef brisket, a pork chop with bordelaise, and the enormous trout Basquet with crabmeat and lemon butter sauce. Don't forget the bread pudding for dessert.

deli/sandwiches... Beebo's (*7329 Freret St.* 504/866–6692 $) is popular with the Tulane/Loyola crowd, drawing both students and professors as well as locals with

its patio dining and knockout sandwiches. The New Orleans steak sandwich is a favorite, along with the grilled-meatloaf sandwich and something called the Swiss Garden meltdown, which almost defies description. Apparently someone raided the garden for a concoction of grilled zucchini, roasted eggplant, tomatoes, mushrooms, onions, and bell peppers, tossed in some melted Swiss cheese, slathered it with a tomato-pesto cream cheese and crammed it inside French bread. This is all dished up in, of all places, a former gas station.

Audubon Market (*1901 Audubon St. 504/866–0064 $*) is a neighborhood standard, with homemade sausages hot enough to set your mouth ablaze and traditional New Orleans sno-balls to cool it off. Their sandwiches are stellar, but don't miss the boneless stuffed chicken filled with your choice of spinach Florentine or crabmeat.

down-home...
Arguably the most famous down-home eatery in the city, **Camellia Grill** (*626 S. Carrollton Ave. 504/866–9573 $*) can be the best of times or only a memory of them. The quality of both the legendary food and super service at those 29 coveted counter stools is slipping these days, which is a real shame considering such past glory. All that having been said, try the big burgers, pecan waffles, chili-cheese omelette, club sandwich, or flavored freeze. You're still given a crisp linen napkin and served by waiters in tuxes, and that surely counts for something.

Probably only a handful of wayward tourists have darkened the nondescript door of **Franky & Johnny's** (*321 Arabella St. 504/899–9146 $–$$*), but they'd be the lucky ones. The ancient place is dimly lit, never heard the term "interior design," and needs a serious scouring, but if that doesn't tweak your aesthetic sensibilities, order the fabulous stuffed artichoke and hush up. Once you've had a bite, you'll be a believer and that means you can progress to the crawfish and (yes, indeedy) alligator pie, fried-oyster platter, and savory red beans and rice. If you want to look like a typically cholesterol-defiant local, hide your camera and order the roast beef po' boy, which slides onto your plate in a lake of gravy. Now you're cookin'!

eclectic... Suits and other locals love **Cannon's (4141 St. Charles Ave. 504/891–3200 $–$$)** for both lunch and dinner. The reason is simple: a lot of good food at reasonable prices. The salads are enormous and well done, especially the Cajun popcorn shrimp number. There's lots of basic fare like fried seafood, pasta jambalaya, and hickory-grilled pork chops, but there's also eggplant pasta marinara with pesto sauce and a delicious grilled salmon with tomatoes and red onions with a sun-dried-tomato remoulade. Before dinner, settle into one of the high-backed leather chairs and enjoy a drink at the massive mahogany bar. **O'Henry's Foods & Spirits (634 S. Carrollton Ave. 504/866–9741 $–$$)** is a branch of the popular kid-friendly local chain. The fare is hearty: burgers, obscenely overloaded cheese fries, Cajun grilled tuna steak, garlic shrimp pasta, etc.

french... Terribly French and terribly atmospheric, **La Crêpe Nanou (1410 Robert St. 504/899–2670 $$–$$$)** is hot and heavy with the pretty Uptown set who keep the place so packed you'd best be prepared to wait a bit. The decor is very rive-gauche, albeit somewhat preciously calculated, with mismatched materials, but why not. It's fine for savoring the salade Niçoise, grilled quail with mushrooms, roast chicken, grilled lamb, or moules marinières served in an onion-and-white-wine sauce with a touch of cream. The grilled salmon with béarnaise is well executed, as is the filet mignon with green-peppercorn sauce. The crêpes, especially the crêpe au crabe with spinach, are probably the best in town. Wash it all down with a good selection of wines by the glass, or spring for a bottle from their fine cellar.

international... The menu at **Upperline** (*1413 Upperline St. 504/891–9822 $$$–$$$$*) really defies categorization, as it includes Creole, seafood, and international dishes. The clientele is just as unfused, smoothly mixing right-wing politicos and left-wing artists with plenty in between to spice the social gumbo. Drawing them in is a chic bistro fit snugly into an 1877 town house—an almost instant tradition, steered by the knowing hands of owner JoAnn Clevenger and chef Richard Benz. The adventurously catholic menu includes a divine duck confit served with glazed turnips with blackberry port jam; and a braised lamb shank, very slowly cooked, presented with a soupçon of *gremolata*. The Bombay shrimp curry with jasmine rice and Indian condiments is a melange of exotic tastes. The appropriately adventurous finale would be the ice cream sauced with garlic chutney. In the past, Upperline has created inspired theme dinners honoring such luminaries as Jane Austen and Thomas Jefferson, the latter dinner accompanied by special Riedel wine glasses. This place is a true New Orleans experience.

italian... At first glance, it's reminiscent of an art-nouveau entrance to the Paris Metro, but there's nothing French about **Rustica** (*3442 St. Charles Ave. 504/899–1570 $$–$$$*). This peculiar oblong structure with a narrow end on the avenue is about as purely Florentine as you can get. The signature eggplant Rigatoni is a mini-masterpiece of rich tomato sauce, parsley, garlic, and Parmesan cheese baked to golden perfection. If you're really in the mood for indulgence, try the creamy gnocchi.

Cafe Nino (*1510 S. Carrollton Ave. 504/865–9200 $*) is a no-frills, cozy space that'll fill your senses with the smells of a Sicilian *cucina* the minute you walk in, and the service is speedy. The packed-with-cheese calzones are good, as is the anise-rich Italian sausage baked in a roll. The pizzas also shine in a town where good pizza is as rare as low humidity, but the real star is the Philly cheese steak: thin sliced beef freshly grilled with peppers, onions, and cheese and served like a po' boy—if you're from south Philly, it's enough to make you homesick. And don't forget the nicely spiced Chicken Marsala with fresh mushrooms and marsala butter.

For a dose of retro, try **Vincent's** (*7839 St. Charles Ave. 504/866–9313 $$–$$$$*), a neighborhood family restaurant with no-nonsense decor and service to match. You can feel all tension ease the moment you walk in and are enveloped in comfy cooking smells. Start with the silky corn-and-crabmeat bisque served in a fresh-baked bread cup, or the sautéed mushrooms with seafood stuffing. You can always tell a good Italian restaurant by the osso bucco, and here it's sublime, served over angel-hair pasta and crowned with a rich brown demiglace. The house-made cannelloni is also a knockout, filled with ground veal, puréed spinach, and Parmesan cheese, baked in Alfredo cream and topped with a delicate red sauce; don't overlook the sautéed Parmesan chicken breast served on a bed of spinach with a beurre blanc and a shot of champagne. Got room for dessert? Go light with the ethereal tiramisù or old reliable lemon ice. If you're lucky, your waiter will be Johnny, who, if you ask nicely, will treat you to the sound of his fine tenor voice as you savor the food.

Another local legend is **Pascal's Manale** (1838 *Napoleon Ave.* 504/895–4877 $$–$$$), which has been around since 1913. Manale's is famous for originating barbecued shrimp and it's still delicious, although purists claim it's better elsewhere. You can't go wrong with any of the three ways they serve oysters—on the half shell with a biting pepper sauce, Rockefeller, or Bienville. The combination pan roast and stuffed eggplant is also good, as is the crab-and-oyster combo pan roast. Beneath the bustle, the place is laid-back, and the portions are enormous.

Figaro's Pizzerie (7900 *Maple St.* 504/866–0100 $–$$) is a longtime favorite of Uptowners and college students. Everything's made from scratch and run through a conveyor-belt oven, ensuring perfect crusts. They're all good, but the ones made with tomato and basil or garlic-herb butter are super. The possible combinations and permutations for toppings would give a math student pause, but consider the quattro stagioni, with different toppings on each of the four quarters—tomato and basil; spinach and feta; artichoke, tomato, and Italian sausage; and white pizza. Wow! Pizza takes center stage, but you might try the shrimp Carrie, which is Gulf shrimp, tomatoes, green onions, mushrooms, and garlic tossed with fusilli in a tangy cream sauce, or the sherried chicken linguine with fresh mushrooms. Most seats are outdoors, but there is a smallish indoor dining room for inclement weather.

This location of **Café Roma** (*1901 Sophie Wright Place 504/524–2419 $–$$*) is one of four in the city, all of which make deliveries. There's a comfy dining area where you can enjoy the savory Italian smells while enjoying the feta rolls, chicken pasta, or a wide choice of pizzas with spinach, artichokes, feta, you name it. Cheap and cheerful.

japanese... It seems a bit strange, Japanese food in a tiny New Orleans cottage, but that's the experience at **Ninja** (*8115 Jeanette St. 504/866–1119 $–$$$*). Fact is, this is one of the top sushi bars in the city, and you have a choice between the 10-seat sushi bar or one of six tables in a separate room. Decor is minimal—some Japanese photos and the ubiquitous sushi posters—but that's okay. Owner/sushi chef Momo Young makes a mean California roll. The crawfish roll is a must-try, combining asparagus, green onion, smelt roe, and chunks of crawfish with Young's zesty house-made egg sauce. Along with the Ninja cartoon logo, sushi and sashimi are the stars here, but there's also barbecued eel, tempura shrimp, teriyaki beef and fish, and a delicious variety of mushrooms. Wash it down with hot or cold sake, plum wine, or Japanese beer.

The fish on the sign outside tells you what to expect at **Hana** (*8116 Hampson St. 504/865–1634 $–$$$*), another Riverbend sushi/sashimi joint. The sushi salads are winners, as are the fresh yellowtail sushi special and the tuna *tataki*. Unfortunately, the service can be chaotic and/or nonexistent, due in part to the servers' unfamiliarity with English. Be prepared to get to know your neighbors, as the tables are small and too numerous.

steak...

No one's really sure how much **Charlie's Steak House** *(4510 Dryades St. 504/895–9705 $$–$$$)* cleaned up after a bad fire over 30 years ago, but if you value food way, way above atmosphere, give it a shot. A visit here is like a day without sunshine, but who cares about sleaze when you can get one of the best T-bones and maybe *the* best fried onion rings in town? And when was the last time you saw a lettuce wedge for a salad? Take a tip from the raucous, virtually all-male clientele and don't ask about the grade of the steak you order. Just do it.

tunisian...

One of the most beguiling eateries in the Riverbend area is **Jamila's Cafe** *(7808 Maple St. 504/ 866–4366 $$)*, which serves delicious Tunisian fare. The place is a family endeavor, with mom, dad, and sons happily determined to make sure you like their food and enjoy yourself. It's certainly hard not to, with the charmingly small dining room, helpful service, and traditional Middle Eastern dishes like the couscous with lamb. The salade Tunisienne has apples, peppers, tuna, and cucumbers. If you feel like venturing into the exotic, order the calamari maison: squid stuffed with shrimp, bulgur wheat, parsley, and onions and served over linguine with a tomato-garlic sauce. The makroud, a semolina cake with dates and orange-blossom syrup, makes an interesting finish.

vegetarian... Eve's Market *(7700 Cohn St. 504/861–1626 $)* puts a tasty spin on veggie food. No doubt the fresh ingredients help. The sandwiches are filling, especially when augmented with a bag of organic corn chips. The salads are good too. Try the pesto rice salad combining brown rice, basil pesto, black olives, red bell peppers, walnuts, toasted pignolis, and balsamic vinegar.

bars/music/clubs

Uptown is blessed with enough outstanding music venues to draw jaded French Quarterites from their embarrassment of musical riches. You can hear some of the finest jamming in town, hang with the college crowd, mix with a cigar-smoking majority, or just groove with the locals. You'll find a club for almost everyone here.

Leading the list is **Tipitina's** *(501 Napoleon Ave. 504/897–3943)*, one of the oldest and most revered clubs in the city, where the lingering funk is almost palpable. Made even more famous by the movie *The Big Easy*, it was named for an old Professor Longhair song, and indeed you'll find a statuette here of the legendary musician himself. Tip's, as the locals call it, has hosted plenty of the R&B great ones, and their memories fairly ooze from the sagging ceiling and tired walls. This is one of several spots where, if you're lucky, you'll catch native sons like the Neville Brothers, or maybe you'll discover some new alternative group. Always call ahead for scheduled performers.

Maple Leaf Bar *(8316 Oak St. 504/866–5323)*, another Uptown institution, began as a music and chess club (two chess tables linger in the back room) and has atmosphere dripping from the ancient tin ceiling. The ghost of the peerless pianist James Booker hovers, now kept company by a worthy successor, pianist Henry Butler. You'll find more of the city's crazy musical gumbo—R&B, zydeco, Latin, funk, brass bands, and pure New Orleans rock. Saturdays are traditional piano nights and Sunday afternoons you can catch a poetry reading.

Carrollton Station Bar (8140 Willow St. 504/865–9190) is a local hangout where you can check out Twangorama or John Mooney & Bluesiana while choosing from a terrific selection of draft beers and top-shelf liquors. Not far away is **Jimmy's Music Club & Patio Bar** (8200 Willow St. 504/861–8200), which draws a younger crowd, but welcomes everyone to enjoy the sounds of ska bands like the Toasters.

The quirky shack with the outsized Christmas wreath is **Snake & Jake's Christmas Club Lounge** (7612 Oak St. 504/861–2802), every college drinking dive you've ever been in, and then some. The mood is friendly, the drinks cheap, and the crowd eager to rock with funk and reggae. Proprietress Miss Elaine keeps things vaguely in check, although regulars are quick to tell you about the time when male nudity was all the rage. Why? Because if you were bare-assed, you drank for free. Patrons work hard at being on the edge and usually succeed, so if you're not ready for college raunch and rowdiness, head out around ten.

Bruno's Bar (7601 Maple St. 504/861–7615) is another popular student hangout, no doubt attracting them with $2.50 pitchers on Monday nights and double-call brands and free food on Fridays. The late-night happy hour runs from midnight until you're blind. This is the place for that hard-to-find keg-to-go. Noisy, smoky, and bustling, just like you remember it. Still more college guys and gals hang out at **Cooter Brown's Tavern** (*509 South Carrollton Ave. 504/866–9104*), which keeps the crowd occupied with over a thousand different beers.

The city's first and one of the most popular of the trendy cigar bars, **Dos Jefes** (*5700 Tchoupitoulas St. 504/899–3030*) combines smoking, drinking, music, and eating in a pleasant, albeit smoky, environment. Smokers can select from over 40 cigar brands, with all the requisite merchandise for enjoying them, while drinkers pick from 20 wines and a good range of top-shelf whiskies, brandies, and ports. Light food is also available. Jazz is provided by Cadillac Red and his Uptown Cigar Band.

buying stuff

Uptown is far more residential than retail, but the concentration of one-of-a-kind shops in Riverbend makes it well worth a visit. This is also a logical spot to break the St. Charles streetcar ride, shop or browse a bit, grab a bite and head back to town or to that fabulous zoo.

antiques... **Driscoll Antiques** (*8118 Oak St. 504/866–7795*) showcases 18th- and 19th-century antiques, researched and beautifully restored. These people are experts at traditional French polishing, gilding, and upholstering and also work in leaded and stained glass.

books... Great Acquisitions Books (8120 Hampson St. 504/861–8707) is one of the city's favorite spots for finding rare, out-of-print, and downright unusual books. You never know what you're going to find in this colorful place, so allow yourself some time for browsing. The staff is always happy to help. **Maple Leaf Book Shop** (7523 Maple St. 504/866–4916) has been around since the '60s and has a comfy warmth you'll feel when you walk in. It stocks current best sellers, as well as books on New Orleans and the region. Local authors love to have signings here. Next door is **The Children's Book Shop** (200 Metairie St. 504/832–8937), which has—natch—books for kids.

clothing/shoes... Azby's (605 Dublin St. 504/866–1971) has a rep for selling entire outfits rather than individual items. They carry clothing for teens and women's sizes 1–12. Fine designer clothing and some shoes. **Ballin's Limited** (721 Dante St. 504/866–4367) has designer clothing, from dressy to casual wear. They also have a nice selection of shoes, accessories, and gifts. **Catalogue Collection** (8141 Maple St. 504/861–5002) carries men's and women's brand-name casual clothing and shoes. **Dunbar & Company** (8209 Hampson St. 504/897–3050) has some great clothing and unusual accessories ranging from the Gay '90s to the fabulous '50s. You'll find vintage beaded purses, evening gowns, costume jewelry, and more. **Gae-Tana's** (7732 Maple St. 504/865–9625) says they have "urban playclothes" for women along with lots of fun accessories, such as their whimsical bug hair clips.

Haase Shoe Store and Young Folks Shop (*8119 Oak St.* 504/866–9944, 504/866–3946) has been a local tradition for over 75 years. It's well known for fine shoes for the whole family and for classic children's clothing. **Lollipop Shoppe** (*8125 Hampson St.* 504/865–1014) has children's clothing and shares space with a ladies' shoe store called **Shoetique**. **On the Other Hand Exclusive** (*8126 Hampson St.* 504/861–0159) has second-hand women's clothing and accessories. **Perossi Clothing** (*7725 Maple St.* 504/866–9438) carries ladies' clothing that's definitely upscale but not outrageously priced. **Priorities** (*8128 Hampson St.* 504/861–8780) carries women's clothing for work, play, and working out. **Victoria's Uptown** (*7725 Maple St.* 504/861–8861) has the newest in designer shoes, plus handbags, belts, and designer jewelry—there can be savings of up to 80 percent on designer shoes. **Yvonne LaFleur** (*8131 Hampson St.* 504/866–9666) is a bona fide New Orleans experience for ladies. The word here is luxe, with Madam LaFleur's silky dresses and gowns, lingerie, custom millinery, and her own signature perfume. She also has imported wedding gowns, in case New Orleans puts you into a *really* romantic mood.

fabric/needlepoint... Meisel's Fabric Shop

(*8225 Oak St.* 504/866–9438) is an old family business carrying fabrics for clothing and interior decorating. **Persian Cat** (*8211 Hampson St.* 504/864–1908) carries a complete line of needlepoint necessities, from kits and canvases to cross-stitch supplies, lots of yarn, and pattern books to inspire you. They'll ship anywhere in the world.

home furnishings... White Pillars Emporium
(8312 Oak St. 504/861–7113) carries some beautiful and whimsical statuary and patio furniture, lampposts, outdoor wall hangings, park benches, and more.

galleries... House of 10,000 Picture Frames (8216 Oak St. 504/865–7255) does framing and exhibits a limited amount of artwork in a quaint old camelback house.

glass... Nuance Blown Glass Studio (728 Dublin St. 504/865–8463) sells fine blown-glass items, fun lightswitch plates designed to resemble historic New Orleans buildings, and eclectic glassware. The place doubles as the Louisiana Artists' Gallery, where local artists show work.

jewelry... Mignon Faget (710 Dublin St. 504/865–7361) is the famed New Orleans designer with an international rep for beautiful designs inspired by architecture, streetcars, crawfish, red beans, etc. **Simply Gold** (7113 Maple St. 504/866–5433) is a direct importer of fine Japanese pearls, and they design and make gold and platinum jewelry. They also carry the works of Ken Friend. **Symmetry Jewelers & Designers** (8138 Hampson St. 504/861–9925) is the place to find pieces by local, national, and international designers, both contemporary and antique-style. They also have in-house designers who will custom-design for you.

toys... Kid's Stuff, Ltd. (714 Dublin St. 504/866–8697) has an amazing array of toys and playthings, domestic and imported. You'll find games, gifts, dollhouses, educational

toys, and specialty items. This place proves that browsing can be fun.

sleeping

The paucity of hotels and B&Bs reflects the reality that, except for the zoo and St. Charles Avenue, Uptown is not an area heavily frequented by tourists. Some visitors prefer it because it's off the beaten track and a place to meet locals. It's also quieter than most other neighborhoods.

Cost Range for double occupancy per night on a weeknight. Call to verify prices.
$/under 100 dollars
$$/100–150 dollars
$$$/150–200 dollars
$$$$/200+ dollars

Doubling as a bordello in the then-scandalous film *Pretty Baby* starring the prepubescent Brooke Shields, **The Columns Hotel** (3811 *St. Charles Ave.* 504/899–9308, 800/445–9308 $–$$$) may be Hollywood's idea of a pillared Southern mansion, but in truth, this 1883 Victorian-style hotel, listed on the National Register of Historic Places, has an extravagant staircase leading to ten surprisingly spartan rooms. There are nine more, even sparser, accommodations for budget travelers who don't mind sharing baths. None have TVs. On those rare cold winter nights, fires crackle in two fireplaces in the cozy lounge, where there's live progressive jazz every Thursday. On

Sundays there's a popular jazz brunch in the restaurant [see **eating/coffee**] with dining indoors or on the veranda overlooking St. Charles Avenue with its clanging streetcars. This is a classic Uptown experience.

An 1892 Victorian splashed in the purples, golds, and greens of Mardi Gras, **Maison Perrier** (4117 *Perrier St.* 504/897–1807 $$–$$$$) is rumored to have been a bordello where a certain Miss Charlotte entertained with her six "nieces." Recently renovated, it has 13-foot ceilings, hardwood floors, period furnishings, and a parlor, game room, and library for your pleasure. There's even a study with large-screen TV and a bar with cold beer always on tap. The rosy Jasmine's Suite has a Victorian mahogany bed and Jacuzzi, and Dolly's Room is a rhapsody in blue with a bed so big you'll need the steps. Both have balcony access. All rooms and suites have phones and voice mail, data port, cable TV, and even blackout shades. These people seem to have thought of everything.

Mandevilla (7716 *St. Charles Ave.* 504/862–6396, 504/ 865–1000 $$–$$$) is a mid-19th century Greek revival beauty tucked behind an imposing iron fence. Guest rooms have high ceilings, delicate moldings, private galleries and baths, and antique beds. Afternoon tea may be taken on the pillared gallery facing the tree-lined avenue.

Château du Louisiane (1216 *Louisiana Ave.* 504/ 269–2600, 800/734–0137 $$) is a Victorian mansion with the usual high ceilings, hardwood floors, and period furnishings. Rooms are decorated and named for famous Louisianians (Louis Armstrong, Huey Long, etc.) and all have private baths, phones with voice mail, and cable TV.

A continental breakfast is served in the Sun Room. The Garden District begins just across leafy Louisiana Avenue.

Southern Nights B&B (1827 *South Carrollton Ave.* 504/861–7187 $–$$) is bound to be an experience. This three-story 1890s house has high ceilings, crown moldings, wood floors, and 13 fireplaces. Romance is clearly a theme, with rooms like the Desire Suite, the Loveswept Room, the Temptation Room, and so on. All have private baths and are furnished with a mixture of European and Louisiana antiques. The continental breakfast is served in a formal dining room, in the tropical courtyard, or in bed. The house specializes in haunted and murder-mystery weekends.

doing stuff

Most everything of interest Uptown is on or near the **St. Charles Streetcar** line. You can continue the ride begun in the Garden Districts [see **garden districts** chapter], or board at Louisiana Avenue. You'll pass **The Columns Hotel** at No. 3811 [see **sleeping**]. **The Sully House**, No. 4010, is a gingerbread extravaganza designed by famed architect Thomas Sully. Dating from 1908, **Touro Synagogue**, No. 4238, is named for one of the city's prominent philanthropists, Judah Touro.

One more block ahead is Napoleon Avenue. To the left one block, at the corner of Prytania Street, is **St. Elizabeth's Orphanage** (1314 *Napoleon Ave.* 504/899–6450), the Anne Rice compound that's home to both 800 dolls and a big chunk of her kinfolk. The white-columned, red-brick structure with its trademark angels dates from the mid-19th century, and for 118 years it was a girl's orphanage run by the Daughters of Charity of St. Vincent de Paul. It covers an astonishing 55,000 square feet and includes a glorious chapel with stained-glass windows (visible from Prytania Street), galleries for both religious and secular art, and one exclusively for the works of Anne's husband, Stan. The famous dolls comfort, inspire, and repulse as they hold mute court in a string of rooms. There are antique porcelain beauties, quaint Creole figures, a Wall of Nuns, a grotesque Pumpkinhead towering eight feet, and of course, the ever-popular Vampire Barbie. Your $7 donation goes to the St. Alphonsus Grammar School and St. Mary's Assumption Church. Except for in the dead of winter, a colorful farmer's truck is always parked outside selling Creole tomatoes, mirlitons, berries, and other local Louisiana produce.

The **Church of the Covenant Presbyterian** at No. 4422 dates from around 1900 and draws from the Colonial revival style. At No. 4521 is the grandiose **Sacred Hearts Academy**, built in 1899 and one of the city's most prestigious girls' schools. The galleries and colonnades are truly spectacular. The Romanesque **St. George's Episcopal Church** at No. 4600 dates from 1900. The **Brown-Villere House** at No. 4717 is the biggest house on the avenue, and ran up an imposing tab of $250,000 when it was built in 1905. Done in the rugged, high Victorian/ medieval style, it stuns passersby with grandeur literally heightened with a foundation atop a man-made mound. Since there are no stones in a river delta, every one of those massive stones had to be brought in.

At No. 5005 is the **Orleans Club**, built in 1868 as a residence, and which has been home to one of the city's oldest women's organizations since 1925. Sprawling over a whole city block, the monumental beaux arts **Milton H. Latter Memorial Library**, No. 5120, was built in 1907 as a residence. Silent-film siren Marguerite Clark married the owner and donated the house to the city in 1947. You may think you're seeing things at No. 5705, but, yes indeed, it's **Tara**! An exact replica of the O'Hara plantation house in the film version of *Gone With the Wind*, it's a favorite of photographers. If you want to see a real original, check out the so-called **Wedding Cake House** at No. 5809, a Georgian revival humdinger and another much-photographed house. It takes a while to digest all the fine detailing, which indeed suggests an elaborate multi-tiered wedding cake with oodles of icing. Another Georgian revival beauty is the 1896 **Castle's House**, No. 6000. It was designed by Thomas Sully and inspired by the 1759 Longfellow House in Massachusetts.

Loyola University, No. 6363, occupies an entire block of St. Charles Avenue and is the largest Catholic university in the South. The buildings are a striking mixture of Gothic and Tudor styles. The college dates from 1904, when it merged with the Jesuit College of the Immaculate Conception downtown. Next door is **Tulane University**, No. 6823, a handsome Romanesque complex dating to 1884. It's noted for its medical and law schools and the oldest college of commerce in America.

Across the avenue from the schools is **Audubon Park**, named for John James Audubon, the great bird painter who lived and worked for a time in New Orleans. Cars are banned in the 340-acre park, originally the plantation of

Etienne Boré, father of Louisiana's granulated-sugar industry. It was created for the 1884–85 World's Industrial and
Cotton Centennial Exposition and remains one of
America's biggest and most celebrated green spaces.
Designed by Frederick Law Olmsted of Central Park fame,
it's dotted with centuries-old live oaks dripping with
Spanish moss, free-form lagoons, statues, gazebos, and
fountains. In addition to the zoo, there's a golf course, riding stables, swimming pool, tennis courts, biking trails,
picnic areas, and jogging paths. Perhaps the strangest fea-
ture is Monkey Hill, built so New Orleans children would
know what a hill looks like—south Louisiana is as flat as a
tabletop.

The **Audubon Zoological Gardens** contain one of the
best zoos in the world. Over 1,500 different critters live
on 53 acres, and are displayed in a variety of imaginative
ways. Sections include the Asian Domain, Flamingo
Lagoon, Australian Outback, Louisiana Swamp, and the
newest, Jaguar Jungle. The popular Louisiana Swamp is a
real cypress swamp where you can watch alligators feed,
see a Cajun trapper's shack and taste some spicy Cajun
food. The Louisiana Swamp section has the distinction of
being a naturally primitive environment in an urban setting. Don't miss the rare and endangered white tiger, the
Asian hornbills, cheetahs, western lowland gorillas,
Sumatran orangs, albino alligators, and the exotic little
golden lion tamarin monkeys. Once you enter the park,
it's about a 20-minute walk to the zoo gates, or you can
catch a free shuttle. It's also accessible via the Cotton
Blossom, which sails to and from the Aquarium of the
Americas.

Just past Tulane on St. Charles Avenue is a rather forbid-
ding stone archway marking the entrance to **Audubon
Place.** James Bond himself would probably have trouble
getting into this ritzy residential enclave, which is guarded
around the clock. Its two blocks contain an awesome assortment of mansions, but the only one you'll get a really good
look at is the **Zemurray House**, facing the entrance at No.
2 Audubon Place. This white-columned stunner was built
in 1907 by the president of United Fruit Company and
today is the home for Tulane's president.

The Tudor-style **Doll House**, No. 7209, is a wee reflec-
tion of the big house beside it. It was built for the daughter
of a former owner and is probably the smallest house in
town with its own mailing address. **St. Mary's Dominican College for Women**, No. 7124, is a glorious Italianate structure dating from 1882. It was a girl's school,
then a women's college, and is now part of the Loyola University School of Law.

At the end of St. Charles Avenue, the streetcar veers right
onto Carrollton Avenue. Get off at the first stop, Maple
Street, and cross the tracks into Riverbend. The glamour of
St. Charles Avenue is left behind in this solid, somewhat
eclectic neighborhood of families, college students,
artists, and working-class folks. Hampson, Dublin, Maple,
and Oak streets have a rewarding cluster of shops and
restaurants worth browsing. The unofficial center is
Hampson between Dublin and Maple streets, a pleasant
boulevard with palms and benches that serves as the front
yard for a number of interesting stores.

The levee is some 60 feet high just across Leake Street, a
grassy slope deflecting a million gallons of water a

minute. Every so often you'll see the tops of smokestacks, an imposing reminder of the Mississippi's omnipresence. Climb up to the levee to drive the point home. This is a splendid place to stroll and take your time before hopping back on the streetcar downtown.

spectating... Tulane University Theater (6823 St. Charles Ave. 504/865–5265) puts on some amazingly good performances, although they do not have a regularly scheduled season. The **Summer Shakespeare Festival** (504/865–5105) is always a big deal, a collaboration of local and traveling talent. The theater is available for non-university productions, meaning local and quirky productions will sometimes be showcased here.

6 lakeside/west end

Lake Pontchartrain was named for Louis de Phlypeaux, Comte de Pontchartrain, as payback for being one of the Sieur d'Iberville's wealthier backers. It forms the northern border of New Orleans and, at 630 square miles, is the eighth-largest lake in the country. In truth, it's no lake at all, but rather an inland bay and brackish estuary of the Gulf of Mexico. The world's longest multispan bridge traverses 24 miles of the lake, connecting the city with the suburban north shore.

turn page for map key

New Orleanians have always loved their lake. The early Creoles built summer cottages there to take advantage of the cooling breezes, and in 1831 a rail line opened along Elysian Fields Avenue, linking the city to a lake town called Milneburg. Hotels and homes arose, along with restaurants, bathing facilities, and shooting galleries. The trains stopped running in 1932, and Milneburg was eventually buried beneath Pontchartrain Beach amusement park, now closed. After World War II, the lakeshore boomed with marinas, fishing camps, boat houses and house boats, high-rises, luxury homes, parks, and even an airport. The Orleans Marina and Southern Yacht Club are there, as is the Intracoastal waterway, a U.S. Coast Guard Station, the University of New Orleans, and a colorful entertainment called the Mardi Gras Fountains. A 5.5-mile-long seawall pretty much ensures that everything stays put.

The city was so busy protecting itself from the lake's occasional ferocious storms that it forgot to protect the lake in return. By the mid-'60s, Pontchartrain was so fouled that it was closed to swimmers. The good news is that it's making a comeback, and strict anti-pollution controls are making the water clean and clear again. The return of absentee pelicans is the sign of a healthy ecological balance, and officials are promising the lake will reopen to swimming in just a few more years.

map key

1 Bruning's
2 Sid -Mar's
3 U.S. Coast Guard Station and Lighthouse
4 Mardi Gras Fountains
5 The Kiefer University of New Orleans Lakefront Arena
6 Bally's Lakefront Resort & Casino

eating/coffee

Seafood unquestionably rules this part of town, as well it should. Visitors inevitably revel in the experience of lakeshore dining with the requisite trimmings—pelicans and gulls, sailboats, comfy breezes, and briny smells sure to whet your appetite.

> **Cost Range** per entree
> $/under 10 dollars
> $$/10–15 dollars
> $$$/15–20 dollars
> $$$$/20+ dollars

chinese... **China Rose** (125 Robert E. Lee Blvd. 504/283–2800 $-$$) is for lakeshore people who want a culinary change of pace, and it's been tastefully delivering that for years. Instead of egg rolls, start with the crab Ragoon, a creamy crab concoction in crisp shells. The beef in garlic sauce is a winner, and so is the dazzling Triple Dragon with chicken, roast pork, and shrimp, served with sautéed mushrooms and veggies in a tangy sauce.

creole... **Barataria** (900 Harrison Ave. 504/488–7474 $$-$$$) specializes in oysters brought in from the owner's private beds down in Barataria Bay—talk about fresh! Surprisingly, there's no oyster bar, but you can have them cooked in a variety of ways: grilled, in milk soup, smoky roasted just out of the wood-burning oven, or oysters Ralphie—half a dozen crowned with Asiago, Parmesan, and Romano cheeses, plus a little beer and herbs. Did you save room for the white-chocolate cheesecake?

Frankie's Cafe (324 Hammond Hwy. 504/838–8064 $–$$$) is a newcomer to the neighborhood, occupying a roomy old house with a history of restaurants. Start with the succulent crab fingers and turtle soup, then move on to the crawfish fajitas or doorstop pork chop. The fettuccine Frankie with tasso and cream sauce is another good choice, made with either chicken or shrimp.

down-home...

For most New Orleanians, lakeside dining is defined by **Sid-Mar's** (1824 Orpheum St. 504/831–9541 $–$$) in Bucktown. There's nothing like peeling shrimp on a screened-in porch right on the water while a fishing boat ties up just a few feet away. The dining rooms inside have an endearingly corny nautical theme. The Burgess family has been cooking here for over 30 years and they know people come for the food and the lake, not for decorating trends. This is definitely the spot to indulge in fried seafood. The oysters are flavorful puffs of gold, succulent perfection when zapped with a kiss of Tabasco, and the seafood platters are heroically portioned. The oyster soup and seafood bisques are sublime, as is the stuffed artichoke with a serious touch of garlic and that local curiosity known as "wop salad." (No one should be offended, since it's an Italian-immigrant concoction popular since the early 1900s.) The service is competent and warm, another ingredient making this place an absolute must. Just ask the locals who bring their own "crab-crackers" in order to access every fragment of crab!

Landry's (789 Harrison Ave. 504/488–6496 $-$$) is

another family-run local tradition. Regulars swear by the Pasta Landry, which is tossed with crawfish, shrimp, catfish or oysters. If soft-shell crab is in season, try this battered and fried version on angel-hair pasta garnished with a crawfish mixture. Also recommended are the chicken and sausage gumbo, grilled ham po' boy (a rarity) and a surprisingly good country breakfast.

eclectic... Breakwater Bistro & Bar (8550 Pontchartrain Blvd. 504/283–8301 $-$$$) is a spacious local hangout, largely patronized by an over-30 crowd looking for fun. The menu is mostly surf and turf, with a very good pepper-seared yellowfin tuna and a splendid prime rib. The tangy, honey-glazed babyback ribs are another good choice. The service is swift, efficient and friendly.

italian... Look carefully to spot the small wooden sign announcing Tony Angelo's Restaurant (6262 Fleur de Lis Dr. 504/488–0888 $$-$$$), located in an enormous one-story house in an otherwise residential neighborhood. There's a large main dining room and smaller private rooms nicely appointed with paintings and comfortable chairs. The food is superb and there is plenty of it, from angel-hair pasta with seafood gravy to a divine osso bucco. The "feed me" special costs $35 and includes a mind-boggling parade of chef's favorites that you think will never end.

mediterranean... Odyssey Grill (6264 Argonne Blvd. 504/482–4092 $$) is a tight ship run by chef Rosita Skias, who owned several restaurants before scoring big

with this one. The food is influenced by several cuisines, including Greek, Italian, Egyptian, Lebanese, and Moroccan, just to name a few. The whole fish, "étouféed" with garlic, herbs, and crabmeat, is delicious, as are the hummus, spinach pie, moussaka, and the souvlaki. Rosita does wonders with the Moroccan chicken that's spice-rubbed, grilled, and presented with couscous and veggies. And for calamari lovers, this place is heaven.

seafood... Many of the lakefront restaurants are legends simply because they've been around so long. **Deanie's** (1713 Lake Ave. 504/831–4141 $-$$) is a prime example. Seafood is king here, served in generous portions in one huge dining room that's always humming. Deanie's barbecue sauce is famed in these parts, as is the awesome size of the platters. The broiled, stuffed flounder is always good, and the fried artichokes are a special treat.

Bruning's (1924 West End Ave. 504/288–4521 $-$$) is another lakeside legend, and the oldest seafood restaurant in America. It's been dishing up seafood since 1859. Recently, Hurricane Georges smashed the back half of the restaurant right into the water, but within months Bruning's was back, with their phenomenal seafood platter erupting with shrimp, oysters, catfish, and soft-shell crab crisped to perfection. And for seven generations, the Bruning family has been guarding a secret that keeps their fried or broiled flounder incredibly moist. Get there before dusk to catch one of Pontchartrain's scarlet sunsets.

Jaeger's Seafood Beer Garden on the Lake (1928 West End Park 504/283–7585 $-$$) has been pleasing palates for almost half a century. Check out the "Big A" seafood platter, a veritable Alp of fried stuff that will fill half a dozen hungry folks for $48. Local musicians provide some hopping live entertainment Wednesdays through Sundays.

steaks/creole... The Steak Knife (888 Harrison Ave. 504/488–8981 $$–$$$) serves an interesting mix of beef and seafood, Creole-style. The place used to be a bank, which accounts for the marble floors and columns, and it's a pretty imaginative conversion. The steaks are USDA prime and served to order. The fragrant lamb, roasted with herbs, is just as good, and the osso bucco is also a tasty surprise.

sleeping

Cost Range for double occupancy per night on a weeknight. Call to verify prices.
$/under 100 dollars
$$/100–150 dollars
$$$/150–200 dollars
$$$$/200+ dollars

Tourists drawn to the lakefront are usually aboard their boats, so accommodations are minimal. A notable exception is **The Rose Manor Bed & Breakfast Inn** (7214 Pontchartrain Blvd. 504/282–8200, 888/608–7673 $-$$), a block from the Southern Yacht Club. You might expect a two-storied, pillared home near the shores of a Louisiana lake, but the interior is a psuedo-English hoot in rose, from the Lily Room to the Magnolia Suite. The three

tours

New Orleans has more specialized tours than any American city its size. Whether you want to explore our exotic Cities of the Dead, touch the Creole past, soar in a seaplane or get up close and personal with an alligator, it's all here. You can tour by bus, carriage, paddle wheeler, swamp boat, seaplane—or on foot. New tours appear constantly, usually attempting to cash in on Anne Rice's portraits of New Orleans as a city teeming with the supernatural. Prices, duration, packages, and scope vary considerably, so call for details.

The highly qualified guides of **Friends of the Cabildo**, (504/523–3939) have a colorful two-hour walking tour leaving no important French Quarter stone unturned. **Le Monde Creole** (504/568–1901) offers the best look into the vanished Creole world of New Orleans. **Voodoo Walking Tours** (504/523–7685) focuses on folklore in the Quarter, and **Heritage Tours** (504/949–9805) showcases important literary sites, notably those frequented by Tennessee Williams. All are walking tours.

A good bet for a knowledgeable Quarter carriage driver is **Royal Carriages, Inc.** (504/495–8273), which has been around since 1941. The only free French Quarter walking tour, offered by the **Jean Lafitte National Historic Park and Preserve** (504/589–2636), is also one of the best. Their knowledgeable park rangers also offer a fine, free tour of the Garden District. Many of the haunted/vampire/ghost tours are so gimmicky they're laughable, but a few are worth mentioning. **Magic Walking Tours** (504/588–9693) is one of the oldest spook tours and still one of the best. **New Orleans Spirits Tours** (504/566–9877) will take you in search of vampires, ghosts, and voodoo. The **New Orleans Ghost Tour** (504/944–7424) is so silly it's fun. All are walking tours.

New Orleans Tours (504/592–0560) and **Gray Line** (504/587–0861) are the grandes dames of city tours and offer all sorts of convenient combination packages aboard big tour buses. **Tours by Isabelle** (504/391–3544) do the same, but with comfy vans; their tours are far more personalized. Fans of the Battle of New Orleans can visit the Chalmette site aboard the *Creole Queen* (504/529–4567). Harbor tours are available aboard the *Natchez* and *Cotton Blossom* (504/586–8777).

Swamp tours are as plentiful as mosquitoes. **Honey Island Swamp Tours** (504/242–5877) is superb, hosted by wetland ecologists who know their stuff and can spot wildlife when you see nothing. **Jean Lafitte Swamp Tours** (504/592–0560) is another good bet, as is **Tours By Cypress** (504/581–4501), which has some good city/swamp/plantation combo tours. If you've never ridden an airboat, try **Bayou Gauche Tours** (toll-free 877/247–2628). **Air Tours on the Bayou** (504/394–8458) takes you up in a seaplane for a pelican's-eye view of the bayous and includes one memorable water landing in the marsh. For cemetery tours, see **cemeteries** sidebar.

rooms and two suites are a study in Victoriana, with tester and four-poster beds, mirrored armoires, marble-topped dressers, and overhead fans. The Georgian dining room manages to be formal and comfy at the same time. Guests receive complimentary passes to the West End Tennis Club, which has a pool, sauna, weight room, hot tub, and smoothie bar, in addition to the tennis courts.

doing stuff

The best way to enjoy the lake is to take a drive along Lakeshore Drive, which runs roughly from the Lakefront Airport to the Orleans/Jefferson Parish line. A car is indispensable in these parts. At 41 miles wide and 25 miles across, Pontchartrain is an imposing expanse, big enough to make the opposite shore invisible. Because it's so shallow— no deeper than 15 feet, depending on whom you ask—it's subject to windy mood swings, glassy one moment and churning with whitecaps the next. "Moderate to heavy chop on the lake" is a frequent part of the local weather report. The city's insurance is the seawall, those stone steps lining the shore built by the U.S. Army Corps of Engineers in the '40s. They most recently held their own against Hurricane Georges.

The drive is dotted with parks and picnic areas with benches for watching sailboats or the lake's changing moods. Near Marconi Drive are the **Mardi Gras Fountains**, built in the '60s. Tile plaques commemorate the various carnival krewes, and the triple fountains shoot some 60 feet high, illuminated at night by the Mardi Gras colors: purple, gold, and green, symbolizing justice, power, and faith, respectively.

Near the western end of the drive is the white, red-roofed U.S. Coast Guard Station and Lighthouse, and just across the inlet is the Southern Yacht Club, founded in 1840 and the second oldest in the country. This is West End, dotted with seafood restaurants and clubs drawing lakeshore residents as well as other locals wanting to be near the water. It's a perfect place to catch that famous breeze, listen to the hungry seagulls, and watch a sunset that'll knock your socks off. There are more good seafood restaurants in Bucktown, a fishing community right next door. Just follow the setting sun.

Bally's Lakefront Resort & Casino (1 *Stars & Stripes Blvd.* 800/572–2559) is just another riverboat aiming to separate fools from their money. It's fun, of course, and the views of the lake are nice. Serious gamblers will be interested to know there are two decks with 30,000 square feet of full gaming facilities.

spectating... Ranked among the top ten arenas in the U.S., **The Kiefer University of New Orleans Lakefront Arena** (6801 *Franklin Ave.* 504/280–7222) has a seating capacity of 10,000. It's used for sporting events and concerts, drawing folks like Elton John and Tina Turner.

MAGAZINE ST

NAL ST

magazine street/ irish channel

Roughly paralleling the
Mississippi, running from the CBD
through the Garden Districts into
Uptown, Magazine Street is one of
the truly great shopping thoroughfares in the country. From Canal
Street to Audubon Park, roughly
six miles of boutiques, galleries,
coffeehouses, and antiques stores
are housed in every sort of building imaginable. For the serious
shopper, this can give the French
Quarter a run

TCHOUPITOULAS ST

6

5

turn page for map key

for its retail dollar. It's no accident that the street's original French name, *magasin*, means shop.

Hugging the lower reaches of Magazine is one of the city's most colorful neighborhoods, the Irish Channel, which began in the mid-19th century as a working-class community. Settled by Irish peasants fleeing the potato famine, it steadily swelled upriver with an unending wave of immigrants (by 1840, New Orleans had 102,000 Irish—more than Boston). There were equally large waves of Germans, but the area was nicknamed for the Irish. The legacy of these two disparate groups is a 104-block area dotted with rows of identical single and double shotgun cottages with modest front yards and generous back yards. The original residents have been largely displaced by lower-income African-Americans and Hispanics. Active churches and schools make this a viable, breathing neighborhood, albeit a depressed and sometimes dangerous one.

eating/coffee

With few exceptions, Magazine Street is the area to rub elbows with the hoi polloi and get some decent, no-frills grub. Much of the fun of New Orleans dining is exploring beyond the grand cuisines of the French Quarter, and this

map key		
	1 Stan Levy Imports, Inc.	4 As You Like It
	2 Joey K's	5 St. Alphonsus Church
	3 Grand Antiques	6 Antebellum Antiques

is a fine place to start. Dinner at Joey K's is definitely a non-tourist experience, and probably one you'll never forget.

Cost Range per entree
$/under 10 dollars
$$/10–15 dollars
$$$/15–20 dollars
$$$$/20+ dollars

cafes/grills... If you don't love the name of **Igor's Buddha Belly Burger Bar** (4437 *Magazine St.* 504/891–6105 $), you gotta love the decor, with old LP covers splashed on the walls. The menu's full of standard stuff, none of it spectacular, but all pretty tasty. There's the garden burger, steak sandwich, fish and chips, and a grilled chicken breast heavy on the oregano and cheese. This place has 'em coming in at all hours, and serves until around four in the morning.

Believe it or not, **The Bulldog Bar & Grill** (3236 *Magazine St.* 504/891–1516 $) has 250 beers on draught and over 200 in bottles. This English-style pub is a fave with locals who get together for a few brews while enjoying the blackened voodoo chicken sandwich or green chilis stuffed with cheese and deep-fried.

coffee... A very popular local chain, **Rue de la Course** (1500 *Magazine St.* 504/529–1455, 3128 *Magazine St.* 504/899–0242 $) is known for fine coffee in a town where the competition is ferocious. The latte and cappuccino are delish, and the secret to the espresso is a gourmet bean blended, micro-roasted, and brewed with care. The fluffy French croissants have that special je ne sais quoi, probably because they're baked by a Frenchman! There are more Rues in the CBD and French Quarter.

The Secret Gardens Tea Room & Cafe (3626 *Magazine* St. 504/895–2913 $) is the perfect place to break your Magazine Street shopping marathon. Choose from a selection of gourmet quiches, soups, salads, and sandwiches, or indulge in a three-course classic tea complete with scones, tea cakes, and the rest of the trimmings.

creole... Local lore has it that **Kevin's** (5538 *Magazine* St. 504/895–5000 $$–$$$), with its quaint porthole windows, was once an old river brothel. Perhaps that shady past inspired artist Beth Lambert to create those wonderfully startling masked nudes teasing from the walls, and prompted chef Kevin Vizard to serve sensual delights that are carnal in the other sense. Consider the oyster brochette with prosciutto or the T-bone with Kevin's own garlic bordelaise. The space is a little cramped for 90 seats, sometimes making for an intense noise level, but the food is good, the prices reasonable, and the service clipped.

Kevin's second restaurant, **Vizard's** (3226 *Magazine* St. 504/895–3030 $$$) is far more upscale, with valet parking and a touch of attitude. It offers panéed rabbit with garlic mashed potatoes and fried Louisiana oysters with apple-smoked bacon, brie, and ravigote sauce, tucked between layers of fried eggplant. There's also whole calamari stuffed with Gulf shrimp, goat cheese, basil, and green onions, fried and served with a roasted-tomato salsa. Crêpe lovers will drool over fillings made with roasted duck and portabello mushrooms with a sun-dried cherry and pistachio demiglace. What dampens the experience is the lack of competent staff to deliver the goods. Maybe they're blinded by the startlingly white-white room complete with a white marble bar with white wood trim. The food may be terrific, but the service blows.

down-home... Joey K's (3001 Magazine St. 504/891–0997 $$) is the quintessential Irish Channel restaurant, a proud, working-class joint where you can forget about cholesterol and calories. Like, when was the last time you saw all-you-can-eat fried catfish on a menu? Other dishes for the hearty appetite include brisket, chicken-fried steak po' boy, and red beans and rice. The famous shrimp Magazine is angel-hair pasta tossed with shrimp sautéed with ham and artichoke hearts in olive oil and garlic butter. Don't overlook those 18-ounce frozen schooners of beer and margaritas.

eclectic... Named for the chef/owner's daughter, Kelsey's (3923 Magazine St. 504/897–6722 $$–$$$) has some truly creative Louisiana cuisine with a contemporary flair. Chef Randy Barlow, a Paul Prudhomme protégé, draws from the master but shows a sure touch in his own earthy, robust dishes. Try the oyster pie, poached oysters in a champagne cream sauce sparked with brie and dill, then covered in a flaky pastry; then proceed to the pecan-encrusted pan-fried trout with crabmeat dressing and the chef's own hollandaise. One of his signature dishes is Eggplant Kelsey, an eggplant pirogue (boat) stuffed with seafood and sprinkled with Parmesan cheese. He also does wondrous things with veal chops and deboned roasted

duck, and his superb sauces include artichoke-caper lemon cream, dill butter cream, brandy peppercorn, and cilantro mousseline.

You'll find more fusion run deliciously amok at **Semolina** (3242 *Magazine St.* 504/895–4260 **$$**), where pasta rules beside all sorts of international consorts, and noodle madness knows no bounds. Check out the double-cheeseburger pasta or macaroni & cheese cake. Or go for the delicate shrimp Bangkok on ultrathin angel-hair pasta, the brassy Santa Fe pasta on linguine or the peanut-encrusted Java pork chop in a tangy marinade served with angel-hair pasta, braised onions, and snow peas. There's even whole-wheat pasta for calorie counters loopy enough to wander into this carbo paradise. New Orleans has nine of these zany joints, and they all do a bustling biz. One taste and you'll know why the buzz.

Le Bon Temps Roule (4801 *Magazine St.* 504/895–8117 **$**) has a busy bar, live music, and is known locally as sandwich heaven. Standards like the burgers, turkey club, and Philly cheese steak are super, but live a little and try the gator sausage po' boy. Late-night music lovers are fond of the grilled quesadillas with two cheeses, black olives, mushrooms, and a good pico de gallo. Stuff yourself silly; this place is laid-back city.

mediterranean...
The tidy **Cafe Angeli** (1818 *Magazine St.* 504/524–1414 **$**) is operated by Turkish chef/owner Ayse Abbott, whose angel theme descends from the heavenly mural right onto the menu. Granted, names like Cherub Chicken, Celestial Artichoke, and Virtuous Vegetarian are cutesy and sound silly when you're order-

ing, but they sure do taste good. The Celestial Eggplant is a sandwich: fried eggplant rounds, roasted peppers, feta cheese, fresh tomatoes, and mozzarella zapped with a downright potent pesto sauce. The Angeli pie is a pizza with garlic sauce garnished with goat cheese, mozzarella, spinach, fresh tomatoes, and artichokes. Veggie pizzas are available with a variety of toppings, and the salads are abundant, fresh, and very reasonably priced.

Another pleasant, slightly pricier ethnic eatery is **Mystic Cafe** (3226 *Magazine* St. 504/891–1992 $$). Their grilled-chicken roll is exceptional, made with slow-cooked chicken, roasted red peppers, mixed greens, feta cheese, tomatoes, and pesto aioli. It's rolled in lavash and accompanied by a fresh bowtie pasta salad. Other notables include the shrimp pesto pasta, spinach and feta triangles, and Mediterranean pizza, all served with a smile.

mexican... About the only thing the diverse clientele has in common at the modest **Taqueria Corona** (5932 *Magazine* St. 504/897–3974 $) is a love for authentic Mexican food heaped up in large portions. Operated by the Mendez family for over a decade, it draws college students, cheap daters, gays, artists, musicians, and a handful of wayward tourists. The ubiquitous sombreros need a good dusting, and who knows the meaning behind those old photos, but if the image of the Virgin Mary doesn't relax you, the tacos will. They're the hit of the house, a soft tortilla stuffed with standard fillings or the far more imaginative char-broiled pork, beef tongue, or a chorizo sausage so zippy, it threatens to bite back. Or maybe you want one filled with highly spiced fried fish topped with red cabbage and tartar sauce. If you're watching your pennies, the combo plates are mucho grande indeed, all served with generous portions of yellow rice and hearty black beans. Tables are fine, but it's much more atmospheric to sit at the counter and watch the staff tearing around the open kitchen.

take-out... Chez Nous Charcuterie (5701 *Magazine St.* 504/899–7303 $$) was a smash from day one. Part of the success came from the richness and authenticity of such local favorites as seafood gumbo, made with a mahogany roux your Creole grandmother would love. Their other brilliant idea was take-out service. Word spread fast, and soon locals were zipping over from work, picking up something special for dinner at home. Other popular entrees include the tangy grillades with cheese grits and chicken crêpes.

buying stuff

Magazine Street may be short on historic sights and places to stay, but when it comes to shopping it holds its own just fine, thank you. The easiest way to explore this shopper's paradise is to begin at one end and work your way to the other, stopping in between for coffee, tea, or lunch. If you don't have a car, cut a deal with a cabbie who'll trail along and tote your packages for a negotiable hourly rate. Better yet, call **Let's Go Antiquing** (1424 4th St. 504/899–3027), which has conducted customized shopping trips for years. Proprietor/antiques maven

Macon Riddle can help find that one elusive item or provide a thorough investigation of the shops of Magazine Street and its side streets.

antiques... Aaron's Antique Mall (2014 *Magazine St.* 504/523–0630) showcases over 30 dealers with 8,000 square feet on two floors. There's good stuff and junk, antiques and old tools, fine sterling silver and tacky bric-a-brac. If you've got the time to explore, this place may turn up a treasure or two.

The 19th century is spotlighted at **Antebellum Antiques** (2011 *Magazine St.* 504/558–0208)—especially American, Empire, and Victorian furnishings and the decorative arts. This is the place to find that gorgeous old rosewood bed, mahogany armoire, or vintage Victorian wicker item. Period accessories such as gold-leafed mirrors are also available.

Antiques Magazine (2028 *Magazine St.* 504/522–2043, 800/264–2043) has everything from antebellum Americana to art deco, with plenty in between. There are also art glass and cut-glass items, silver, costume jewelry, gold-leafed mirrors, and more. Some intriguing lighting fixtures.

Audubon Antiques (2025 *Magazine St.* 504/581–5704) has two floors of trash and treasures just waiting to be explored. Prices vary wildly. They buy as well as sell. **Antique Vault** (2123 *Magazine St.* 504/523–8888) carries American, European, and Asian goods. **Antiquities Les Oliviers** (2138 *Magazine St.* 504/525–1294) is the place for 18th- and 19th-century French and Louisiana furniture, but don't overlook the clocks, coins, religious art, and highly collectible Old Paris porcelains.

Bep's Antiques Inc. (2051 *Magazine* St. 504/525–7726) has an unusual collection of English and French furniture, plus china, bottles, tiles, Imari, redware, medical tools, crockery, antique boxes, and corkscrews. And for some inexplicable reason, over 800 New Age and Celtic CDs and candles. **Blackamoor** (3433 *Magazine* St. 504/897–2711) carries Chinese antiquities, English and Asian porcelains, and more. **British Antiques** (5415 *Magazine* St. 504 895–3716) has an interesting mixture of English, French, and Asian antiques.

Bush Antiques (2109–11 *Magazine* St. 504/581–3518) says it specializes in antique beds for sweet dreams. It also carries religious art, armoires and chairs, unusual lighting, iron, and lots of accessories.

Dodge Fjeld Antiques (2033 *Magazine* St. 504/581–6930) specializes in carefully selected American and European pieces and carries an interesting choice of clocks. **Empire Antiques** (3420 *Magazine* St. 504/897–0252) has some stunning 18th- and 19th-century European furnishings, formal and provincial pieces, and a must-see selection of bronze Doré mantle clocks and candlesticks. **Fairman-McKinney Antiques** (3636 *Magazine* St. 504/269–4888, 504/528–1811) has French, English, and Italian antiques and some repros. **French Collectibles** (3424 *Magazine* St. 504/897–9020) specializes in 18th- and 19th-century French antiques, but has Italian and English as well. **Gloria Slater Antiques** (2115 *Magazine* St. 504/561–5738) shows fine English, French, and Continental 18th- and 19th-century furniture. Also chandeliers and mirrors. If you're looking for an antique piano, **Grand Antiques** (3125 *Magazine* St. 504/897–3179) has 19th-century models with rosewood veneers, inlaid brass, and exquisitely executed fretwork. **Hands** (2042 *Magazine St.* 504/522–2590) features pre-Columbian artworks, plus furniture, china, silver, and religious art from the 1700s to the present. Also some Latin American handicrafts.

Java Nola (1313 *Magazine St.* 504/558–0369) imports exotica from Southeast Asia with a focus on antiques and Dutch colonial furniture from Indonesia. They also carry hand-crafted accessories made from bronze, ceramics, stone, and wood and an interesting selection of textiles. Pottery is the focus at **Jean Bragg Antiques** (3901 *Magazine St.* 504/895–7375), which carries superb Newcomb, Ohr, Rookwood, and Roseville pieces. There are also vintage linens, paintings, and some furniture. **Jon Antiques** (4605 *Magazine St.* 504/899–4482) has some stunning English and French pieces, showcased in a historic home. **Home, Hook and Ladder** (4100 *Magazine St.* 504/895–4480) carries mostly French and English antiques with some very special accessories. **Karla Katz & Co.** (4017 *Magazine St.* 504/897–0061) has 18th- & 19th-century Empire, Italian, and French antiques. **Kohlmaier and Kohlmaier** (1018 *Harmony St.* 504/895–6394) is the place for rare and unique antique clocks.

Magazine Arcade Antiques (3017 *Magazine St.* 504/895–5451) is one of the area's largest antiques emporiums, representing a number of dealers. You'll find furniture, clocks, porcelain, glassware, music boxes, dolls and dollhouses, European and Asian art, and Asian furniture. **Miss Edna's Antiques** (2035 *Magazine St.* 504/524–1897) has a pretty good selection of furniture and fine paintings. She can also help with restoration of that damaged old

cemeteries

The reason cemeteries are so special here has to do with the notoriously high water table of southern Louisiana in general, and New Orleans in particular. You only have to dig a few feet before hitting water. The early French settlers quickly discovered the problem when they tried to bury their dead, only to have the wooden coffins pop right back up. The only workable alternative was "burying" the body on top of the ground. As the city grew and prospered, those crude plaster crypts metamorphosed into grand mausoleums. To conserve space in a land-scarce city, the smaller crypts were stacked, earning them the nickname "ovens" because they resembled bread ovens. In an early effort at recycling, they could be rented for a year and a day, after which time old bones were crunched aside as a new body was shoved in to replace it. The city's first real cemetery, **St. Louis No. 1**, was built in 1796 just across Rampart Street from the original planned settlement. It was soon dubbed "City of the Dead" because the neat rows of white-washed tombs gave it the look of a small village. Some of the monuments are dazzling, including those of Governor Claiborne's family, designed by Benjamin Latrobe in 1811, but the real draw is its most infamous tenant, Marie Laveau, the undisputed 19th-century voodoo queen. Marie's triple-tiered tomb is near the Basin Street entrance and gashed with the X's of admirers. It says Marie Philomen Glapion décédé le 11 Juin 1897. Her daughter, Marie II, who legend says passed herself off as her mother in a peculiar and partially successful stab at immortality, is interred four blocks away in **St. Louis No. 2** on Claiborne Avenue. No. 2 also holds the crypt of infamous pirate Dominique You.

By far the largest is **Metairie Cemetery**, a 133-acre graveyard humdinger built on the site of the old Jockey Club. When Charles T. Howard was denied membership in the exclusive club, he retaliated by buying the racetrack and turning it into a cemetery. Some of the grandiose mausoleums are as flamboyantly competitive as the new Las Vegas mega-hotels. There's an Egyptian pyramid, an Irish castle, and even a version of the Greek Temple of Nike. By far the largest is that of Irish immigrant Mary Moriarty, whose grieving husband raised a granite monument flanked by four figures: Faith, Hope, Charity and... Mrs. Moriarity! Free self-guided walking/driving tours are available. Just pick up a tape player at the adjacent **Lake Lawn Metairie Funeral Home** office.

A word of warning. The cemeteries are a must-see, but, Metairie excepted, they're dangerous to visit alone. Go in a group or, better yet, take a tour. For information, call the non-profit group that keeps watch over this precious heritage, **Save Our Cemeteries** (305 Baronne St. 504/525–3377). **The New Orleans Historic Voodoo Museum** (724 Dumaine St. 504/523–7685) also offers cemetery tours. If your group comprises ten or more, they can arrange a jazz funeral.

painting. For fine art and antiques, **Neal Auction Company** (4038 Magazine St. 504/899–5329) is one of the top auction houses in the country—'nuff said. **Passages Antiques** (3939 Magazine St. 504/899–3883) means 18th- and 19th-century European and Asian works, plus some intriguing objets d'art. **Petite Pence** (4904 Magazine St. 504/891–3353) showcases English and French imports in a Victorian cottage atmosphere. **Prince & Pauper** (3308 Magazine St. 504/899–2378) carries furniture, antiques, and silver at prices that won't bankrupt you. **Private Connection** (3927 Magazine St. 504/899–4944) specializes in Indonesian imports, antiques, architectural pieces, and contemporary works. Also handcrafted gifts and jewelry. **Renaissance Shop** (2104 Magazine St. 504/525–8568) has repros as well as the real thing, and does restoration work. **Sister Agnes, Ltd.** (3450 Magazine St. 504/269–9444) is an interesting amalgam of old and new home furnishings, including hand-crafted ceramic lights, silver tea sippers, and other fun stuff. **Stan Levy Imports, Inc.** (1028 Louisiana Ave. 504/899–6384) receives container shipments from England and France with emphasis on 17th-, 18th-, and 19th-century antiques. One of the largest dealers on Magazine Street, Levy has furniture, china, silver, copper, brass, paintings, cut glass, art deco, and more.

Sigi Russell Antiques (4304 Magazine St. 504/891–5390) has both American and European antiques, with some interesting religious art, chandeliers, and armoires. **Top Drawer Auction & Appraisal Company** (4310 Magazine St. 504/832–9080) has over 7,000 square feet of antiques and repros, china, paintings, pottery, and more. **Uptowner Antiques** (3828 Magazine St. 504/891–7700) imports 18th- and 19th-century French and Italian pieces. They also carry antique mirrors and accessories. **Wirthmore Antiques** (3727 Magazine St. 504/269–0660, 3900 Magazine St. 504/899–9888) showcases French provincial antiques and accessories, with a limited number of other Continental and English pieces.

brass... Accessories in Brass (3112 Magazine St. 504/899–6237) specializes in brass architectural reproductions and decorative hardware, plus bath and fireplace accessories. It's one of the biggest solid-brass inventories in the Gulf South. **Brass Image** (3801 Magazine St. 504/897–1861) has an enormous choice of antique and repro brass beds and iron beds in neoclassical finishes. Also linens and bedding. **Brass Menagerie** (2105 Magazine St. 504/524–5445) has a spacious showroom filled with, well, brass—and lots of it. Chandeliers, lanterns, decorative and antique hardware, bathroom faucets, and accessories. There's also some iron hardware.

carpets... Dombourian Oriental Rugs (2841 Magazine St. 504/891–6601) has been selling fine quality oriental rugs, both antique and new, for over 80 years. They also do carpet restoration. **Jacqueline Vance Rugs** (3944 Magazine St. 504/891–3304) carries a large and varied selection of tapestries, contemporary carpets, and antique and new oriental rugs, all handmade. **Talebloo Oriental Rugs** (4130 Magazine St. 504/899–8114) focuses on antique and recent Persian rugs and carpets.

clothing... **ah-ha** (3119 Magazine St. 504/269–2442) has hot women's clothes at cool prices. **Joan Vass** (2917 Magazine St. 504/891–4502) carries smart women's fashions by the local designer, known for her incredibly soft cotton knits. This is America's only exclusively Joan Vass store. **Mariposa Vintage Clothes** (2038 Magazine St. 504/523–3037) has reasonably priced vintage duds from the '40s to the '70s. If you're gonna keep that promise to learn swing dancing, here are the clothes to get you started. **Perlis** (6070 Magazine St. 504/895–8661) carries the Cajun Clothing Company line: sports shirts with a crawfish where you usually see an alligator. They also appear on ties, boxers, and more.

eclectic... **Aux Belles Choses** (3912 Magazine St. 504/891–1009) spotlights imported French and English accessories for home and garden. **Aesthetics & Antiques** (3122 Magazine St. 504/895–7011) is made for lazy browsing. There's jewelry, art, furniture, deco stuff, sports things, quirky treasures, and much more. Check it out. **Louisianian Angéle Parlange** (5419 Magazine St. 504/897–6511) has received national acclaim for her fanciful designs for hand-printed fabrics, pillows, furniture, and bedding. Her showroom is a study in luxe taffetas, chiffons, and dupioni silks.

Bianca's (5509 Magazine St. 504/891–4533) has jewelry, accessories, clothes, and vintage stuff. You just might find that special gift in here. **Custom Linens** (3638 Magazine St. 504/899–0604) has fine linens for bed, bath, and table. **Gerrie Bremermann** (3806 Magazine St. 504/899–0212, 3943 Magazine St. 504/891–7763) has antiques, French decorative accessories, and works by local artists. **Janet**

Molero (*3935 Magazine St. 504/269–8305*) carries fine furniture and accessories. Check out the Rue Orleans tables, made from a vintage shutter atop a custom metal base. Obviously no two are alike. **Orient Expressed** (*3905 Magazine St. 504/899–3060*) is everyone's favorite shop for antique santos, Chinese funerary figures, Thai bronzes, excellent repro paintings from the Cuzco School, and much more. Don't miss the hand-smocked children's clothing and toys in the back. **Out of Focus** (*1119–A St. Mary St. 504/586–1888*) is a funky little spot with photography by local artists plus an odd assortment of jewelry, candles, incense, tin work, and lots more.

Pied Nu (*5521 Magazine St. 504/899–4118*) can dress both a lady and her home. There's everything from lighting and linens to designer duds. They also offer a fine line of skin-care products. **The Private Connection** (*3927 Magazine St. 504/899–4944*) carries a wide range of Indonesian imports, including furniture, carvings, umbrellas, even a gamelan or two. **The Quilt Cottage** (*801 Nashville Ave. 504/895–3791*) carries new and antique quilts, plus everything you need to make your own, including books, notions, and over a thousand bolts of pure cotton. **Scriptura** (*5423 Magazine St. 504/897–1555*) is a fascinating little shop with just about everything related to paper. Aside from stationery, you'll find pens, fab wrapping papers, wax seals, lamps, photo albums, and paper-related home furnishings. **Shop of the Two Sisters** (*1800 Magazine St. 504/525–2747*) is a warm, sumptuous haven brimming with pretty things collected by sisters Lee and Rose Ali. There's some furniture, although accessories clearly dominate. You'll find luxe throw pillows, fine linens, mirrors, lighting fixtures, unusual candlesticks, and much more. They also carry frames and artwork. **Sitting Duck Gallery (3953 Magazine St. 504/899–2007)** is famed for furniture created from salvaged architectural cypress pieces. **Utopia (5408 Magazine St. 504/899–8488)** has contemporary casual clothing, jewelry, candles, hand-blocked pillows, and housewares, plus the hand-painted furniture of Louisiana artist David Marsh. **Villa Vicci** (2930 Magazine St. 504/ 899–2931) carries a fine line of home furnishings with a focus on bed and bath.

furniture... Cirello's Furniture Company (1115 St. Mary St. 504/523–3491) is the place for furniture restoration, old and new, specializing in colored crackled lacquer and exotic finishes. They also carry a limited amount of furniture and collectibles. **New Orleans Cypress Works (3105 Magazine St. 504/891–0001)** does custom furniture work in cypress and heart of pine. **Le Wicker Gazebo (3715 Magazine St. 504/899–1355)** carries antique, new, and custom-made wicker furniture, and does wicker repairs and painting. **The Shaker Shop** (3029 Magazine St. 504/895–8646) has old and new rustic furniture with an emphasis on cypress. **The Tulip Tree** (5831 Magazine St. 504/895–3748, 504/865–1551) has an enormous selection of antique golden oak furniture plus accessories, pottery, collectibles, and more. **Wilkerson Row** (3137 Magazine St. 504/899–3311) is a showcase for the Alpha Award-winning designs of Shaun Wilkerson. His fine works are imaginatively inspired by 19th-century New Orleans architecture. He also does custom designs.

galleries... Artifacts (5515 Magazine St. 504/899–5505) exhibits local and national artists, along with unique furniture, lamps, mirrors, candles, ornaments, and a big selection of decorative hardware. This place is a hoot! **Astoria Fine Art Gallery** (1817 Magazine St. 504/527–0032) shows paintings, prints, and metal sculpture, and offers custom-designed light fixtures, tables, chairs, beds, and more. At **Berta's and Mina's Antiquities** (4138 Magazine St. 504/895–6201) you'll find folk art by self-taught Louisiana artists Nilo and Mina Lanzas. There are also duck decoys and other collectibles. **Carol Robinson Gallery** (4537 Magazine St. 504/895–6130) showcases Southern contemporary works including paintings, sculpture, ceramics, jewelry, and wearable art. You can watch a potter at work at **Casey Willems Pottery** (3919 Magazine St. 504/899–1174) and choose from bowls, lamps, vases, planters, and much more. **Davis Gallery** (3964 Magazine St. 504/897–0780) has a fine collection of authentic African tribal art, including jewelry, baskets, weapons, costumes, and sculpture. **Cole Pratt Gallery** (3800 Magazine St. 504/891–6789) represents over 30 contemporary regional artists working in various media. **Cone 10** (5015 Magazine St. 504/895–3909) exhibits the works of local potter Catherine Cashio and contemporary jewelry designer Dominique Giordano. **Diva Gallery/Studio** (1110 Antonine St. 504/899–0275) shows works by a large number of local artists and craftspeople in virtually every medium, including glass beads, stained glass, and mosaics. They're not all divas, but definitely worth a look. **Morgan-West Studio Gallery** (3326 Magazine St. 504/895–7976) show-

cases Alpha Award-winning artist Perry Morgan III, who works in silk, clay, and wood. Other local and regional crafts artists are also exhibited. **The New Orleans School of Glassworks and Printmaking Studio** (727 Magazine St. 504/529–7277) is the South's largest hot-glass, printmaking, and bookbinding studio. Pieces by local and visiting artists who work in these media are exhibited. **Reina Gallery** (4132 Magazine St. 504/ 895–0022) exhibits local and regional artists with an emphasis on etchings, watercolors, ceramic jewelry, masks, and textile art. **Shadyside Pottery Shop** (3823 Magazine St. 504/897–1710) is the place to see master potter Charles Bohn at work. Custom pottery is available, or you can choose from a handsome selection on exhibit; ancient Japanese raku pottery is a specialty.

jewelry... **Anne Pratt** (3937 Magazine St. 504/891–2227) struts her talent in iron furniture designs and unique jewelry designs of silver and vermeil. **The Bead Shop** (4612 Magazine St. 504/895–6161) is where you'll find materials from all over the world for making your own jewelry, including books, supplies, and tools. The store doubles as a gallery for potter Nancy Campbell. **C. Susman** (3933 Magazine St. 504/897–9144) has the largest selection of estate jewelry on the street. You'll also find unique antique collectibles in silver, art pottery, and art glass. **Katy Ben** (3701 Magazine St. 504/896–9600) carries limited-edition fine silver and gold jewelry and represents Reinstein-Ross, Michael Good, and Barbara Heinrich. **Ruby Ann Tobar-Blanco** (3005 Magazine St. 504/897–0811, 800/826–7282) showcases her innovative designs in pins, necklaces, earrings, and bracelets.

kids... **Big Life Toys** (3117 *Magazine St.* 504/895–8695, 5430 *Magazine St.* 504/899–8697) has something for children of all ages. Your child will love the lunch boxes, stuffed animals, puzzles, and more, plus some retro stuff you may want as collectibles. When was the last time you saw a Curious George lunch box?

lighting... **Eclectique Antiques** (2112 *Magazine St.* 504/524–6500) has one-of-a-kind lamps by designer David A. Donovan. There are also lampshades, antiques, and unusual accessories. **New Orleans Lighting & Antiques** (3634 *Magazine St.* 504/891–1090) has a wonderful selection of antique and repro chandeliers, lamps, and sconces, plus some antique furniture and nauticals.

silver... In business more than 30 years, **As You Like It** (3025 *Magazine St.* 504/897–6915, 800/828–2311) is a splendiferous showcase for silver. They have sterling-silver flatware and hollowware in active, inactive, and obsolete patterns. **Melange Sterling** (5421 *Magazine St.* 504/899–4796, 800/513–3991) specializes in pattern matching, with a wide selection of active, inactive, and obsolete sterling flatware from America and Europe. Also estate and antique hollowware.

sleeping

Since Magazine Street cuts through the designated neighborhoods here, the two following spots are actually located in the Lower Garden District and the Garden District respectively.

Cost Range for double occupancy per night on a weeknight. Call to verify prices.
$/under 100 dollars
$$/100–150 dollars
$$$/150–200 dollars
$$$$/200+ dollars

The 1860s **McKendrick-Breaux House B&B** (*1474 Magazine St. 504/586–1700, 888/570–1700* $$–$$$) is another charming restoration in the Lower Garden District. All rooms have private baths, and the attention to detail is impressive.

The Garden District Bed & Breakfast (*2418 Magazine St. 504/895–4302* $) is a 1880s Victorian town house with 12-foot ceilings, antique furnishings, fireplaces in all 16 rooms and a patio for guests only. Joe and Flo do their best to make you feel at home. Four units with kitchens.

doing stuff

The Irish Channel is defined by Magazine, Tchoupitoulas, and Delachaise streets and Jackson Avenue. With the exception of Magazine Street, the area is generally too risky for exploring, but there's little to see anyway. Notable exceptions are magnificent churches representing two of the three groups that settled the area. **St. Alphonsus Church** (*2029 Constance St. 504/522–6748*) was built by the Irish in 1855, and services were conducted in English. Although its bell towers were never completed, its facade is reminiscent of St. Louis Cathedral. The grandiose Renaissance interior will stir your soul as surely as the peeling frescoes will break your heart. Closed for many years, it's one of author Anne Rice's pet restoration projects, and may be visited by special arrangement. Dating from 1858, the German Baroque **St. Mary's Assumption** (*2030 Constance St.*) just across the street originally held services in German, and has a magnificent tower visible for miles. Its high altar is slightly less lavish than its decaying neighbor's. These sites should be visited only by day and only in groups. The nearby St. Thomas Housing Projects turn the area deadly after dark, and sometimes even before.

The handsome **Bertucci-Schmaltz Building** (*1500–04 Magazine St.*) was built in 1870 and is headquarters for Operation Comeback, which is responsible for the remarkable restorations in this area.

body

Belladonna (*2900 Magazine St. 504/891–4393*) is one of the city's top full-service spas, offering a wide range of massages (including shiatsu), body wraps, hair treatments, and facials. Don't miss the gift shop, which has everything from vitamins and aromatherapy items to bed linens. Incidentally, Belladonna's awesome seaweed body wrap can make you tingle in places you didn't know existed.

off the edge

the river road plantations

New Orleans has always owed its wealth to the Mississippi. By the 1850s it was the nation's largest port in terms of export, wharves sagging beneath tons of cotton, rice, and sugar. With a slave-based economy, planters between New Orleans and Natchez attained vertiginous levels of wealth, boasting more millionaires than the rest of America combined. They lived like kings and built accordingly. Their grand Greek revival homes lined both sides of the river in an almost unbroken line of columns. They graced their mansions with French furniture and statuary from Italy and Greece and secured the newest creature comforts, including indoor plumbing, hot running water and even their own gas plants to light their gasoliers.

The Civil War vanquished that lifestyle forever, and most of the plantation homes with it, but some remain to paint a fair picture of the grandeur that was. Most are located on or near the historic River Road paralleling both banks of the Mississippi between New Orleans and Baton Rouge. There are bridges at Destrehan, Gramercy-Wallace and the Sunshine Bridge, Highway 70, and scattered ferries whose erratic operating schedules will make you nuts. Get a map and cross at your whim. The closest and oldest plantation house, Destrehan, is just eight miles from the airport, while the grandest and most distant, Nottoway, is an hour and a half away, near Donaldsonville. The ten listed here were chosen for their historical or architectural merit, or because of something special. Try to come calling in the late fall or spring when the cane fields are burning.

Built in 1787, **Destrehan** (13034 River Road, Destrehan, 504/764–9315) is one of the oldest homes in the Louisiana Purchase and noteworthy for the West Indies-style roof, hand-hewn cypress timbers, and walls made of bousillage, a hardened mixture of mud and Spanish moss. It's one of many plantations nearly destroyed by petroleum companies. In this happy scenario, American Oil Company shut down in 1959 and donated the badly damaged house and four acres to the River Road Historical Society in 1972. Nicely restored, its grounds are popular for concerts.

Twenty minutes upriver is **San Francisco** (River Road in Reserve, 504/535–2341), unique because of an architecturally flamboyant style called Steamboat Gothic. It was built in 1853 by Edward Bozonier Marmillion, whose fortunes were so drained by the house, he complained that he was "*sans fruscin*," meaning without a cent. Over the years that lamentation became "San Francisco." The house originally had several hundred yards of grand gardens, but the encroaching river forced several levee setbacks and eventually brought the levee right to the front door.

On the West Bank is **Laura** (2247 Hwy. 18, Vacherie, 225/265–7690), one of the most unique restorations, because it's a Creole, not an American, plantation. Built in 1805, the many surviving outbuildings afford a good look at plantation life. It was the American home of B'rer Rabbit.

Not far upriver is **Oak Alley** (3645 Hwy. 18, Vacherie,

225/265–2151), probably the most photographed plantation home in the South. Justifiable fame comes from the
double row of 28 gigantic live oaks which perfectly frame
the house. The oaks were planted by an early French settler
whose modest home at the end of the allée was razed by
planter Jacques Télesphore Roman III, who completed the
present house in 1839. For a spectacular view, climb the
levee and look back. Brad Pitt rode a horse here in *Interview
with the Vampire*. You can get breakfast or lunch at the plantation restaurant and overnight in cottages on the property.

On the East Bank again is **Tezcuco** (3138 Hwy. 44, Darrow,
225/562–3929), which means "resting place" in Aztec, a
handsomely restored raised cottage with deceptive dimen-
sions. The interior has 15-foot ceilings! Tezcuco is now
operated as a B&B, and has a restaurant serving buffet
lunches. A small Civil War museum is also on the grounds.

If you're hungry, **The Cabin** (Hwy. 44 at Hwy. 22, Burnside,
225/473–3007 $) will satisfy you with hearty Cajun fare.
An old slave cabin that's been expanded and modernized,
it's a historical experience in itself. Try the crab fingers,
chicken-fried steak or gumbo, and delicious dirty rice.
Reasonable and friendly, and the rest rooms are a trip.

Just upriver from The Cabin and named for a vanished
Indian tribe is **Houmas House** (40136 Hwy. 942, Darrow,
225/473–7841), built in 1800 and incorporated into the
much larger Greek revival home in 1840. It's a two-and-a-
half-story temple surrounded by Doric columns on three
sides and flanked by hexagonal *garçonnieres*—quarters for
unmarried men when unmarried girls were in the Big
House. *Hush, Hush, Sweet Charlotte* was filmed here.

Continuing upriver on the East Bank Highway 942 (River

Road) are three historic houses not open to the public but certainly worth a look. All have historical markers. The first is **Bocage**, something of a novelty with its different-sized columns and a large pediment completely concealing the roof. It was built in 1801 by Marius Pons Bringier as a wedding present for his daughter, Françoise.

Next is **L'Hermitage**, another of Bringier's wedding gifts. This one went to son Michel, who fought alongside Andy Jackson in the Battle of New Orleans and honored the great general by naming his house after Jackson's Tennessee home. It's a majestic Greek revival temple built in 1812, with broad galleries supported by Doric columns.

The **Ashland-Belle Hélène**, between Darrow and Geismar, was built in 1841 by Duncan Kenner, the Confederate minister to France and Louisiana's great sugar king. Massive square columns, 4 feet square, 30 feet tall and eight to a side, surround enormous galleries 20 feet wide. The house is a Hollywood fave, and was used in the filming of *Band of Angels*, *Beguiled*, *Mandingo*, and *Fletch Lives*.

Across the river lies **Nottoway** *(River Road, White Castle, 225/545–2730)*, 1859, the South's largest surviving plantation, with 22 towering columns, over 60 rooms and 53,000 square feet. The interior is more Tara than traditional, and it's fun—if you take the tour with a grain of salt. The white ballroom is a highlight, with its white floors, Corinthian columns and plaster cornices and moldings. The windows were flung high during a ball so belles and their beaux could waltz out onto the galleries for some fresh air. Sugar fields come to the back door. It's operated today as a restaurant and B&B.

phone numbers

transportation
airport: New Orleans International Airport (also known as Moissant Airport), 504/464–0831; **New Orleans Lakefront Airport**, 504/242–5483; **Heliport New Orleans Downtown** (public use) 1500 Poydras St., 504/586–0055.

ships: Port of New Orleans, 504/243–4010

buses out of town: Greyhound Bus Lines, 1001 Loyola Avenue, 504/524–3136 or 800/231–2222

public transportation: Regional Transit Authority, 800/872–7245 or 504/242–2600, schedules, 504/248–3900; **Para-Transit,** 504/827–7433; **Ferries,** (run 24 Hours), 504/248–3900 or 800/231–2222

taxis: United Cabs, Inc., 504/522–9771; **White Fleet Cabs**, 504/948–6605; **Yellow-Checker Cabs**, 504/525–3311.

trains: Amtrak, 800/USA-RAIL or 504/528–1610

car rental: Enterprise Rent-A-Car, 504/486–3723; **Hertz Rent A Car—Downtown**, 504/568–1645; **National Car Rental**, 504/525–0416; **Payless Car Rental**, 504/441–5700

emergency/health
police, fire, and ambulance: 911; non-emergency police, 504/821–2222; non-emergency fire, 504/581–3473

pharmacies: Walgreens Drug Store (24 hr. locations) 504/822–1003, 504/242–0566, 504/368–8171

hospitals: Charity Hospital, 1541 Tulane Ave., 504/588–3000; **Tulane University Hospital**, 1415 Tulane Ave., 504/588–5263; **Touro Infirmiry**, 1401 Foucher St., 540/897–7011

boating: US Coast Guard, 504/589–2332

car breakdowns: AAA Emergency Road Service, 800/222–4357

credit-card emergencies: American Express 800/528–4800; **Mastercard** 800/826–2181; Visa 800/336–8472
travelers aid society: 504/525–8726
crime stoppers: 504/822–1111

media/information

newspapers: Times-Picayune (daily) 504/822–6660 or 800/925–0000; **Gambit** (weekly) 504/486–5900

radio stations: WRBH(88.3) Radio for the Blind; WWNO(89.9/90.5) Classical, PBS Affiliate; WTUL (91.5) Educational/Non-commercial; WCKW(92.3) Classic and New Rock; WEZB(97.1) Adult Contemporary; WLMG(101.9) Adult Contemporary; WNOE (101.1) Country; WRNO(99.5) Rock; WWL(870AM) Sports/News/Talk; WWOZ(90.7) Jazz/Local/Eclectic

tv stations: CBS, WWL Ch. 4; **NBC,** WDSU Ch. 6; **FOX,** WVUE Ch. 8; **PBS,** WYES Ch. 12; **ABC,** WGNO Ch. 26; **WB,** WNOL Ch. 38

convention and visitors bureau: New Orleans Metro-politan Convention and Visitors Bureau, Inc., 529 St. Ann Street, 504/566–5031; **New Orleans Visitors Info Center**, 7450 Paris Road, 504/246–5666; **US Passport Agency**, 701 Loyola Avenue, 504/589–6161

gay resources: The Lesbian, Gay, Community Center of New Orleans, 816 N. Rampart St., 504/522–1103

tickets: Ticketmaster, 504/522–5555

time & weather: 504/828–4000

January: **NOKIA Sugar Bowl**, Louisiana Superdome, 504/525–8573:College football fans cram the city for this event. **Jan. 6: Mardi Gras Season Begins**: It is the duty of the Krewe of Phorty Phunny Phellows to ride streetcar lines announcing the beginning of the revelry. **Krewe of Kids**: A visually spectacular performance in the spirit of Mardi Gras. **Battle of New Orleans Celebration**, Chalmette National Park, 504/589–4426: Reenactment of the 1812 Battle of New Orleans.

February: **Mardi Gras**, 800/672–6124 or 504/566–5019: New Orleans' legendary holiday. Celebrations in the streets to formal masquerade balls. Parades begin early and continue past sundown. **SweetArts Ball**, Contemporary Arts Center, 504/523–1216: The place to connect with New Orleans' patrons of the arts.

March: **Music at the Mint:** The Old U.S. Mint is bound to wake up after local musicians fill the place with sound. **Tennessee Williams Literary Festival**, 504/581–1144: A series of events honoring the author. **Shotgun Showhouse Tour Preservation Resource Center**, 504/581–7032: One of the city's distinctive styles of architecture enjoys the spotlight for this springtime tour. **Children's World's Fair,** Louisiana Children's Museum, 504/523–1357: An international exhibition featuring music, literature, native attire, inventions, crafts, and food. **Art In Bloom**, New Orleans Museum of Art, 504/488–2631: Floral exhibits including birdhouses designed by local architectural firms, lectures, workshops and a silent auction. **Louisiana Black Heritage**

Festival, Audubon Zoo, Riverwalk and Louisiana State Museum, 504/827–5771: Features food, music, arts and crafts. **Spring Fiesta**, 504/581–1367: Tours of historic homes and courtyards. Begins with presentation of the Spring Fiesta Queen and a horse-drawn parade.

April: French Quarter Festival, 504/522–5730: This free annual event celebrates the food and music of the city with fireworks, tours, and the "world's largest jazz brunch." **New Orleans Jazz and Heritage Festival (Jazzfest)**, New Orleans Fair Grounds, 504/522–4786: Over 4,000 musicians and hundreds of cooks and crafts-people gather at the Fair Grounds by day and through-out the clubs and restaurants during the evenings of this wonderful 10-day festival. **Zoo-To-Do for Kids**, Audubon Zoo, 504/861–2537: The combination of food, music, clowns, mimes, face painters and a petting zoo makes this a special event. **Symphony Swing in the Oaks**, City Park, 504/523–6530: Featuring the Louisiana Philharmonic Orchestra. **Crescent City Classic**, 504/861–8686: This 10K race draws runners from all over the world. **NO/AIDS Hair Raiser**, 504/945–4000: Salons and spas throughout New Orleans dedicate proceeds of one day's business to NO/AIDS Task Force. The day ends with a cocktail party and fash-ion show. **New Orleans Gay & Lesbian Film Festival,** Prytania Theatre, 504/488–3700: Featuring quality films not available for screening in mainstream theaters. **Big Easy Entertainment Awards**, 504/486–5900: New Orleans' premier event honoring the musical and the-atrical talent of the city.

May: **Funky Butt Bash**, Contemporary Arts Center, 504/523–1216. **Greek Festival**, Hellenic Cultural Center, 504/282–0259: Greek entertainment, music, cuisine, and crafts. **Jazzfest** continues (see April). **Bank One Zoo-To-Do**, Audubon Zoo, 504/861–2537: One of the most popular social events of the year. Features live entertainment, decorations by local designers, and delicacies supplied by leading restaurants. **Freeport-McDermott Golf Classic**, English Turn Country Club, 504/831–4653. **Cinco De Mayo Festival**, Warehouse District, 504/347–1540: Celebrates Latin culture in New Orleans.

June: **Great French Market Tomato Festival**, French Market, 504/522–2621: Cooking demonstrations, tomato tasting, music, and entertainment. **Absolut New Orleans**, Contemporary Arts Center, 504/ 523–1216: Features New Orleans top chefs making cocktails and concoctions that you can devour while viewing C.A.C.'s acclaimed art collection. **Reggae Riddums Festival**, 504/367–1313: A three-day celebration of the Caribbean featuring international reggae, calypso, and ska bands.

July: **Go 4th on the River**, 504/528–9994: Activities, entertainment, and fireworks for the entire family along the riverfront. **Essence Music Festival**, Louisiana Superdome, 800/ESSENCE: Nighttime performances of jazz and blues, and daytime seminars on spirituality and empowerment. **New Orleans Wine & Food Experience**, 504/529–9462: Features wine dinners, seminars and tastings in restaurants, galleries, and shops citywide. **Dining For Life**, 504/945–4000: Restaurants throughout New Orleans donate the proceeds of one day's business to NO/AIDS Task Force.

August: **White Linen Night**, Contemporary Arts Center, 504/523–1216: This open-air event features over a dozen gallery exhibit openings throughout the Warehouse Arts District, with performance stages set up on Julia Street.

September: **Southern Decadence**: This Labor Day gay weekend event commences with a kickoff party toasting over 60,000 revelers. **Cutting Edge Music Conference**, U.S. Mint and music clubs citywide, 504/945–1800: Features seminars, band showcases, and new-product trials. **Louisiana Restaurant Association Canal Street Classic**, 504/454–2277: This 5K race and party benefit LRA's Education Foundation. **NO/AIDS Walk**, Audubon Park, 504/945–4000: This 3.5-mile walk benefits NO/AIDS Task Force. **MOJO Music Festival**, City Park, 504/482–8211: The biggest alternative music festival of the year. **Southern Comfort Rocks the Blues**, Audubon Park: A day-long outdoor music festival.

October: **Art for Art's Sake**, Contemporary Arts Center: This benefit bash marks the opening of the city's visual arts season. **Weindorf Festival New Orleans**, Washington Square, 504/522–5730: This festival has authentic German cuisine provided by noted local chefs, folkloric dancers, yodeling and chicken dance contests. **Okto-**

berfest, Deutsches Haus, 504/522–8014: German food, beer, and polka music. **Lark in the Park**, City Park, 504/483–9376: Gala including cuisine from more than 50 local restaurants, open bar and silent auction. **Lesbian/Gay Pride Celebration. Swamp Fest**, Audubon Zoo and Woldenberg Park, 504/581–4629: Food, music, crafts and hands-on contact with live Louisiana swamp animals. **New Orleans Film & Video Festival**, Canal Place Cinema and other venues, 504/523–3818: World and local premieres and award-winning films and videos. **Halloween Circuit Weekend**: A four-day gay celebration benefiting the NO/AIDS Task Force.

November: **Celebration in the Oaks**, City Park, 504/483–9415: More than one million sparkling lights decorate the ancient oak trees in the park. **Crescent City Fall Classic**, Audubon Park, 504/861–8686: 5K race. **Bayou Classic Football Game**, Louisiana Superdome, 504/523–5652: Southern University and Grambling University come together for their end-of-season game.

December: **Christmas, New Orleans Style:** Réveillon dinners, productions of the Nutcracker and the Messiah, candlelight caroling in Jackson Square, street-theater productions, Christmas Eve bonfires along the Mississippi, and more. **Odyssey Ball**, New Orleans Museum of Art, 504/488–2631: Black-tie gala fundraiser. **New Year's Eve**: The coming of the new year is always a blast in New Orleans. Watch the ball drop from Jax Brewery, wander down to Woldenburg Park to watch the fireworks extravaganza, or just join the party in the streets.

eating/coffee

Acme Oyster House, 37
Alex Patout's Louisiana
    Restaurant, 21
Angelo Brocato's, 172
Anthony's Seafood House, 148
Antione's, 27
Arnaud's, 28
Audubon Market, 201
Avenue Pub, 118
Bacco, 35, 73
Bangkok Cuisine, 180
Barataria, 225
Bayona, 32
Beebo's, 200
Bella Luna, 33
Bistro at Maison de Ville, The, 33
Bizou, 141
Bluebird Cafe, 111
Bon Temps Roule, Le, 240
Bouchon, 117
Bravo, 119
Breakwater Bisto & Bar, 227
Brennan's, 29
Brightsen's, 198
Broussard's, 29
Bruning's, 228
Buffa's, 94
Bulldog Bar & Grill, 237
Cabin, The, 260
Cafe Angeli, 240
Cafe Atchafalaya, 115
Café Beignet, 25
Café Degas, 176
Café Du Monde, 24
Cafe Havana, 27
Cafe Marigny, 93
Café Maspero, 20
Cafe Nino, 204
Café Roma, 206
Café Volage, 200
Camellia Grill, 201
Cannon's, 202
Caribbean Room, The, 115
CC's Gourmet Coffeehouse, 25
Charlie's Steak House, 207
Chef's Table, The, 115
Chez Nous Charcuterie, 242
China Rose, 225
Christian's, 174
Clancy's, 199
Clover Grill, 18
Coffee, Tea, Or..., 26
Columns Hotel, 198
Commander's Palace, 111
Country Flame, 36
Court of Two Sisters, 31
Crêpe Nanou, La, 202
Crescent City Steakhouse, 179
Croissant d'Or Patisserie, 26
Cubanacan Restaurant, 142
Deanie's, 228
Delmonico, 114
DiPiazza's, 32
Dooky Chase, 173
Dream Palace Reality Grill, 93
Emeril's, 146
Ernst Cafe, 136
Eve's Market, 208
Feelings, 92
Felix's Restaurant & Oyster Bar,
    37
Figaro's Pizzerie, 205
Fiorella's, 19
Five Happiness, 172
Frankie's Cafe, 226
Franky & Johnny's, 201
G&E Courtyard Grill, 34
Gabrielle, 173

Galatoire's, 28

Gauloise Bistro, La, 145

Genghis Kahn, 177

Grill Room, The, 146, 156, 160

Gumbo Shop, The, 30

Hana, 206

Hard Rock Café, 20

House of Blues, 35

Hummingbird Grill, 143

Igor's Buddha Belly Burger Bar, 237

Igor's Garlic Clove Restaurant, 119

Irene's Cuisine, 36

Jacques-Imo, 197

Jaeger's Seafood Beer Garden on the Lake, 228

Jamila's Cafe, 207

Joey K's, 239

K-Paul's Louisiana Kitchen, 20

Kabby's Restaurant & Sports Edition, 148

Kaldi's Coffee Museum and Coffee House, 25

Kelsey's, 239

Kevin's, 238

Kung's Dynasty, 199

Landry's, 226

Lemon Grass Cafe, 180

Liborio, 142

Liuzza's By TheTracks, 174

Liuzza's, 175

Lola's, 178

Louis XVI, 31

Lucky Cheng's, 18

Lucy's Retired Surfer's Bar & Restaurant, 144

Madeleine, La, 20

Mandina's, 176

Mat & Naddie's Cafe, 197

Metro Bistro, 145

Michael's Mid-City Grill, 171

Michaud's on St. Charles, 137

Mike's on the Avenue, 118

Mr. B's Bistro, 29

Mona Lisa, 36

Mother's Restaurant, 143

Mulate's, 136

Mystic Cafe, 241

Napoleon House, The, 23

New City Diner, 142

Ninja, 206

NOLA, 30

O'Henry's Foods & Spirits, 144, 202

Odyssey Gril, 227

Original Pierre Maspero's, 23

P.J.'s Coffee & Tea Café, 92, 199

Palace Café, 141

Palm Court Jazz Cafe, 21

Palmer's, 177

Pascal's Manale, 205

Patout's, 21

Pelian Club, 31

Péniche, La, 94

Père Antoine Restaurant & Bar, 22

Peristyle, 34

Planet Hollywood, 35

Poppy's Grill, 19

Praline Connection, The, 95

Quarter Scene, 22

Ralph & Kacoo's, 38, 65

Ralph Brennan's Redfish Grill, 37

Red Bike Bakery & Cafe, 135

Red Room, The, 117

Rib Room, The, 33

Riverview, 144

Robin's On Canal, 171

Rock-N-Sake, 147

Royal Blend Coffee & Tea House, 26
Royal Cafe, 22
Rue de la Course, 237
Rustica, 204
Ruth's Chris Steakhouse, 179
St. Charles Tavern, 119
Samuel's Avenue Pub, 118
Santa Fe, 95
Sazerac, 140
Secret Gardens Tea Room & Cafe, 238
Semolina, 240
Siam Café, 96
Sid-Mar's, 226
Snug Harbor, 92
Steak Knife, The, 229
Steak Pit, The, 23
Straya, 116
Sugar House, The, 147
Taqueria Corona, 241
Tennessee Williams, 122, 123
Tony Angelo's Restaurant, 227
Top of the Dome, 149
Tourist Trap, The, 19
Trolley Stop Cafe, 172
True Brew, 137
Tujague's, 30
Ugleschi's, 137
Upperline, 203
Vaquero's, 122
Venezia, 177
Veranda, 138
Vic's Kangaroo Cafe, 136
Vincent's, 204
Vizard's, 238
Warehouse District Pizza, 148
Whole Foods Market, 178
Ye Olde College Inn, 175
Zachary's Restaurant, 200

bars/music/clubs

Andrew Jaeger's House of Seafood, 43
Apple Barrell Bar, 98
Arnaud's Cigar Bar, 42
Bombay Club and Martini Bar, The, 39
Bourbon Pub, 45
Bowl Me Under, 181
Bruno's Bar, 209
Buffa's, 98
Cafe Brasil, 97
Canal Bus Stop Bar & Grill, 181
Carrolton Station Bar, 209
Cooter Brown's Tavern, 210
Corner Club, 44
Daquiri Shoppe, 39
Donna's Bar and Grill, 44
Dos Jefes, 210
Dream Palace, The, 97
Fleur de Lee, 149
Fritzel's, 43
Funky Butt at Congo Square, 45
Funky Pirate, 43
Good Friends, 46
House of Blues, 43
Howlin' Wolf, 44
Jazz Alley, 44
Jimmy's Music Club & Patio Bar, 209
Lafitte's Blacksmith Shop, 39
Lafitte's-in-Exile, 46
Maison Bourbon Dedicated to the Preservation of Jazz, 43
Maple Leaf Bar, 208
Margaritaville, 45
Mermaid Lounge, The, 149
Mid-City Lanes, 181
Oz, 45

Palm Court Jazz Café, 42
Parade Disco, 46
Parlor Room, 44
Pat O'Brien's, 39
Preservation Hall, 42
Rawhide 2010, 46
Red Room, The, 122
Sazerac Bar, The, 149, 161
Snake & Jake's Christmas Club
    Lounge, 209
Snug Harbor, 97
Storyville District, 44
Tipitina's French Quarter, 45
Tipitina's, 208
21 Supper Club, 43
Vaughn's, 98

buying stuff

Aaron's Antique Mall, 243
Accent Annex Mardi Gras
    Headquarters, 62
Accessories in Brass, 249
Adler's, 151
Aesthetics & Antiques, 250
ah-ha, 250
Angel Wings, 54
Animal Art Antiques, 49
Anne Pratt, 254
Antebellum Antiques, 243
Antique Vault, 243
Antiques Magazine, 243
Antiquities Les Oliviers, 243
Ariondante Contemporary Craft
    Gallery, 152
Arthur Roger Gallery, 152
Artifacts, 253
Artworks of Lousiana, 154
As You Like It, 255

Astoria Fine Art Gallery, 253
Audubon Antiques, 243
Aunt Sally's Original Creole
    Pralines, 55
Aux Belles Choses, 250
Azby's, 211
Ballin's Limited, 211
Barakat, 52
Barrister's Gallery, 59
Bayou Bangles, 154
Bayou Trading Co., 154
Bead Shop, The, 254
Beckham's Bookshop, 49
Bedazzle, 60
Bep's Antiques Inc., 244
Bergen Galleries, 59
Berta's and Mina's Anitquities,
    253
Bianca's, 250
Big Life Toys, 255
Black Art Collection, 59
Black Butterfly, 54
Blackamoor, 244
Bourbon French Parfums, 63
Brass Image, 249
Brass Lion, 60
Brass Menagerie, 249
British Antiques, 244
Bush Antiques, 244
C. Susman, 254
Café Du Monde Shop, 55
California Drawstrings, 52
Canal Place, 150
Carol Robinson Gallery, 253
Casa del Corazon, 52
Casey Willems Pottery, 253
Catalogue Collection, 211
Central Grocery, 55
Children's Book Shop, The, 211
Cirello's Furniture Company, 252

Civil War Store, 53
Coghlan Gallery, 66
Cole Pratt Gallery, 253
Concepts, 54
Cone 10, 253
Contemporary Arts Center, 152
Cotton Market, 52
Crafty Louisianians, 53
Creole Delicacies, 56
Creole Delicacies Gourmet Shop, 155
Crescent City Books, 50
Custom Linens, 250
Custom Shop, The, 151
D.O.C.S., 152
Dashka Roth Contemporary Jewelry, 61
Dauphine Street Books, 50
Davis Gallery, 253
DeVille Books & Prints, 154
Different Approach, A, 53
Diva Gallery/Studio, 253
Dixon & Dixon, 48
Dodge Fjeld Antiques, 244
Dombourian Oriental Rugs, 249
Donna Browne, 151
Driscoll Antiques, 210
Dunbar & Company, 211
Earl Hébert Gallery, 59
Eclectique Antiques, 255
Empire Antiques, 244
Eye on the Square, 59
Fairman-McKinney Antiques, 244
Farmer's Market, 57
Faubourg Marigny Bookstore, 99
Faulkner House Books, 50
Fifi Mahoney's, 64
Fischer Gambino, 54
Flea Market, 57
Fleur de Paris, 50

Frame Shop & Gallery, 60
French Antique Shop, Inc., 48
French Collectibles, 244
French Connection, 51
French Quarter Postal Emporium, 66
Fudgery, The, 155
Gae-Tana's, 211
Garage, Le, 53
Gargoyle's, 61
Gentleman's Quarter, Ltd. and Ladies Quarter, 50
Gerald D. Katz, 48
Gerrie Bremermann, 250
Gloria Slater Antiques, 244
Gothic Shop, The, 66
Grace Note, 63
Grand Antiques, 244
Great Acquisitions Books, 211
Greek Designs, 154
Haase Shoe Store and Young Folks Shop, 212
Hands, 245
Hanson Galleries, 59
Harper's, 48
Harris Antiques, 48
Hello Dolly, 54
Hombres, The, 53
Home, Hook, and Ladder, 245
House of 10,000 Picture Frames, 213
Hové Parfeumeur, Ltd., 62
Idea Factory, 64
Image Gallery, 55
Importicos, 53
James H. Cohen & Sons, 53
Janet Molero, 250
Jacqueline Vance Rugs, 249
Java Nola, 154, 245
Jazzin' on the River, 154

Jean Bragg Antiques, 245
Joan Good Antiques, 60
Joan Vass, 250
Jon Antiques, 245
Judy's Collage, 99
Kaboom Books, 50
Karla Katz & Co., 245
Katy Ben, 254
Keil's, 48
Kid's Stuff, Ltd., 213
Kite Shop at Jackson Square, The, 66
Kohlmaier and Kohlmaier, 245
Kurt E. Shon, Ltd., 59
L.M.S. Fine Arts and Antiques, 49
Ladies Quarter, 50
Laura's Candies & Creole Gourmet, 55
Lemieux Galleries, 152
Let's Go Antiquing, 242
Libraire, La, 49
Little Mex, 63
Lollipop Shoppe, 212
Lord & Taylor, 153
Lord Jim, 53
Louisiana Loom Works, 64
Louisianian Angelé Parlange, 250
Lucullus, 49
M.S. Rau, 48
Ma Sherie Amour, 64
Macy's, 153
Madam Laveau's Antiques, 49
Magazine Arcade Antiques, 245
Manheim Galleries, 48
Maple Leaf Book Shop, 211
Marceline Bonorden Gallery, 152
Mardi Gras Madness, 155
Mardis Gras Center, 62
Marguerite Oestreicher Fine Art, 152

Marie Laveau's House of Voodoo, 67
Mariposa Vintage Clothes, 250
Marquise Pastry Shop, La, 56
Masks and Make-Believe, 155
Masquerade Fantasy, 61
Meisel's Fabric Shop, 212
Melange Sterling, 255
Michalopoulos, 58
Mignon Faget, 150, 213
Miss Edna's Antiques, 245
Morgan-West Studio Gallery, 253
Mystic Curio, 64
Neal Auction Company, 248
New Orleans Centre, 153
New Orleans Cypress Works, 252
New Orleans Lighting & Antques, 255
New Orleans School of Glassworks and Printmaking Studio, The, 254
Nuance Blown Glass Studio, 213
Oh, Susannah, 54
On the Other Hand Exclusive, 212
Orient Expressed, 251
Out of Focus, 251
Passages Antiques, 248
Perlis, 250
Perossi Clothing, 212
Persian Cat, 212
Petit Soldier Shop, La, 53
Petite Pence, 248
Photo Works, 59
Pied Nu, 251
Pierre Crawdeaux, 154
Pippin Lane, 51
Postmark New Orleans, 63
Prince & Pauper, 248
Priorities, 212
Private Connectiion, The, 248, 251

Quarter Moon, 63
Quarter Stitch, 66
Quilt Cottage, The, 251
Reina Gallery, 254
Renaissance Shop, 248
Rendezvous Linen & Lace, 66
Reverand Zombie's House of
    Voodoo, 67
Rhino Contemporary Crafts Co.,
    151
Rine Chapeux, 154
Riverwalk, 153
Rodrigue Studios, 58
Royal Ltd., 51
Royal Rags, 51
Rubenstein Bros., 151
Ruby Ann Tobar-Blanco, 254
Rumors, 60
Rumors-Too, 60
Sabai Jewlery/Gallery, 61
Salloum's Contemporary Jewlery,
    61
Santa's Quarters, 64
Scriptura, 251
Second Skin, 61
Serendipitous Masks, 61
Shadyside Pottery Shop, 254
Shaker Shop, The, 252
Shoetique, 212
Shop of the Two Sisters, 251
Shushan's Ltd., 52
Sigi Russell Antiques, 248
Sigle's Antiques and Metalcraft, 52
Simply Gold, 213
Sister Agnes, Ltd., 248
Sitting Duck Gallery, 252
Southern Expressions, 59
Southwest Design, 67
Spice, Inc., 151
Spilled Ink, 60

Stan Levy Imports, Ltd., 248
Still-Zinsel, 153
Street Scene Gallery, 154
Sugar & Spice Company, 56
Symmetry Jewelers & Designers,
    213
Tabasco Country Store, 155
Talebloo, 249
Three Dog Bakery, 56
Top Drawer Auction & Appraisal
    Company, 248
Trashy Diva, 51
Tulip Tree, The, 252
Uptowner Antiques, 249
Utopia, 252
Victoria's Secret, 216
Victoria's Uptown, 212
Vieux Carré Hair Store, The, 62
Villa Vicci, 252
Vintage 429, 53
Violet's, 51
Vision Quest, 67
Voo Doo New Orleans, 154
Voodoo Museum, 67
White Pillars Emporium, 213
Wicker Gazebo, Le, 252
Wilkerson Row, 252
Wirthmore Antiques, 249
Wise Buys, 51
Wyndy Morehead Fine Arts, 153
Yvonne LaFleur, 212

sleeping

Bourbon Orleans Hotel, 72
Bourgoyne House, The, 74
Château du Louisiane, 215
Claiborne Mansion, 101
Columns Hotel, The, 214

Cornstalk Hotel, 72
Dauphine Orleans, The, 71
Degas House, 184
Esplanade Villa, 185
Fairmont Hotel, The, 157
Frenchmen, The, 104
Garden District Bed & Breakfast,
  The, 256
Holiday Inn Downtown-
  Superdome, 160
Hotel de la Monnaie, 101
Hotel de la Poste, 73
Hotel Inter-Continental, 157
Hotel Monteleone, 69
Hotel St. Louis, 69
Hotel Villa Convento, 73
House on Bayou Road, The, 186
Hyatt Regency New Orleans, 157
Inn on Bourbon Street, The, 71
Josephine Guest House, 124
Lafitte Gueast House, 72
Lamonthe House Hotel, 185
Maison de Ville, 68
Maison Esplanade Guest House,
  185
Maison Perrier, 215
Mandevilla, 215
McKendrick-Breaux House B&B,
  256
Melrose Mansion Hotel, 100
Meridien New Orleans, Le, 158
New Orleans Marriott Hotel, 164
Olivier House Hotel, The, 71
Omni Royal Orleans, The, 69
Parkview Marginy B&B, 104
Pavillion Hotel, Le, 159
Pelham Hotel, 159
Pontchartain Hotel, The, 123
Quality Inn Maison St. Charles,
  124

Queen & Crescent Hotel, The,
  159
Ramada Plaza Hotel-St. Charles,
  124
Richelieu, Le, 71
Rose Manor Bed & Breakfast Inn,
  229
Royal Sonesta Hotel, The, 70
Rue Royale Inn, The, 73
Sheraton New Orleans, The, 163
Soniat House & Maisonettes, 70
Southern Nights B&B, 216
St. Charles Guest House B&B,
  124
Ursuline Guest House, The, 74
Westin Canal Place, 158
Windsor Court, 156

doing stuff

Air Tours on the Bayou, 231
Aquarium of the Americas, 83
Ashland-Belle Hélène, 261
Audubon Park, 218
Audubon Place, 220
Audubon Zoological Gardens,
  219
Bally's Lakefront Resort &
  Casino, 233
Bayou Gauche Tours, 231
Beauregard-Keyes House, 77
Bertucci-Schmaltz Building, 257
Blaine Kern's Mardi Gras World,
  65
Blanc House, 191
Bocage, 261
Boston Club, 161
Botanical Gardens, 192
Bourbon Orleans Hotel, The, 80

Bradish Johnson House, 128
Brown-Villere House, 217
Bultman Funeral Home, 129
Bultman House, 129
Cabildo, 75, 112
Cajun Queen, 169
Canal Place Cinema, 167
Castle's House, 218
Christ Church Cathedral, 129
Church of the Covenant
   Presbyterian, The, 217
City Park, 191
Civil Courts Building, 79
Claiborne Mansion, 106
Colonel Short's Villa, 129
Confederate Museum, 162
Congo Square, 83
Contemporary Arts Center
   (C.A.C.), 163, 166, 170
Cotton Blossom, 84, 231
Creole Queen, 169, 231
Destrehan, 259
Doll House, 220
Dolliole-Davis Cottage, 105
Dueling Oaks, 193
Dufour-Baldwin House, 188
1850 House, 77
1852 Degas House, 189
Entergy IMAX Theater, 84
Evariste Blanc House, 191
Fair Grounds, 193
Fairchild Guesthouse, 125
Flettrich House, 105
Friends of the Cabildo, 230
Gallery Row, 163
Gallier Hall, 164
Gallier House, 78
Gardette-Le Prête House, 79
Gauche Villa, 81
Germaine Cazenave Wells Mardi
   Gras Museum, 65
Geron-Edwards-St. Martin
   House, 125
Gray Line, 231
Hackett House, 127
Hancock Building, 162
Heritage Tours, 230
Hermann-Grima House, 78
Historic New Orleans
   Collections, The, 80
Honey Island Swamp Tours, 231
Houmas House, 260
Hula Mae's Tropical Wash, 83
if you miss the carnival, 65
Jazzfest, 182
Jean Lafitte National Historic
   Park and Preserve, 230
Jean Lafitte Swamp Tours, 231
Julia Place Apartments, 163
Julia Row, 113, 163
Kiefer University of New
   Orleans Lakefront Arena, 233
L'Hermitage, 261
Lafayette Cemetery No.1, 129
Lafayette Park, 164
Lafitte's Blacksmith, 112
Lake Lawn Metairie Funeral
   Home, 247
Laura, 259
Lee Circle, 162
Louis Armstrong Park, 82
Louisiana Superdome, 167
Loyola University, 218
Luling Mansion, 189
Madame John's Legacy, 77, 112
Magic Walking Tours, 231
Mahalia Jackson Center for the
   Performing Arts, 82
Mardi Gras, 40
Mardi Gras Fountains, 232

Mardi Gras Museum at Rivertown, 65

Maspero's Exchznge, 79

Metairie Cemetary, 247

Miltenberger House, 78

Milton H. Latter Memorial Library, 218

Monde Creole, Le, 230

Moon Walk, 84

Municipal Auditorium, 82

Musée Conti Wax Museum of Louisiana Legends, 80

Musgrove-Wilkinson House, 191

Musson House, The, 128

Natchez, 84, 231

Nathan-Lewis-Cizek House, 105

New Orleans Ghost Tour, 231

New Orleans Historic Voodoo Museum, 247

New Orleans Museum of Art, 189, 192

New Orleans Opera, 82

New Orleans Pharmacy Museum, The, 80

New Orleans Spirits Tours, 231

New Orleans Steamboat Company, 84

New Orleans Tours, 231

1916 Jerusalem Temple No.1137, 129

Nottoway, 261

Oak Alley, 259

Ogden Museum of Southern Art, 162

Old U.S. Mint, 81

1035 Royal Street, 80

1140 Royal Street, 80

Orleans Ballroom, 80

Orleans Club, 217

Orpheum Theater, 161

Our Lady of Guadaloupe Chapel, 83

Our Lady of Victory, 81

Pavilion of Two Sisters, 192

Payne-Strachan House, 128

Peristyle, The, 192

Petit Théâtre du Vieux Carré, Le, 85

Piazza d'Italia, 164

Pitot House, 112, 191

Place d'Armes, 76

Presbytère, 75, 112

Preservation Resources Center, 163

Robinson-Jordan House, 129

Royal Carriages, Inc., 230

Royal Street after dark, 85

Sacred Hearts Academy, 217

Saegner Theater, 161

St. Alphonsus Church, 256

St. Anna's Asylum, 125

St. Charles Streetcar, 84, 127, 216

St. Elizabeth Orphanage, 216

St. George's Episcopal Church, 217

St. Louis Cathedral, 75, 112

St. Louis Cemetary No. III, 190

St. Louis No.1 (Cemetary), 246

St. Louis No.2 (Cemetary), 247

St. Mary's Assumption, 257

St. Mary's Dominican College for Women, 220

St. Patrick's Church, 163

San Francisco, 259

Save Our Cemeteries, 247

Seven Sisters, 128

Southern Decadence Day, 102

Southern Repertory Theater Company, The, 166

Spanish Custom House, 191
Square before the Cathedral and
    the steps on the Decatur
    Street side, The, 77
Stanley House, 126
Storyland, 192
Sully House, The, 216
Summer Shakespeare Festival,
    221
Tara, 218
Tezcuco, 260
Toby-Westfeldt House, 128
Touro Synagogue, 216
Tours By Cypress, 231
Tours By Isabelle, 231
True Brew, 165
Tulane University Theater, 221
Tulane University, 218
U.S. Customs House, 161
Ursuline Convent, 81
Voodoo Walking Tours, 230
Wedding Cake House, 218
Woldenberg Park, 84
World Trade Center, 165
Zemurray House, 220

Mr. Jack's Louisiana Haircutters,
    87
New Orleans Athletic Club, 85
Orleans Ink Tattoos and Body
    Piercing, 107
Salon, Le, (French Quarter)86
Salon, Le, (CBD/ Warehouse)156
Warlocks, 87

body

Aart Accent Tat-2 Café, 87
Arthur's House of Glamour, 87
Belladonna, 257
Earthsavers, 86
Eclipse Salon, 87
Fountain of Beauty, 87
Guy Keefer Salons, 87
Happiness Hair Salon, 87
Headquarters, 87
Ivette Keller, 87
Moulin Rouge Beauty Salon, 86

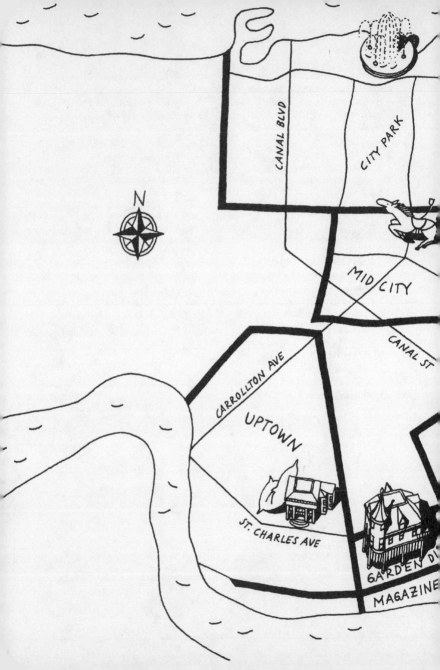